NATHANIEL HAWTHORNE: A CRITICAL STUDY

Encyclopaedia of World Great Novelists Series

Nathaniel Hawthorne

A Critical Study

Edited by

Robert Hudson

Edwin Arnold

ANMOL PUBLICATIONS PVT. LTD.

NEW DELHI - 110 002 (INDIA)

ANMOL PUBLICATIONS PVT. LTD.
4374/4B, Ansari Road, Daryaganj
New Delhi - 110 002
Ph.: 23261597, 23278000
Visit us at: www.anmolpublications.com

Nathaniel Hawthorne: A Critical Study

First Published, 2005

ISBN 81-261-2065-7

PRINTED IN INDIA

Published by J.L. Kumar for Anmol Publications Pvt. Ltd., New Delhi - 110 002 and Printed at Mehra Offset Press, Delhi.

Contents

Preface

Novelist and short story writer, a central figure in the American Renaissance. Nathaniel Hawthorne's best-known works include *The Scarlet Letter* (1850) and *The House of the Seven Gables* (1851). Like Edgar Allan Poe, Hawthorne took a dark view of human nature.

Nathaniel Hawthorne was born in Salem, Massachusetts. His father, also Nathaniel, was a sea captain and descendent of John Hawthorne, one of the judges in the Salem witchcraft trials of 1692. He died when the young Nathaniel was four year old. Hawthorne grew up in seclusion with his widowed mother Elizabeth—and for the rest of her life they relied on each other for emotional solace. Later he wrote to his friend Henry Wadsworth Longfellow: "I have locked myself in a dungeon and I can't find the key to get out." Hawthorne was educated at the Bowdoin College in Maine (1821-24). In the school among his friends were Longfellow and Franklin Pierce, who became the 14th president of the U.S.

The work was based on his college life. It did not receive much attention and the author burned the unsold copies. However, the book initiated a friendship between Hawthorne and the publisher Samuel Goodrich. He edited in 1836 the *American Magazine of Useful and Entertaining Knowledge* in Boston, and compiled in 1837 *Peter Parley's Universal History* for children. In was followed by a series of books for children—*Grandfather's Chair* (1841), *Famous Old People* (1841), *Liberty Tree* (1841), and *Biographical Stories for Children* (1842). The second, expanded edition of *Twice Told Tales* (1837), was praised by Edgar Allan Poe in *Graham's Magazine*.

Hawthorne was one of the first American writers to explore the hidden motivations of his characters. Among his allegorical stories is 'The Artist of the Beautiful' (1844) in which his protagonist creates an insect, perhaps a steam-driven butterfly. A girl he admires asks whether he made it, and he answers: "Wherefore ask who created it, so it be beautiful?" Eventually the insect is killed by an unfeeling child. Hawthorne once wrote of his workroom: "This deserves to be called a haunted chamber, for thousands and thousands of visions have appeared to me in it."

This book gives a vivid account of his life events and critique of his literary works by various commentators on him. Certainly this will be useful and informative for students, researchers and teachers besides the general readers.

—Editors

1

Nathaniel Hawthorne: An Overview

Before 1830 the New England scene had degenerated into a despondent and fossilized spectacle. Two hundred years of pioneering effort, of land-clearing and upbuilding in the materialistic sense, of Indian wars and revolution, and of a thin semi-bitter social coagulation had resulted in a superficially unified community that rested upon the dark foundation of the so-called Puritan tradition. This tradition, bulwarked by an intense religious dogma, was not strong enough in itself to outlast the peculiar circumstances that brought it into being. So long as ethical rules dominated the daily life of the community just so long would the tradition last as a living thing, a phenomenon not without its admirable qualities in a New World that demanded an invincible front of its conquerors; and for some years it did so last, growing, however, more dry and shell-like as the seasons succeeded one another. But with the crumbling of the religious bulwark, with the splitting apart of an heretofore unified moral impulse, with the cessation of primitive building-up and the incursion of a more elaborate material development, with the first faint hints of commercial intercourse as possible Big Business, and with the tardy realization of the arts as forces in themselves (and how vaguely this was suspected!), the tradition was steadily undermined and its collapse became a matter of decades.

After 1830 life changed in New England. The change was gradual except for the sudden outburst of literary expression, but it grew more and more apparent as the years crept on toward the Civil War. Economic shifts followed hard upon one another and a fever of unrest that expressed itself in countless political parties and cliques and circles ran through the community. The towns grew so large that they became menaces to the country and the old scheme of existence was consequently partially demolished. A great influx of Irish immigrants streamed through the gateways of New England and with them, of course, came increased activities of the Roman Catholic Church. A state of ill-feeling which sometimes erupted in riots developed between the lower-class Protestants and these Irish. Unitarianism became the fashionable religion of the older New England families, thrusting into the background the ancient fierce and emotional Calvinism. It was Calvinism that had molded the Puritan tradition and with the desertion of it in favor of a dogma that expounded an easy optimistic faith in the inherent goodness of mankind the moral features of New England suffered a sea-change. Instead of Jonathan Edwards, that curious religious sadist, bellowing that God would make blood squirt out of sinners, that He would hold them over the mouth of Hell as one holds a spider over a fire, the gentler William Ellery Channing soothed his circumspect congregation with fairer aspects.

Into this shifting and inchoate reorganization of sociological, economic, and religious urges came the writers, a sudden streaming wave of them, the vanguard of intellectual progress. The *Quaker Whittier* appeared first in 1831 and then in rapid succession appeared the first volume of Bancroft *"History of the United States"* in 1834,

Emerson *"Nature"* in 1836, Hawthorne *"Twice Told Tales"* in 1837, Prescott *"Ferdinand and Isabella"* in 1838, and Longfellow *"Voices of the Night"* in 1839. It was an auspicious flowering and it kept up without abatement until the muttering guns of the Civil War startled the minds of men into more terrible channels. There were other than material reasons for this bourgeoning of the intellectual life and one of these reasons is implicit in foreign influences. There had always been foreign influences in New England but heretofore they had come mainly from England. Now they came from Spain, from France, and, especially, from Germany. Then, too, a new race of scholars had sprung into existence, men who had traveled and knew whereof they spoke, men who had grown up, perhaps, in the Puritan tradition not much questioning it during their early years but now acutely aware of it because of its very weakening. It is true that a man may live intimately with a scene for ages and not be too aware of it because it is so much a part of the air he breathes and the life he absorbs through all his faculties; then, when this scene is shaken by the incursion of foreign urges, the native suddenly becomes aware of his environment and is moved to speculations concerning its adjuncts and drawbacks. The present becomes a perspective against which he may set the past. He has a standard for comparison. So the intelligent New Englander after 1830 could (vaguely and, at times, subconsciously) see the multifarious aspects of his environment and seize upon them for that rather mellow and innocuous but demonstrable ratiocination that lay clutched in the chaste arms of morality at the bottom of the cool and contemplative lake of his native literature. After 1830 the New Englander stumbled upon the history of his own mind's development and revealed it both consciously and unconsciously in a gathering flood of books.

Literature for New England ceased to be almost wholly a matter of piracy from England. It is true that for some time the publishers continued to steal the books of the Mother Country with a fine Puritanical abandonment, but a thin stream of native products trickled through these foreign works, a stream that steadily widened and became, before long, a river important in itself and furnishing some degree of sustenance to the country adjacent to its limpid current. Men and women in the smaller as well as the larger towns found a satisfaction of the mind in these native works for they as well as the authors were riding this current of new endeavors. Though the material birth of New England had taken place two centuries before accompanied by more or less severe pains it was not until this era whose advent is set at 1830 (although this is an arbitrary date, for all eras overlap) that the literary birth of New England may be affirmed to have taken place. In the quiet parlors of hundreds of substantial homes calm-eyed women and politically-excited men were turning over pages fresh from the presses of Boston and New York. An activity, not too feverish, to be sure, animated the literary phenomena of the times. It would be pleasant now to pass into one of those old-fashioned homes slumbering in the sun beneath its huge shade-tree and partake of the atmosphere of the period, to talk for a moment with the inmates about the lamentable riot in Boston between the firemen and the Irish and the subsequent calling-out of the militia, for instance, or Washington Allston's paintings that were so much better than the work of Michael Angelo, or Mr. Emerson's latest lecture, or the newly-arrived bundle of books, or some vexed aspect of the religious problems of the day. But this is impossible. Some of these old houses still exist but their inhabitants are almost as far from us to-day as Caesar and his Legions or Washington's Continentals. There is nothing but the galvanized corpse of a tradition that twitches infrequently, some crumbling edifices about which Time has wrapped a faint historical aroma, a few pictures and wood cuts out of which peer strange and calm eyes, and a bundle of books and letters and diaries left to remind us that between 1830 and the

Civil War New England passed through a flowering era of rather circumspect literary gentility.

One man stands both in and aside from this genteel flowering. He was unquestionably a part of it but he was so unlike his contemporaries as to fit into no groove. He was neither of the Concord group although he lived there for a while nor of the Cambridge group although he called some of them his friends. He cannot be classified as a Transcendental although he was intimate with the leaders of that foggy idealism. He was a man whose mood was essentially dark, who was visited by small daemons, who was haunted by spectres, who saw in Time the horrors of eternity and yet who, in himself, was a dull, shy, quiet relic of iron-minded Puritan forebears. We may approach him through the alert mind of Miss Elizabeth Peabody of Salem, Massachusetts. In 1837 that strong-minded young lady happened upon a small book called *"Twice Told Tales,"* published by the American Stationers' Company, Boston, read it from cover to cover, recognized some of the narratives as matter that had arrested her attention before in the columns of the *New England Magazine* (indeed, she had written, but never sent, a letter to the "supposed old man" responsible for them) and discovered (for Miss Peabody appears to have been a ubiquitous "educated" lady) that the mysterious scribbler was Madame Hawthorne's son. Now Madame Hawthorne's son lived very near Miss Peabody in an old house on Herbert Street, but propinquity of residence proved no particular aid to access. It was a year before Madame Hawthorne's son, accompanied by his two sisters, was inveigled into a visit to the Peabody house. He was a painfully shy young man almost antagonistic because of an acute realization of his accursed bashfulness. Miss Peabody thought him handsomer than Lord Byron. What he thought of her is not on record. Upstairs the invalid sister of Miss Elizabeth Peabody kept to her chamber and refused to come down even though the visitor were handsomer than Lord Byron.

This sister, Sophia by name, had suffered from headaches for years. The visit ended on a better note than it began for Madame Hawthorne's son lost some of his shyness as the conversation proceeded and his two sisters, Elizabeth and Louisa, proved agreeable enough. At the conclusion of the call the young man and his two sisters directed their steps toward home, toward Madame Hawthorne's house on Herbert Street. With them walked the ghosts of old New England.

Nathaniel Hawthorne walked arm in arm with solitude. During the later years of his life when public offices and his fame had forced him somewhat into the world of affairs and friendships he ceased to lead an hermit-like existence. But even in the jolliest gatherings he was an hermit appearing in public. There was a difference between him and those friends of his who enjoyed laudation and the social amenities. The sweet urbanity of Longfellow, the gentle friendliness of Emerson, the vivid argumentativeness of Margaret Fuller, these things were not for Hawthorne. He could meet these people and talk with some degree of animation, he could attend dinners and literary gatherings and business conferences, he could frequent taverns and wharves, he could administrate a consular office, he could travel through England and France and Italy; all these things he could do and yet it was impossible for him to appear anywhere without the impalpable specter of solitude fondly hanging to his arm. It has been asserted by people who ought to know that Hawthorne's withdrawal from the world has been over-emphasized and in a physical sense this is undoubtedly so. He did see people and go about. He was disposed in a friendly enough fashion to the world around him. Yet in the spiritual sense his withdrawal from the world has not been over-emphasized. He was never a part of the social surface of his environment although the roots of his personality sank deeper into that environment, perhaps, than those of any of the more vivid figures of the period. From one point of view he was nearer Jonathan Edwards than Ellery Channing and yet he was not actually a Puritan of the old type. But the somberness of the ancient Puritans stayed with him as a dark cloak through all his days and though it was often lightened by an intelligence quite aware of the fairer vistas of existence, these brief illuminations were not sufficient to dissipate the aura of dusk that clung about him so tenaciously. His early inclinations, his literary gift to the very last, and the essential timbre of his mentality were tinged with an autumn hue. There were obvious reasons for this and the two principal ones were his life to maturity and for some years beyond, and the hampering power over his intelligence of Puritanism, Calvinism, and tradition.

The mature man is always the child of his youth to some degree. During those early formative years that approach puberty and extend beyond it for some time the nervous processes of the youth are shaping the quality and measure of the intelligence. It was so in the case of Hawthorne. His youth and early manhood were passed in such surroundings that he was flung directly into the arms of solitude. A naturally sensitive temperament was withdrawn from the world by an impossible arrangement of days. He saw solitude sitting beside his curious mother and dogging the steps of his two reticent sisters. He found solitude in the lonely byways he walked, on the midnight expanse of Lake Sebago where he skated across the pale ice in the moonlight, and in the haunted chamber under the eaves on Herbert Street where he pored over old Puritan chronicles and learned of the Salem witches. His imagination, fostered in such silence, lifted the gray wings of the moth and circled about this native Salem of his where his forefathers had dwelt for so many decades. He lived in the Past, as it were, and the Past is, after all, a solitary place peopled only with ghosts. Flung so upon himself he grew reticent but not morose, shy but not *gauche*, for the elements of the gentleman were born in him. Then, aiding and abetting this instinct for solitude, were the looming wraiths of Puritanism, Calvinism and tradition. Hawthorne did not move out from their shadow until it was too late in life and then his days became an uncertain rebellion against them. He carried an abiding realization of his descent and his blood-relationship with the old Salem Hawthornes and though he knew that he was quite unlike them and that they probably would have snorted a bit at him yet he understood only too well that their huge shadows hung over his days.

It has been pointed out that life changed in New England after 1830 and that a new race of writers was the direct result of the crumbling scene. Hawthorne was of these new writers (he could not have existed as a force before 1830) and yet he was not like them. He, alone, of the New England group came from a home that had been absolutely untouched by the new spirit in the air. It was both his fortune and his misfortune to drink more deeply the essential spirit of the old Puritan tradition than any of the others, Longfellow, Emerson, Thoreau, Lowell, or Holmes. These men were all in the current of daily life, moving along with it at greater or lesser speed, while Hawthorne was sitting in his room in Salem and fashioning tales out of old chronicles. He was therefore maladjusted to the urbane talkative Cambridge and Concord men, and though they respected him none of them ever got very close to him. It was impossible because he was a figure who had drunk at more solitary springs. Hawthorne was vaguely at odds with this old spirit that had watched over his youth but he did not possess the requisite pugnacity to fight quite clear of it. He was never quite sure of his own strength. He felt the past stretching out at him like a ghostly hand to be placed on his shoulder. The sense of this past, therefore, informed most of his work. While Longfellow, for instance, was ransacking the romantic stores of Europe Hawthorne was lifting skeletons from the old Puritan annals and clothing them in a shadowy flesh.

While Emerson was preaching his great new doctrine of spiritual and intellectual self-reliance Hawthorne was remolding the old Puritan sense of the burden of sin with an artistic delicacy almost foreign to the contemporary scene. And while Thoreau was seeking in nature by the silent waters of Walden Pond the desirable simplifications of life, Hawthorne was clothing the dim figments of ancient New England ghosts and "essences" with the suave cloaks of his shadowy meditations. In one sense of the word he was not of the New England Renaissance. He was not a part of that gallant and contained group who thrust open the long closed doors into an unprejudiced life that was unridden by semi-defunct tradition. He hardly ever stepped outside of himself as Emerson did or became an epitome in himself of the new Simple Man, the Rousseau *de nos jours*, as Thoreau.

Instead of this, he shut himself in with his soul "and the shapes came eddying forth." But in another sense of the word he did belong to this Renaissance of the mind in New England. He, like the others, succeeded in regarding his environment with a certain degree of objectivity. The historical sense was fecund in him and he could take the burden of the Puritan (and what was that burden but the omnipresent sense of man's inborn sinfulness) and examine it with a semi-detached aesthetic interest. He was the foremost artist of his day if we consider him from this point of view, more natural than Poe if not so bold and thoroughly capable of comprehending the aesthetic nuances of the material which he shaped so patiently.

One must travel back in Time to find the real Nathaniel Hawthorne and yet this journey will discover no more than a few frightful ghosts, a greater number of inconsequential phantoms, and the spent luster of a scene that reflects a comfortless sun shining through biting autumn weather. The locale is Salem always, a Salem of ferocious urges that quickly spend themselves, a Salem that becomes a long drab vista of unsightly houses and rusty people. Hawthorne was born in this New England town on the Fourth of July, 1804, as Henry James declared, "on the day on which of all days in the year the great Republic enjoys her acutest fit of self-consciousness." Hawthorne was hardly self-conscious at his birth but it is obvious that he grew self-conscious as to his place in life and the reason for his birth in after-years. The frowning shadow of his ancestors permeated his youth and early manhood, and, indeed, haunted him to the end of his life. To understand him one must understand these ancestors. They were the dark shadowed spring of icy water out of which rose the coldly delicate flower that was Hawthorne's mind. At the same time one must not overestimate the influence of these vanished progenitors on the writer, for though he was blood of their blood and bone of their bone it is a matter of perplexed and complicated argument to assert that he was brain of their brain. As a matter of fact he was not. Hawthorne reached that plane in the progress of a family where he could observe his ancestors detachedly.

The first of these ancestors was Major William Hathorne (it was Nathaniel Hawthorne himself who introduced the W into the name although the pronunciation remained unchanged) and he appears in New England history about 1630. He was the typical Puritan of the period, a fighter of Indians and a persecutor of Quakers. Like all typical Puritans he became a magistrate. Nathaniel Hawthorne pictured him in the introduction to *"The Scarlet Letter."* "The figure of that first ancestor, invested by family tradition with a dim and dusky grandeur, was present to my boyish imagination as far back as I can remember. It still haunts me, and induces a sort of home-feeling with the past, which I scarcely claim in reference to the present, phase of the town. I seem to have a stronger claim to a residence here on account of this grave, bearded, sable-cloaked and steeple-crowned progenitor—who came so early, with his Bible and his sword, and trod the unworn street with such a stately port, and made so large a figure as a man of war and peace-a stronger claim than for myself, whose name is seldom heard and my face scarcely known. He was a soldier, legislator, judge; he was a ruler in the church; he had all the Puritanic traits, both good and evil. He was likewise a bitter persecutor, as witness the Quakers, who have remembered him in their histories, and relate an incident of his hard severity towards a woman of their sect which will last longer, it is to be feared, than any of his better deeds, though these were many."

If this man (who died in 1681) was fierce, his son, John, was even fiercer for that worthy comes down through history as one of the witch persecutors. The witchcraft delusion hangs like a pall over early Puritan chronicles and somewhere in that pall a small daemon (perhaps the one at which Martin Luther flung his ink bottle) laughs shrilly. It was the last madness of Puritanism, the complete orgy of a sin-crazed conscience. To understand the Puritan conscience, to comprehend from what unyielding iron it was forged, to realize the *reductio ad absurdum* of fanaticism, one must acquaint oneself with the Salem witch trials. It is an unbelievable dip back into the medieval age, perhaps even the Black Age, and it illustrates only too clearly how close religious exultation is to complete madness, how faith may be translated into mad delusion, and how often dogmatic conviction becomes bloody tyranny. Gallows Hill in Salem is the Golgotha from whence come streaming all the spearmen of intolerant American reform. The men who put the nooses about the necks of the distraught "witches" were the progenitors of the more sly and less stark prophets of prohibitions who bluster through American life to-day. Hawthorne, in his day, recognized the curse of intolerance and it is manifested more than once in his own writings. Even his family was supposed to labor under a malediction directed upon it by one of Colonel John Hathorne's witch victims. Whether or not there was an historic curse it is obvious that after the civic prominence of the first two Hawthornes, William and John, the family subsided into the completest silence and obscurity. They became a race of seafarers, skippers of merchant vessels and whalers, and this vocation continued down to the time of Nathaniel Hawthorne's father, another Nathaniel, who died of fever in Surinam in 1808 when the future novelist was but four years old.

It would be an easy matter to indulge in all sorts of suppositions regarding the influence of Hawthorne's family upon him. However, the main inferences may be stated in a very few sentences. Hawthorne's hereditary endowment included, first of all, an obsession with the influence of conscience on character. It adumbrated sin as a vital essence to be combatted wherever possible, and, curiously enough, Hawthorne, like his ancestors (although in a different and more objective way) was fascinated by the aspect of sin. It lurked in the back of his mind and forced its way constantly into his fictions. Whether it was the unforgivable sin of Ethan Brand or the scarlet letter of Hester Prynne or the ghost of old Maule hovering over the House of the Seven Gables or the murder festering in Donatello's faunlike soul it was always present as a dark elixir imbuing its victims with a wild life that was somehow outside of life. Together with this consciousness of sin went a fastidiousness that bordered on squeamishness. Hawthorne, for instance, disapproved mightily of nude statues and who can affirm that this is not a throwback to that old Puritanical point of view that regards the body, first of all, as the potential house of evil? So far as Hawthorne's inclination for solitude went it must be considered as almost overwhelmingly due to his immediate environment, his home which was conducted as few homes have ever been conducted and his locale which bound him to it only through ghostly connections with the past. These questions may be taken up in their proper order. His hereditary temperament, of course, played some part in this leaning toward solitude, for the Puritan mind was far from a social mind and its ubiquitous urge was decidedly limited. But the case of Hawthorne was unusual and he can hardly be regarded as a type.

The early years of the boy offer a curious study in family morbidity. After the death of Captain Hawthorne at Surinam Madame Hawthorne (she was born Elizabeth Clark Manning) withdrew from the world in the fullest meaning of the word. She shut herself up in the Herbert Street house with her three children and in so doing shut the world away from these children when they most needed it. It is true that the earlier years of confinement did not prove too onerous. While Madame Hawthorne sat in her chamber like the mourning widow of an Indian rajah her children played and had some schooling. Hawthorne himself read *"The Faery Queene," "Pilgrim's Progress,"* some of Scott, and the usual inept school books of the period. He went to school. He was taught by Dr. Joseph Worcester, the lexicographer. He played with other children. Elizabeth Peabody remembered playing with him when he was a small boy. In 1813, when he was nine years old, he injured his foot while playing ball and it was several years before he recovered fully and was able to fling his crutches away. During these years of convalescence he fed to the full on the loneliness of his home, a home where the inmates did not live but merely existed as silent growths in an almost-vacuum. It is easy to recapture the "feel" of this shadowy house. In one chamber Madame Hawthorne, still in her early thirties, sat, her life having passed away beneath the hot sun of Surinam. In another chamber the quiet daughters reposed. And in still another chamber the lame boy lingered, turning the pages of books, drinking in the essence of silence, and growing more and more like the owl that loves darkness best of all. Outside the cold sun filtered through the heavy branches of the ancient trees above the deserted town street. The ugly white houses pushed abjectly against Time and got nowhere at all. In the harbor a creaking schooner unloaded firewood from Nova Scotia. The men abroad walked slowly. Birds twittered in the trees. The peaceful and despondent end of an era was slowly, almost slumberously, drawing to a close.

Later when Hawthorne was fourteen years old the family removed to Raymond, Maine, where they dwelt in "Manning's Folly," the home of Robert Manning, one of Madame Hawthorne's brothers. Near by was Lake Sebago and about this quiet expanse of water the boy, now recovered from his injury, wandered. It was here and at this time, according to Hawthorne himself, that he first got his "cursed habits of solitude." It is to be suspected, however, that these habits had already been planted and that only at this time did they begin to sprout noticeably. The young boy does not notice how cut off he is from the world as much as the older boy who feels the need of comradeship, as curiosity and an urge for conversation boil up within his mind. Hawthorne had been to Raymond before, had gone there during early summers and played beneath the trees, but now he was on the verge of the thinking state and he could better observe the effects of his environment. As he skated by night over the still, icy bosom of Lake Sebago, the steel blades of his skates cutting through the forlorn and desolate silence, he had an opportunity to set himself against the world and compare himself with those few acquaintances he had already made.

The comparison (and it probably did not delve very deeply for, after all, the boy was still but a boy) may not have been odious but it could have presented but few enchanting aspects. What was he, after all? He was the only son of a morbidly-minded widow of a sea-captain. His household was composed entirely of women except when he visited, or was visited by, his uncles. His time was passed between a lonely house in a rather sad New England seaport from whence the greater bulk of ocean-traffic had fled to the more important ports of Boston or

New Bedford or Newburyport and a somewhat primitive Maine town that was still, to all intents and purposes, an outpost of civilization. The enormous cultural awakening of New England hardly permeated these corners. Boston might be active with young men about to break clear of an old tradition but Salem was still the town of the witches and Raymond was practically on the edge of nowhere.

When Hawthorne returned to his native town after a season of the loneliness of Raymond the habit of solitude was indelibly impressed upon his nature. He was unused to the common contact of men, to the daily give and take of personalities, to the excitement of conversation. He was too young to be unhappy at such a predicament and his natural somberness of mood (which appears to have been more of a thoughtful gravity than anything else) sustained him as a solitary being. Even the return to school did not lighten him materially. He was of a reflective disposition (as many sensitive boys are) and his chief enjoyment was undoubtedly occasioned by the long tramps through the outskirts of Salem, wanderings which quickened his fancy and opened his eyes to the natural beauties and delicacies of the New England landscape. He saw with a brooding eye, and his Puritan heritage endowed the things he saw with faint moralistic adumbrations. If this was a new world about him he did not see it as such. It was not so much a civilized seaboard snatched from the impenetrable miles of wilderness as an autumn-hued terrain across which swept the crown-hatted and square-shoed ghosts of an earlier era. The rolling voice of William Hathorne ordering that Anne Coleman and four of her Quaker friends be whipped through Salem, Boston, and Dedham sounded in the salty sea-breezes that swept through the streets of the boy's native town. John Hathorne holding court for the hysteric witches and their epileptic victims was an omnipresent specter. There was a distant roll of drums, a whispering of women in the side-lanes, the Black Man waiting in the dark forest clearing for the unholy Sabaoth, the ugly skeleton of the pillory, and, above all, the unsightly fruit hanging from the gibbet on Gallows Hill. These things were undoubtedly in the boy's mind as he completed his primary schooling and bethought himself of the new college in Brunswick, Maine, to which he was to go for that finishing process which was to make an acceptable New Englander of him. But he was not to be an acceptable New Englander, after all, for an underlying independence (fortified to some extent by his solitude) held him above what was already a perishing mass-movement. He was to go his own way unmindful of the gentle cultural urge of New England, and yet, curiously enough, an unwitting exponent of it.

Hawthorne entered Bowdoin College in 1821 when he was seventeen years old. It was a wilderness college, a new venture set somewhat daringly against a background of primitive nature. Across the Androscoggin the lumber mills squealed and bellowed and the huge logs shot down the sluices into the river. The modest buildings upreared themselves doggedly against the huge blizzards that swept down from the north, and the little group of students huddled in the insufficiently heated halls and strove as best they might to swallow the druggets of knowledge prepared for them by the somewhat limited professors. It would be an interesting enough matter to go into the atmosphere of Bowdoin in 1821 with some degree of thoroughness but it is hardly necessary to do so here for it is difficult to perceive that the college influenced Hawthorne in any impressive way. As a matter of fact he kept pretty much to himself, was no more than a fair scholar, and formed but two friendships that were of any importance to him in later life. Longfellow was a college-mate but the connection between the two men who were to loom largest in New England creative literature during their era appears to have been rather fragile. Hawthorne, after all, was not cut from the material of which social undergraduates are made. He was too much on his own, too much of a solitary thinker, and a little too independent for the fastidious youths who composed the "upper set" at Bowdoin. Longfellow might be the dapper young man already convinced of a great future for himself but Hawthorne was more likely to be fined for playing cards at Ward's Tavern or cutting his classes to wander through the surrounding woods. He was not of the urbane academic type and scholarship for its own sake did not appeal to him. It is true that he wrote some verse but that is best forgotten. It was extraordinarily bad verse.

Hawthorne's two particular friends at Bowdoin were Franklin Pierce, later to be President of the United States (perhaps the greatest nonentity who ever became President and that is saying a great deal) and Horatio Bridge. To Bridge, Hawthorne wrote later in an introduction to *"The Snow Image"*: "If anybody is responsible at this day for my being an author, it is yourself. I know not whence your faith came; but while we were lads together at a country college—gathering blueberries in study-hours under those tall Academic pines; or watching the great logs as they tumbled along the current of the Androscoggin; or shooting pigeons and gray squirrels in the woods; or bat-fowling in the summer twilight; or catching trout in that shadowy little stream which, I suppose, is still wandering riverward through the forest—though you and I will never cast a line in it again—two idle lads, in short (as we need not fear to acknowledge now), doing a hundred things the Faculty never heard of, or else it had been worse for us—still it was your prognostic of your friend's destiny that he was to be a writer of fiction." These lines would appear to give a fairly accurate picture of Hawthorne's life at college, a life passed more in the pursuit of diversion than of culture. Although he was quiet and in love with solitude it was not the quietude and silence of the study hall that appealed to him. Rather was it the interrupted silence of the forest while one friend trudged beside him and prognosticated a future of literary eminence for him. That shadowy rebellion against "form" as it was understood in the New England social circle of the 1820s was working like a yeast in Hawthorne. The infraction of rules was a matter of small moment to him because he was self-centered in his solitude. He did not consider himself a part of the life of the day although he walked through it with a shy urbanity. Something called in the distance and perhaps it was literature, but a faintness of virile struggle and an unconscious self-deprecation withheld him from those dominant gestures that might be supposed to forward him on the road to fame. He had lived too long by himself and was too familiar with silence. He could not break free from his essential spiritual loneliness. And yet the pen was already in his hand.

The personal habits of Hawthorne during these college years remains a matter of shadowy conjecture. It is a fact that he played cards for money men drank to some extent there is nothing unusual about this. He was an excellent student in English and it is possible that *"Fanshawe,"* his first romance, was germinating in his mind during these undergraduate years. Perhaps it was the discussion of this book and a draft of a portion of it that aroused in Bridge the encouraging prophecy of Hawthorne's future as an author of fiction. He appears to have taken no part in the religious argumentations of the time (as Longfellow did, for instance) but to have pursued a somewhat lonely way outside of the pale of formalized dogma. We may picture him as a lithe handsome boy, moody of temperament, quiet but sure in humor, uneasy in large gatherings, regardless of regulations, hesitant of putting himself forward in any particular way and yet endowed with a thin steel-like independence. His reserved nature prevented him from making many friends, and, indeed, the bulwark of friends was quite unnecessary to his peculiar cast of individuality. He had no use for them as a general rule. He could not dissipate himself in social amenities.

Longfellow, for instance, made friends right and left and these intimates proved a tower of strength to the poet in later years; but though sensitive and understanding personalities might desire to give themselves more fully to Hawthorne and to receive something in return the Salem recluse could not meet them in the broad sunlight. One or two might walk the shadowy way with him but a congenital reticence debarred Hawthorne from surrounding himself with those many admirers who might have aided him so much during that decade that followed upon his departure from Bowdoin. The truth was that Hawthorne was already—during these college years-walking in that shadowy borderland between this world and the world of his fancy. To all intents and purposes, he was Fanshawe, Fanshawe the pale student who with one stern look and a short, "Retire, Sir!" could discomfit the villain, Fanshawe who could save the woman he loved from the clutches of a scoundrel and then calmly turn her over to a rival, Fanshawe who burned the midnight oil and died at the early age of twenty. Hawthorne, it is to be suspected, romanticized himself a bit from the very first and yet in so vague and delicate a fashion that it is difficult to perceive where romanticization left off and reality began. All imaginative men romanticize themselves to some extent and Hawthorne, conscious at last of his own peculiar solitude, must have dwelt upon it with an increasing moodiness as the years immediately following the Bowdoin interlude passed along, each one more subdued and doleful than the last.

The seasons at college, therefore, were but an interim of tentative associations between two silences. A few friends were made, were, indeed, grappled to his soul with hoops of steel, but the nature of the man did not change. Hawthorne was in no whit drawn out of himself by his education. If anything he was thrust deeper into his own loneliness.

The awareness of literature was, indeed, an added bulwark against the loud, changing, outer world that was shifting its moorings so insensibly at first and so disconcertingly later on. For Hawthorne the world meant not so much a career as a return to the disconsolate, ghost-ridden house on Herbert Street where he was to sit in a haunted chamber under the eaves and meditate on a vague future for a decade or more. The virility of youth seemed lacking from his makeup. He did not desire to dash out into the world and seize Time by the forelock. He would sit by the wayside (and later he was to call one of his homes 'The Wayside') and let the world go by. Longfellow was to cross the seas and study Europe but Hawthorne was to return on the beaten track and study the old-fashioned town where his forefathers had dwelt and ruled with rods of iron. It was a gloomy and dubious aspect induced by lack of aggressiveness, pinched financial means, and a wondering uncertainty.

The return to Salem in 1825 was like a return to the tomb. Hawthorne was morbidly concerned about his future and he sat down to think about it. Year after year he kept on considering what he was fit for and year after year the pen in his hand grew more active and, almost like a somnambulist, he entered upon his career without knowing it. Though he imagined his footsteps to be imprinted not upon the earth but upon the air he was, from the first, walking that oblique devious way through life which he was to pursue all his days. The tomb that had closed upon him after his few years of freedom at Brunswick could not stifle his imagination and his fancy. Though his mother, garmented in antique costumes, might sit solemnly in her high chamber and scorn any intercourse with her relations, though the two daughters, Elizabeth and Louisa, might drift to their private rooms and there immerse themselves in their own strange commerce with life, though Hawthorne himself might hide like a mole in his study by day and take his solitary walks after the darkness had fallen over Salem, the budding writer was already fumbling his way forward. No sooner was he home from college than he began the *"Seven Tales of My Native Land,"* a series of stories which he was to burn later, and *"Fanshawe,"* the curious novelette which he privately published in 1828 and the copies of which he searched out almost immediately after publication for the purpose of destroying them. He was a born writer but he had no confidence in himself. He saw life in terms of the imagination and his solitude developed this imagination along a triple course that was most natural to the anchorite. In the first place this imagination seized upon chronicles for its inspiration. Having no particular knowledge of man as he lived in a modern milieu Hawthorne turned to the historical memorials of his native land. A brooding over moral problems grew up with this aptitude toward revitalizing dead things. And that observance of life from the outside which is so often the peculiar property of the solitary evinced itself in the sketches of fancy.

For a number of years now Hawthorne's life was to follow a steady and uninterrupted course. He studied in the morning, wrote in the afternoon, and read in the evening as a general rule. He made few friends and he did not encourage callers. After the fall of darkness he would sometimes wander forth. Occasionally he would pass the evening playing cards and drinking in the kitchen of Susan Ingersoll's house on Turner Street, together with such acquaintances as Horace Conolly and David Roberts. What did he think of this Salem which had shaped his young mind? Well, not much. He thought he "might as well develop an affection for a checkerboard as this disarranged pattern of ugly wooden houses." Yet a feeling of intimacy persisted in spite of his evident coldness of observance. Salem was the home of his fathers and their dust had become a part of the soil beneath his feet. The blood and bones of vanished Hawthornes were a portion of this quiet town on the edge of the great sea and therefore it was, in a measure, a part of Nathaniel Hawthorne himself. His cold affection for his native town he called "the sensuous sympathy of dust for dust" and there was a deep subtlety in the phrase. He had a home feeling for the past and as the past glimmered up at him out of the heavy tomes he brought to the chamber under the eaves on Herbert Street he experienced that strange mystic feeling that destiny had fastened his roots in the secret soil where the bones of the witches were long since dust. "The old wooden houses, the mud and dust, the dead level of site and sentiment, the chill east wind, and the chilliest of social atmospheres" held and compelled him implacably and his "strange, indolent, unjoyous attachment" was not to be broken through life. Here, if anywhere, the mysteries of sin and tortured conscience and the old Puritan earnestness of concern might strike with a peculiarly vivid fastidiousness upon his artistic consciousness. During the decade or more that he lived for the most part in Salem it was not so much a passion that held Hawthorne stationary as it was the desolate sense that he had nowhere else to go and that his faith either in himself or in the reciprocity of the public was enervated by a hundred and one doubts.

So he idled by the wayside of life very much like a sleeper so far as any energetic actions were concerned. Occasionally he would wander forth by day but mainly in twilight and once a year he would make a trip of some weeks' duration. He was intimate with the neighboring towns, Nahant, Ipswich, Danvers, and he gravitated toward the taverns, perhaps because he found there that unrestricted and natural effervescence of life that was not to be sought out in the more staidly social gatherings of the day. In Boston he knew the Maverick House, the City Tavern, and the Mechanics' Hotel, for instance, and the taste of hot punch was not strange to him. During these days the inborn inclinations for an aesthetic satisfaction crept into his mind and colored his thoughts albeit their manifestations were weak and almost choked by the Puritan heritage that Time had vouchsafed him. He meditated on the grossness of pigs and their lack of beauty, for instance, as he passed a muddy sty, whereas another New Englander would have remarked no more than the possible number of pounds of meat in the swine. Seeing three little girls wading in a stream he instinctively protested at the sight of their unlovely pantalets. On his way to Nahant he searched in vain for a beautiful face amongst the passing pedestrians. He was quick to discern the flaws in people, over-dressed dandies at the Boston hotels, for instance, with worn-out soles to their shoes. All this while meditated on life and scribbled his secret thoughts, his experiments in his voluminous note-books. "The world is so sad and solemn," he noted, "that things meant in jest are liable, by an overpowering influence, to become dreadful earnest,—gayly dressed fantasies turning to ghostly and black-clad images of themselves." He fashioned four precepts for himself: to break off customs, to shake off spirits ill-disposed, to meditate on youth, and to do nothing against one's genius. He never did break off customs although he did manage to view them with some degree of detachment. The ill-disposed spirits haunted his to his grave. His meditations on youth were autumnal in hue and garmented in none of that bright glancing luster that might have leavened his dusky gravity. And he did do things against his genius, things induced mainly by pecuniary necessity as when he became a customs official and so silenced his imagination for several years, or because of friendship as when he wrote his life of Franklin Pierce. But during these early years he followed the still path of meditation and permitted it to lead him wheresoever it chose. Life became a severe monotony. "We sometimes congratulate ourselves at the moment of waking from a troubled dream," he noted in his persistent diary, "it may be so the moment after death." Life was a dream to him but not too much troubled until enough of his stories had appeared in periodicals to arouse him to an active sense of the great outer world that cried about his ivory tower.

Then, as the 1830s gathered speed, a depression settled upon Hawthorne. He knew that he must go out into the world and yet he knew not how to go. He suspected a faithless public as many a young writer suspected it before him and has suspected it since. Though his friend, Horatio Bridge, might insist on telling him how good he was and strive valiantly to dissuade him from morbid frames of mind the rainy weather continued in his spirit.

From 1830 on he contributed his short sketches and tales to a few magazines, but these apparent bits of thistledown settled on stony soil so far as Hawthorne could see. The fame which he won in his dismal chamber was extraordinarily limited and yet he did have a small audience by 1837, one or two editors interested in him, and, for his own part, some degree of awareness of his powers. He desired to have a book published but the obstacles Fate flung in his way were many and it was not until Horatio Bridge guaranteed the publishers against loss that *"Twice Told Tales"* was issued by the American Stationers' Company in 1837. For a year or two before that Hawthorne had some degree of intimate relationship with the journalistic world. S. G. Goodrich, known to New England readers of that era as Peter Parley, had been one of Hawthorne's first friends among magazine editors. He was a promoter of hack writings and the editor of *"The Token"*, a periodical in which some of Hawthorne's first stories appeared. As early as 1830 he had tried to find a publisher for a projected book by the Salem recluse to be called *"Provincial Tales,"* a venture which never materialized. In 1836 he procured for Hawthorne the editorship of a small magazine rejoicing in the astoundingly long name of *"The American Magazine of Useful and Entertaining Knowledge."* The periodical lasted a few months and then blew up as such ventures generally do and Hawthorne was out the greater part of his salary. After working off some irritation at Goodrich, Hawthorne, aided by his sister, Elizabeth, put together *"Peter Parley's Universal History on the Basis of Geography"* for the busy editor and received as a reward the sum of one hundred dollars. The book sold into millions. All of this was most unsatisfactory and Hawthorne, obviously pinched for money, grew more and more depressed. By this time he was thirty-three years old and except for some scattered tales he had nothing to show for the seasons of meditation and voluminous scribbling in the Herbert Street house. Longfellow was already a professor at Harvard, a man who had explored Europe and published several books. The rest of Hawthorne's Bowdoin classmates were moving along with the Time Spirit. Franklin Pierce was a Senator and Jonathan Cilley was a member of Congress. Hawthorne alone sat by the wayside of life, "like a man under enchantment," and the thicket of obscurity grew up about him and hid the world from him and him from the world. To Horatio Bridge he poured out his depression, calling himself "a doomed man." It is a curious spectacle, this of Hawthorne actually too inactive to push his own way and yet bewailing his lot. Whether or not he expected the world to come to him and batter down the closed door of the Herbert Street house is a riddle. It is obvious, however, that he made no vigorous gestures on his own part.

Friends, nevertheless, were about to thrust Hawthorne into that rather weak limelight that was to be his reward until the great days of *"The Scarlet Letter,"* and first among them was the faithful Bridge who made possible the *"Twice Told Tales."* This book was published at a psychological moment for Hawthorne who had been drooping despondently over his miserable fortune. Longfellow, already secure in the adulation of the Cambridge group, was quick to give his old classmate a helping hand by a review that was much more laudatory than critical and the Salem hermit was thus somewhat prodded out of his somber thicket. To Longfellow, shortly before the review appeared, Hawthorne had revealed himself curiously, writing: "By some witchcraft or other—for I really cannot assign any reasonable why and wherefore—I have been carried apart from the main current of life, and find it impossible to get back again. Since we last met, which you remember was in Sawtell's room, where you read a farewell poem to the relics of the class,—ever since that time I have secluded myself from society; and yet I never meant any such thing, nor dreamed what sort of life I was going to lead. I have made a captive of myself, and put me into a dungeon, and now I cannot find the key to let myself out." And again: "For the last ten years, I have not lived, but only dreamt of living." The key, however, had been turned in the lock and Hawthorne was to issue from his dungeon, blinking like a mole in the light of day and inclined, ever and again, to hurry back to that merciful obscurity where he did not need to be on any particular behavior. His solitude, partially congenital, had now been so stamped into his temperament that no vagaries of fortune could destroy his inclination for it. It was his natural state of being and though conditions might thrust him into the midst of life he was always to be a visitor and not a part of the scene.

The work produced by Hawthorne up to the time that he met Sophia Peabody (a meeting which, together with the publication of "Twice Told Tales," may be said to have terminated his dolorous twelve years of solitude and introspection) was not bulky but it was entirely indicative of the author who was to assume so important a place in the annals of New England letters. Three books were the main fruits of this period but two of them, *"Fanshawe,"* and the anonymous *"Peter Parley's Universal History on the Basis of Geography"* are best forgotten. The first was the tentative unfolding of a talent obsessed by Scott's novels and the second was typical hack-work of the era, undistinguished, hurriedly done, and partially the creation of Elizabeth Hawthorne. But the third book, *"Twice Told Tales,"* is a part of the New England heritage today. There were but eighteen stories and sketches in the first series of *"Twice Told Tales"* but Hawthorne had, by the time of its publication, composed nearly forty pieces. He was therefore well set and developed as a writer of short efforts.

To return briefly to *"Fanshawe"* it may be described as a short impossible romance with some fair description and a deal of stuff and nonsense. The scene is Harley College (which was inspired, of course, by Bowdoin College) and the action is concerned with the love of two undergraduates for Ellen, a young woman placed somewhat curiously in the care of Dr. Melmoth, the president of this rural seat of learning. A nefarious villain named Butler conspires to inveigle Ellen away, force her into a marriage, and so secure her wealth, but he is discomfited by Fanshawe. Fanshawe then hands Ellen over to his handsome and wealthy schoolmate, Edward Wolcott. This farrago of nonsense was rightly suppressed by Hawthorne and yet there is some curious matter in it. Fanshawe, a poor recluse already passing into a decline through overmuch study, is a fanciful and romanticized picture of Hawthorne himself. There is the aspect of a hero out of the Gothic romances in this youth who can hold a villain at bay with a burning eye. Edward Wolcott must be regarded as Hawthorne's subconscious romanticization of the luckier, wealthier, more socially-adept scholar of the day at Bowdoin, a Ned Preble, for instance, or a Longfellow. A comparison, unconscious, perhaps, lurked in Hawthorne's mind as he worked on this romance, a comparison of the difference between himself so solitary, so cut off from the social amenities of the times, and the more bland and wealthier students who mingled so happily in the polite gatherings of the institution. Except for what one may so read into *"Fanshawe"* and for the stray descriptions of college life and scenery there is little to hold the reader in this first attempt. The structure creaks abominably and the characterization is too stark and obvious. Hawthorne was on a false scent when he followed this work to the bitter end. It was no more than an exercise and he was perfectly right in destroying whatever copies he could lay his hands on almost immediately after the publication of the book.

But the short stories and sketches are a different matter. Here was the authentic and unmistakable revelation of a talent as extraordinary as it was new in the literary history of the time. It is true that the public paid very little attention, indeed, to this phoenix of form and finished prose that rose so quietly from the ashes of Salem. The tales were dissipated on thin air for the most part and yet their function was assured from the start. They were seeds blown by a new wind and though many of them fluttered to soil as stony as some of the hill farms of New England a few found fallow earth wherein to sprout. The importance of Hawthorne to his day was momentous and yet he stood decidedly aloof from what might be called the main cultural current. This awakened territory that was springing into intellectual action and expressing itself through new voices after 1830 needed the leaven of a painstaking artistry and this was exactly what Hawthorne revealed in the best of his short tales. He could write a delicately suave prose, but, best of all, he was animated by an aesthetic urge that was somewhat alien to the moralistic and in. formative inclinations of his New England. It was true that this urge was choked and hampered by the twisting roots of the old New England itself which was born decidedly in his blood but this interference failed to thwart the half-unconscious purpose of Hawthorne's daemon. Emerson might wear the prophet's mantle and Whittier might express the kindling aspirations for reform and Longfellow might illustrate the academic tendencies of the day and Lowell might develop the contemporary humanism but Hawthorne summed up in himself the sheer artistic impulses of the era. He remained the artist to the last. It was as though he gathered the scattered essences of artistry and aesthetic concern vague-blown and fragile over the New England scene, and from them drew his thin but visible vitality. His solitude aided him in his attitude. He did not have the conflict of men and the perplexities of new outbursts of social endeavor to subvert him from his instinctive course.

The short tales and sketches by Hawthorne which made up the first series of *"Twice Told Tales"* and appeared in various publications from which they were to be rescued for further volumes exhibit the writer's imagination in three distinct manners. There is his imagination in—a creative sense in the fantastic tales, in such efforts as *"The Minister's Black Vei. . . . The Wedding Knell,"* and *"Dr. Heidegger's Experiment."* There is his imagination in a re-creative sense in the historical tales, in such revivifications of past atmospheres and scenes as *"The Gray Champion"* and *"The May-Pole of Merry Mount."* Finally, there is his imagination in an observational sense, in such sketches of manners and contemporary scenes as *"Sunday at Home . . . A Rill From the Town Pump"* and *"Sights From a Steeple."* These works have been commented upon time and again and it would serve no purpose and become merely repetitious to restate their peculiar qualities, indicate their virtues, and glance briefly at their defects. They were the work of a young man of genius, a young man blessed with a flowing and spontaneous fancy, with a curious objective obsession with the sense of sin and its effect on the conscience, and with a purity of selectiveness unique in the letters of his time. Practically all of these pieces were written in the chamber under the eaves on Herbert Street and they are, therefore, reflections of the activities of Hawthorne's mind and impulses during those slow years of early maturity. It is easy enough to relate the simpler classifications to Hawthorne's days.

The essays, the sketches of things seen, are assuredly the product of a lonely man, a man who wandered through the world of his youth torn between shyness and inquisitiveness. He was not the man in the crowd buffeting and being buffeted by the unceasing stream of humanity. Rather was he the town-pump set in the midst of the town and somewhat apart from it and yet observing everything that happens and all who pass with a sort of still curiosity. A brooding contemplation, melancholy or blithe as the occasion might warrant, seizes upon the most natural and slight gestures and reanimates them with a gentle charm that is part of the finest tradition of essay-writing. This drawing of life through the eyes, as it were, was not without its powerful discipline on Hawthorne's selectiveness as a descriptional writer. It taught him arrangement, emphasis, what to retain and what to discard, and unification of impressions. He approached life almost as a painter would, his palette filled with sober pigments and his brushes of a fine feathery order. Nowhere in the crowded library of New England letters can the reader find more delicate, more astute, more *real* descriptions of the native landscape than in the essays and sketches (and, indeed, the novels) of Hawthorne. He fairly captured the native scene, its physical front and, somehow interfused with this, its spiritual emanations. Part of the reason for this was Hawthorne's sensitiveness to the spirit of places. He could feel the scene impinging on his consciousness whether it was a woodland, a country road or a town thoroughfare.

His eyes devoured the life about him but in that life they could find no more than a limited picturesqueness. He had to look further for those unusual elements upon which his spirit was to feed so constantly, and, being a lonely untraveled man, this meant an immersion in books. Being the child of Puritans it was but natural for him to fling himself (if so abrupt a phrase may be applied to Hawthorne at all) upon the chronicles of early New England, the conquest of the wilderness, the fanticisms of religious zeal, and the subdued coloring of infant Salem and Boston. It was from these sources that he drew the many historical tales that form so excellent a proportion of his literary endeavors. These brief flashes of history, miniatures of simplicity and unification, chastely carved and as polished as cameos, were unusual in that they exemplified an urge which was hardly noticeable in the New England of that day. They revealed a distinct creativeness in the handling of historical matter, a sort of humanization of the dry bones of chronicles that anticipated the more important ventures of later eras. Hawthorne's fancy played about the ancient tales of young New England, about Endicott and his flag, about the motley crew that roystered beneath the Maypole at Merry Mount, about the persecuted Quakers, but it played in a restrained and reasonable manner. These gracefully conceived reanimations of history were compact with a rare simplicity and an inborn literary tact that pushed the frontiers of American writing still further back. The skill in selectiveness, the quiet mastery of detail and rare eschewment of nonessentials, the brevity of composition, and, above all, the instinctive comprehension of the period involved combined to fashion these stories into rare fusions of historical fact and delicate imagination. Though the archaic note is persistent in some of these tales to-day, a note emphasized by changing styles, still the best among them continue to live with a quietly tenacious vitality that is unusual. Hawthorne's genius was not at its highest evolvement in these historical tales but it was on a plane peculiarly its own.

To find the man's genius at its highest expression one must turn to the third classification of tales, the stories combining fantasy, allegory, and a sort of tortured reality that trembles between two worlds. Here was the terrain wherein Hawthorne walked most at ease, an autumn land where a dull rain-bloated cloud that might be called the shadow of sin hovered desolately, and weak mortals wandered seeking the outward doors and seeking them in vain. Both the weakness and the strength of Hawthorne's genius were implicit in these tales and this weakness and strength came from the same source,—his Puritan heritage, that still dark blood that flowed so mutely through his veins. The weakness was to be found in an overpowering moralism, a monotonous insistence on ethical illuminations that, often enough, threw his tales out of their proper focus. The source of this urge was, plainly enough, the old New England puritanical attitude toward life that sought the sinful speck in the fruit before it became manifest to the naked eye. However, it was from this same Puritan urge that Hawthorne's genius received its strength, that dark pondering on life, that essential gravity that constantly dug beneath surfaces of the minds of men, that steady twilight glow that gave an almost spectral aspect to the scenery and mortal beings who walked the town-streets of New England. The best of Hawthorne's fantastic short tales are surcharged with an unearthly glow, a brooding sense of the supernatural, a comprehension of the invisible and mystic auras surrounding the soul. They are like spells and if these spells are weakened by an over-obvious moralistic inference the reader must accept them for what they are and reflect that no other type of mind but one intensely susceptible to moralistic conclusions could have created them. They are the late harvest of the Puritan tradition, dark-petaled flowers growing in lonely meadows and more gracious in aspect than the early harvests.

Hawthorne was not a Puritan of the old type but he was obviously the child of those forebears. He had reached a plane where he could view the Puritan conceptions of life and fate with some degree of detachment, where he could take up the ancient urges and beliefs and reshape them with an aesthetic comprehension of their values. Though the shadow of sin hovered over him as it had hovered over his fathers, that shadow did not eat into his soul in quite the same way. It permeated his intelligence but it was impalpable. It was not a grewsome conviction but a somber aspect of living that might be molded into some sort of art. An aesthete came to the surface in

Hawthorne and dominated an obliqueness of mind that had, in other years, dominated its thin-lipped victims.

It is obvious that Hawthorne's peculiarly lonely boyhood, youth, and early manhood had much to do with the shaping of his mind, almost as much, in fact, as his Puritan forebears had to do with it. An ingrowing intelligence surrounded on all sides by the shattered aspects of Puritan life, by Salem with its deserted port and its quiet streets, by a house that was almost a tomb, by the essential "feel" in the air of an ancient way of living, by books that were the histories of old fanaticisms, by ghosts that were the ghosts of one's forefathers, could hardly fight its way clear. New England as a whole might be fighting itself free but Hawthorne's struggle was fiercer and his complete success was dubious. He was not a part of the more or less conscious urge toward liberation which set in with the 1830s and yet his very indication of the limitations of the Puritan attitude with all its maladies of the soul was a distinct aid and adjunct to that urge. He orientated the old Puritanism to some degree and translated it from an invisible essence to a visible and weak-kneed giant that might be combatted by those who desire to lay it low. This peculiar function which Fate had thrust upon him was as unconscious to him as it was to his pitifully small audience.

In 1837 Hawthorne stepped into Time. Before that he had been living outside of Time although for the few seasons immediately previous to that date he had been standing at the door of the world and knocking with some degree of dubious timidity. When *"Twice Told Tales"* was issued the door had opened and when the young man "handsomer than Lord Byron," accompanied by his two sisters, stepped into the house of Elizabeth and Sophia Peabody Hawthorne may be said to have entered the world. His meeting with Sophia Peabody was really the beginning of his worldly life although vague stories connect him with one or two women previous to this encounter. It does not matter whether or not a fickle Boston beauty befooled him into challenging a friend to a duel only to have that friend convince him of the Boston beauty's double-dealing. This story, if it is true, merely shows how badly prepared for life Hawthorne was, how romantically inclined and naïve he could be. But with Sophia Peabody came love and with love came a dozen other things, a refreshened ambition, for instance, and an objective for which to work and make material gains. Hawthorne could no longer sit in the haunted chamber under the eaves on Herbert Street and let the world go by while he read or fashioned his tales from the dark fabric of his fancy. He perceived that he had a possible place in Time, that he must make a home for himself and no longer hide away in the somber house of his mother. Then, too, the publication of *"Twice Told Tales"* was an urge. Although the book had caused no more than a minor ripple that ripple had been sufficient to provoke a few friends to an outspoken declaration of the young man's merits. It was time, therefore, for Hawthorne to step out into the world. Yet he was so unprepared that he did not know how to go about it.

He continued his quiet courtship with some degree of secrecy for he knew that his own sisters were averse to seeing him slip from the sleepy milieu wherein he had existed so many years. Sophia Peabody had been an invalid for long seasons, suffering from terrific headaches, and this, too, was probably an inducement toward quietude. In any case Hawthorne would have been quiet about it, for he was a subdued and silent man as reticent in his passions as he was in his calms. His Puritanical upbringing and his congenital morbidity had convinced him that behind even the most joyous things stood a sad spectre who might, in an instant, translate the brightness into shadow. A man entering life in this way enters it with some degree of armor. He is impervious, to a certain extent, against the barbs of fortune. This was a lucky thing for Hawthorne for he was to know many disappointments in the course of his career. The reality was to fall short constantly of the dream although it was never to do so in the case of his married life. That, at least, was to see him through triumphantly. But the perplexing business of making a living was to continually stare him in the face. He was an artist in a land where artists were a strange sort of phoenix and he was to find that there was no particular sort of preparation for this unusual kind of bird. In 1837, therefore, when he stepped into Time as an author and a lover, he might well have been dubious about his prospects. His friends had sped far ahead of him in the race of life and hero he was, still at scratch, troubled about making a start. All that he possessed was his imagination, a cursed shyness, an incurable addiction to solitude, and some degree—not much—of Yankee common sense. With these weapons he decided to build up a home and a future.

The door into Time opened and Hawthorne diffidently stepped through in 1837; yet it was to be some years before he ventured any great distance. He stood just outside of his hermitage observing the perspective with a rather worried eye. There really was not much to see from his peculiar point of vantage and though rumors may have reached him from a few friends, Bridge or Pierce, for instance, they can hardly have impinged upon his consciousness with any great degree of violence. He knew very well that there was a modern world and he must have realized that that modern world had been uniquely accelerated during the decade that had paralleled his maturity. However, he was not the type of intelligence to get below the surface of his era. He preferred to dodge back into the Past. Now, though the future wore a thinly threatening aspect the immediate present was not without its delicate and composed pleasures. As Sophia Peabody bourgeoned in Hawthorne's mind (and she had a way of flowering that was essentially feminine) his nature thawed to a considerable extent. Days were passed in her company, days in which walks were taken through the well-known Salem scenes and the old surroundings must have taken on new colors. The town put on a brighter aspect, and Hawthorne, only too well aware that joys have a way of shifting into mere mockeries, may well have pondered the durability of this pleasing scene. The somber qualities of the Puritan rose to the surface. He decided to go off by himself, to travel into the Berkshires and Vermont and cut himself loose from every connection, including his mother. It is possible that he desired that solitude wherein he was so emphatically at home, there to ponder over his prospects and adjust himself to the thought of a new order of things.

After his return the two lovers became engaged, although the matter was kept a close secret. There were reasons for this secrecy. Hawthorne was not quite ready to break the news in the Herbert Street house; he sensed there a thin antagonism in his sisters and he feared the effect on his mother. Indeed, his oldest sister, Elizabeth, appears to have suspected the probable trend of his acquaintance with Sophia Peabody from the first and endeavored in some slight ways to obstruct and divert Hawthorne's inclination. He, therefore, maintained a discreet silence as to his purpose. It was not that he was particularly under the influence of his family or dominated by them to any extent for he appears to have been quite the young king in his tiny dusky kingdom; but he was a part of that quiet retired *ménage* and he naturally felt some compunctions at upsetting the equilibrium of the haven that had sheltered him from life for so many years. After all, his prospects were exceedingly dubious. The financial future was a matter of precarious possibilities. He had made no great inroads on popular fame. Reticently, then, like the typical thin-lipped New Englander he kept his counsels to himself until fortune might indicate more clearly his probable path.

Fortune took two years in coming to the point. During this interim he continued the composition of short stories and sketches. While waiting for life to call him into the midst of things he remained stolidly in the shadow of life and occupied his mind with such ghosts as walked through "Howe's Masquerade," "Lady Eleanore's Mantle," and "Old Esther Dudley." The ferocity of the modern scene smashed against his calm only once and that was when his old college-friend, Jonathan Cilley, was killed in a duel. It has been affirmed that Hawthorne took the death of Cilley much to heart in that he suspected his own fire-eating vigor (when he challenged a friend to fight over a legendary vampire-lady from Boston) afforded an example to Cilley. This, however, is in the realms of misty conjecture. If Hawthorne ever did challenge anybody to a duel he didn't fight it and Cilley had but half an example before him. For the most part, then, Hawthorne remained in Salem among his ghosts and peered somewhat uneasily through the fog of existence for the bright beckoning hand of fortune. When that hand did appear through the mist it was blackened with coal-dust. Hawthorne was appointed a measurer in the Boston Custom House at a salary of fifteen hundred dollars a year. Of all the appointments that literary men have ever received this was probably one of the most ridiculous, a direct reflection on the evaluation that New England put on her literary figures. If they could not support themselves as preachers, lawyers or college professors they could go out in Boston Harbor and weigh coal. Hawthorne went to work in January, 1839. He was thirty-five years old and just stepping into life via a coal-barge.

During Hawthorne's twenty-seven months as a measurer he appears to have been painstaking, hardworking, and entirely capable. Flung so into a grossly practical life he welcomed the change, at first, with some degree of pleasure. He felt that he was earning his own salt at last, that he was buffeting his way with the rest of the busy humming New England that was so much more engrossed in business than he had imagined. It was good to tramp the dirty decks of cargo-boats and catch the cold sea-wind on the spray. As he attended to the various details of his business, treated with sinewy captains and sailors, appraised the salt fish and coal and iron and molasses, and sat in tiny cabins drinking his noggin of rum, he felt himself a part of life at last and no longer a dreamer loitering in a shaded chamber just off the high-road of living. There was novelty in the new scene, material for copious notations, and he made the most of it for the better part of a year. After that a weariness, a dispirited acceptance of things, crept over him. The newness had worn off and, at heart, Hawthorne was not at all adapted to this busy intercourse. He was a creature of solitude and though for a time the unique aspects of an unknown scene might carry him on, as soon as it became a regular aspect of living an inborn need for loneliness welled up within him. When the novelty wore off there was no more copy in his occupation, and, though he used it or not, life was always copy to Hawthorne. The practicalities of living were to him no more than the shell of a spiritual life.

His social existence during this period was a matter of vague and tentative gestures. The Peabody family—and Sophia in particular—lured him into an emotional acceptance of life. When, in 1840, they removed from Salem to Boston, the contacts became more intimate. It was no longer a matter of letters but a matter of consistent companionship. Elizabeth Peabody became the administrative head of a shop that combined in itself a library, bookstore and homeopathic drug-store and this place of business speedily developed into a Transcendental center. *"The Dial"* was published there and certain figures, George Ripley and Emerson, for instance, were frequent visitors. Hawthorne began to hear about such things as German philosophy, Fourierism, "the better world," and the complete expression of one's self. It is to be suspected that these things did not concern him too deeply, although he may have accepted some of the radical notions of the time. He was essentially a conservative man, a hard-shell when it came to innovations of any sort. He was never a "come-outer." The world about him was still a semi-alien place and the exuberance of youth was a passion he was never to experience. He was not dull-witted (he was too much the fastidious dreamer for that) but he was disappointingly phlegmatic, a machine-man where politics and reforms were concerned. The idea of adventuring into the arena of life to combat the inimical lions of ancient misconceptions and dogmas never entered his head. This young giant of New England, this awkward Titanchild, might be rising to its feet and staggering after the brave banners of Emerson and a dozen lesser leaders but Hawthorne was not to be found in the vanguard, except by chance. Brook Farm was in the near future but Brook Farm was more a refuge than an experiment to the serious young man already intent on marriage.

In the meanwhile his arduous labors on coal and salt barges dammed his creative work. Except for a single story, *"John Inglefield's Thanksgiving,"* his output was confined to three volumes of children's stories—rehandlings of historic episodes from colonial and revolutionary annals-which were published from the Peabody shop in 1841. His long immersion in the chronicles of New England stood him in good stead here, and *"Grandfather's Chair," "Famous Old People,"* and *"Liberty Tree,"* (the three books to appear later under the collective title of *"The Whole History of Grandfather's Chair"*) reveal how neatly and simply Hawthorne could rewrite history for children. As pleasant as these works are it can hardly be affirmed that they added anything to his literary stature. They were essentially the labor of a man unable to cope with pure creative matter while diverted by a more or less repugnant occupation. He needed solitude, an emancipation from the world, long hours of revery, and the sleepy tedium of rural living, if he was to give the best that was in him.

So time passed to labors in Boston Bay, to the writing of children's histories, to the quiet companionship of Sophia, to the brief meetings with various Transcendentals, and then, in the spring of 1841, the governmental administration changed and Hawthorne (obviously in imminent fear of unceremonious removal) left the Custom House. This was the first of the three departures from governmental appointments endured by Hawthorne because of the ridiculous patronage system which regulated the affairs of the United States. We may guess that he was not too broken hearted over the shift in his fortunes. He had, for long, been quite satiated with his grimy portion of utilitarian life and the idea of pleasant green fields and ploughed acres must have glimmered pleasantly in his mind. But where was he to go? He did not possess enough money or courage to marry and the prospect of a return to Salem must have seemed gloomy enough. In Miss Peabody's shop, however, he had heard all about the new cooperative colony to be started at Brook Farm in Roxbury ("The Brook Farm Institute of Agriculture and Education," to give it its full name) and this appealed to him as an immediate haven. It offered several attractive features. Perhaps cottages would be built there eventually where young couples might live. There would be a fine and distinguished mingling of manual labor and mental development. Above all, it would keep the shy writer from his cursed solitude in the shadowy Salem chamber. So, by April, Hawthorne found himself installed as one of the gentleman-farmers at Brook Farm. Chance had made him one of the laborers for Utopia.

The spectacle of "Nath. Hawthorne, Ploughman," (he signed one of his letters from Brook Farm in that way) is both humorous and anomalous. He was no more adapted to farm-life than he was to the onerous duties of a measurer in the Custom House. In fact, Hawthorne was unfitted for all of the jobs which Fortune vouchsafed him. His place was in a quiet study where he could dream over his books and manuscripts. Yet there was a portion of his brain that recognized the virtues of labor, that-inspired by an old Puritan conception —believed that the sweat of man's brow induced by hard manual work was as admirable—perhaps more so—than the travail of the soul over the fantastic conceptions of fictions. Luckily enough, this portion of Hawthorne's brain was invariably subdued and silenced by the aesthetic consciousness that welled up within him.

It was in the midst of a snow-storm that Hawthorne arrived at Brook Farm and took his place among those idealistic workers who planned so naïvely and superbly a Utopia amidst the New England farms. As usual with him, the novelty of the experience aroused an enthusiasm that abated almost as quickly as it grew: He had put a thousand dollars into the undertaking (the greater part of his savings from the meager Custom House salary) and in the back of his mind always was the idea that here might be reared that little cottage to which he intended to bring a wife. He started work with some gusto, attacking piles of manure with a dung-fork, milking cows in the most inexpert manner, chopping wood, and hoeing beans. The picture of the sensitive writer (no longer young but now thirty-seven years old) clad in a heavy smock and stomping along (in New England they do not stamp but stomp) in tremendous cow-hide boots with soles two inches thick is worth loitering over. He was certainly not unduly feverish about the future of mankind or the ideals behind the Brook Farm experiment. Emerson, who viewed Brook Farm from afar as a Transcendental Picnic, probably understood the futility of the undertaking no better than Hawthorne.

But Hawthorne imagined he had something personal at stake. It was his future. He wanted to marry and in order to marry he needed a home. Brook Farm offered a slim enough opportunity but there was some hope that the colony might last. As time went on, however, Hawthorne grew skeptical. He also grew tired of manual labor and five months after he first picked up the dung-fork he admitted his weariness. "Even my Custom House experience," he noted, "was not such a thraldom and weariness; my mind and heart were free. Oh, labor is the curse of the world, and nobody can meddle with it without becoming proportionably brutified! Is it a praiseworthy matter that I have spent five golden months in providing food for cows and horses? It is not so." This was in August, 1841, and, though with the interruption of a return to Salem and several visits to Boston and nearby towns, Hawthorne was to remain until the spring of 1842, he was, from the time of this first unrest, never a real part of the colony.

He went about his labors doggedly for a time and then eased himself out of them and became more of a boarder than anything else. He made a few friends—not many, and conversed with the dynamic Margaret Fuller, always with a cautious and critical eye cocked at her. He wandered about and saw flowers and woodlands and lonely roads and sunsets. He was, in a last analysis, a lost soul among these wordy theoretical disciples of a foggy Utopia. The unceasing observance that was so much a part of his solitary nature stored up impressions which were to be translated into the pages of *"The Blithedale Romance"* some years later, and that is about all that Hawthorne got from his sojourn at Brook Farm. He was simply not the type of mentality to assist at experiments. He could not let himself go. Self-consciousness undoubtedly played its part in this careful withdrawal of himself from anything that smacked of freakish propensities. "The real Me was never an associate of the community," he noted, "There has been a spectral Appearance there, sounding the horn at daybreak, and milking the cows, and hoeing potatoes, and raking hay, toiling in the sun, and doing me the honour to assume my name. But this spectre was not myself." Like many dreamers he could detach his superior intelligence from his physical manifestations and watch the body at its labors much as one stranger observes another.

Hawthorne's literary work suffered as badly at Brook Farm as it had suffered while he was measuring coal for an ungrateful government. Another children's book was produced, *"Biographical Stories for Children,"* and the enlarged edition of *"Twice Told Tales,"* a volume with twice as many stories included, was ushered from the press of James Munroe and Company in two volumes. That was all. For nearly three years now his creative faculties had lain dormant although the pen had been intermittently busy in his hand with children's stories and the voluminous entries in his note-books. He was waiting for that milieu which would give him the peace he desired to settle down once more to hard literary creation. Of course, this milieu was to include Sophia. She was uppermost in his mind always and now that she had recovered from the invalidism of years, her chronic headaches disappearing at this time, Hawthorne set his heart upon an immediate marriage, be the prospects what they might. If he did not marry he would sink back again into the drab lotos-land of Salem, there to hide in his chamber until the end of time. There is reason to believe that he feared this, that he realized in some measure the ominous threat of his own inclination for solitude. He was also very much in love. It was with some trepidation, then, that he broke the news of his impending marriage to his mother, and his relief must have been great to discover that the wise old lady (for all of her retirement from the world) had long ago observed in what direction things were moving for her son and was quite agreeable to the proposed wedding. Hawthorne was thirty nine years old and Sophia was thirty two. They were no longer in the spring of life when they were married on July 9, 1842, at the Peabody house in Boston. Hawthorne had left Brook Farm with no regrets some months before. He was now on the verge of that decade wherein he was to create all of his best work except *"The Marble Faun."*

Between two tall gate-posts of rough hewn stone (the gate itself having fallen from its hinges at some unknown epoch) Hawthorne and his wife, at the termination of their three hours' honeymoon journey from Boston, saw the home in which they were to spend the first three years of their married life. The gray front of an old parsonage looming at the end of an avenue of black ash trees stood before them. This was the Old Manse, a dwelling set back from the town-street of Concord and waiting patiently for the subdued domesticity that was to inhabit it. The story of Hawthorne's occupancy of this moss-grown building is a story of shadows, of dim figures moving circumspectly and silently through long days of sunshine and rain and snow while the intellectually-enfevered town of Concord pursued a varied orbit in a different direction. It would not be accurate to assert that Hawthorne took no part in the Concord life of his day. Emerson, living nearby, came to converse with him. He wandered about the fields with Ellery Channing. He even went boating with the big-nosed Thoreau. There was Margaret Fuller to perturb him slightly with Transcendental arguments. Inside the Old Manse occasional visitors rippled the calm surface of the days, George Bradford, for instance, or the mildly insane Frank Farley from Brook Farm, or the bustling George Hillard come with news of the more suave Cambridge group which at that time was already dominated by the dapper Professor Longfellow. But these interruptions were no more than slight stones flung into a pool. The tiny concentric circles spread rapidly and merged into the still expanse of lonely living. The confirmed solitary was at peace at last except for the irritating prick of poverty which continued to urge him into gestures of some sort.

Hawthorne's life at the Old Manse, then, was a sort of New England idyl. Although he was very near "the rude bridge that arched the flood" none of the exalted passion that animated those longvanished farmers who treated the British to the smell of gunpowder throbbed in his veins. The Old Manse was a ghostly house to the curious burghers of Concord who passed it always with an eye cocked for the withdrawn inhabitants. The dark windows gloomed across the grass at night with no lights behind them. Now and then the old coachman from the station set down a fare before the posts from which the unused gate had fallen. It was not often, however, and we may be sure that the old ladies of Concord put their heads together over their steaming cups of green tea and conjectured as to whether it was a living man or a phantom that appeared in the market-garden and hoed with the meditative air of a Greek philosopher. The spirit of solitude invested this ancient edifice with an autumn mantle. It was the sort of place that might have inspired a serious-minded romancer to curious thoughts, thoughts not gloomy in themselves, perhaps, but yet touched with that every light which partakes as much of the hidden life beyond the actualities of existence as it does of the daily phenomena of living.

Yet life went on in the Old Manse and sometimes in the fields and on the river. It would never do to give an impression of Hawthorne as a gloomy and embittered solitary hiding from Time in the creaking chambers of a dusty parsonage. The lamp-light glowed brightly enough on the sturdy walls and if the outside world was more or less held at bay this does not predicate that a smaller and more personal world did not exist within the soft ring cast by the yellow flame. Hawthorne, in spite of the mounting irritation of poverty, was as happy as he could be. He had Sophia with him and Sophia adored him. He was her Endymion, her Apollo, and he took a grave joy in pleasing her, in attending to various chores, in washing dishes, in cooking, in reading to her during the long New

England evenings. To sit in the lamp-light and relive the passages of Macaulay, of Shakespeare, of Spenser, was a sort of vicarious existence for him. And when he was writing (for now that he had his freedom from the chains of ulterior obligations he seized his pen again) Sophia could continue her art-work, her sketching and painting and modeling, for she was a confirmed dilettante of the pictorial arts. Thus the quiet household continued its placid way.

Hawthorne had already impressed his subdued personality on his few friends. They understood his strange temperament and accepted his silence and respected his involuntary desire not to be drawn out of himself. Thus one acquaintance speaks of meeting him at Emerson's house about this time: "There were various men and women of note assembled, and I, who listened attentively to all the fine things that were said, was for some time scarcely aware of a man who sat upon the edge of the circle, a little withdrawn, his head slightly thrown forward upon his breast, and his bright eyes clearly burning under his black brow. As I drifted down the stream of talk, this person, who sat silent as a shadow, looked to me, as Webster might have looked, had he been a poet,—a kind of poetic Webster. He rose and walked to the window, and stood quietly there for a long time, watching the dead white landscape. No appeal was made to him, nobody looked after him, the conversation flowed steadily on as if every one understood that his silence was to be respected. It was the same thing at table. In vain the silent man imbibed aesthetic tea. Whatever fancies it inspired did not flower at his lips. But there was a light in his eye which assured me that nothing was lost. So supreme was his silence that it presently engrossed me to the exclusion of everything else. There was very brilliant discourse, but this silence was much more poetic and fascinating. Fine things were said by the philosophers, but much finer things were implied by the dumbness of this gentleman with heavy brows and black hair. When he presently rose and went,

Emerson, with the 'slow, wise smile' that breaks over his face, like day over the sky, said:

> 'Hawthorne rides well his horse of the night.' This was the Hawthorne of the period of the Old Manse, "a man who sat upon the edge of the circle, a little withdrawn." The new spirit of the times was already a noticeable phenomenon and Hawthorne was conscious of it. He was present at its inception and he must have followed its growth for too many of his acquaintances were a part of that brave, often deluded, sometimes freakish group for him not to have been aware of the troubled exalted currents that permeated the chilly air above the bustling New England towns. In a faint, almost lackadaisical, sort of way he was interested and moved by this new spirit. But he could not be a part of it for his solitude restrained him from an immediate mingling in the vexed problems of the day; his sluggishness of temperament so far as the practicalities of living and "causes" were concerned did not possess enough self-volition; and his inborn aesthetic concern with letters lifted him above and apart from any intense humanistic manifestations.

During his three years residence at the Old Manse he fairly exhausted his vein as a narrator of short pieces. The necessity for immediate money was always before him and, as rapidly as he could, he flung his small, polished stones of literature at a somewhat insensitive public. This need for money was aggravated by the birth of his first child, Una, on March 3, 1844. More than ever, it was necessary for him to keep afloat. Therefore he wrote for such varied publications as *"The Boys' and Girls' Magazine," "The Pioneer," "The Democratic Review,"* which, alas, failed, and *"Graham's Magazine."* He edited the *"Papers of an Old Dartmoor Prisoner,"* and he assisted his friend, Horatio Bridge, in revising that naval officer's *"Journal of an*

African Cruiser." The new tales which he wrote were collected under the title of *"Mosses from an Old Manse"* and published by Wiley and Putnam of New York shortly after he left Concord for Salem in 1846. With this book his career as a writer of short sketches may be said to have reached its apogee and end, although he was still to collect another volume of early pieces and give them to the public. By 1846 Hawthorne was forty-two years old, and, though he possessed an unquestioned place as a creator of short tales, those greater works that were to place him quite definitely in the front rank of New England writers were still to be made public. Two-thirds of his life had passed and he was yet to cement his position as a creative genius. How different is the comparison between him and that other fellow-student and writer from Bowdoin, Longfellow. That facile versifier at the age of forty-two had to his credit, omitting translations, eight popular books, including "Evangeline," (the suggestion for which he received from Hawthorne), *"Voices of the Night," "Ballads and Other Poems,"* and *"The Belfry of Bruges and Other Poems."* He had traveled and seen the major part of the European world. He was the friend and intimate of such famous men as Charles Dickens and Washington Irving. And, most important of all, he was esteemed and highly popular with a huge public. In 1846 Longfellow had thirty-six years of adulation before him while Hawthorne had but eighteen years of his life left. It is in such ways that Destiny moves.

Hawthorne's claim to fame at this time was based on (roughly speaking) a hundred short stories and sketches. It had taken him twenty years to write them. If he had never written anything else he would have survived through these stories, survived as a gently growing provincial writer picturing his particular terrain with the cleverness of the solitary observer. The immanence of genius is here but, more often than not, it is but vaguely adumbrated. There are obvious reasons for this vagueness of emphasis. In the first place Hawthorne, as, a young writer, had no peculiar and dominating objective. He wanted to write because writing came to him easily, but, after all, he had nothing especial to say. Therefore he seized upon anything that occurred to him and as nothing occurred to him—rapt away from life as he was and always imbued with a coldness of passion—but the immediate facts of an eventless career in a small town or the dim resuscitations of historical figures out of dusty old chronicles he turned to them and made the most of them. Sometimes his sketches read like the conversation of a man talking softly to himself. As he continued to write he continued to develop and his aesthetic consciousness grew as he matured. A far-away nebulous objective appeared on his intellectual horizon, an objective adumbrated in some of the fantastic tales and receiving its growing urge from that Puritan consciousness of sin and the dark battle of conscience. Hawthorne grew in stature steadily as a writer as the slow seasons passed, and, eventually, he who had merely set down his fancies and observations as a solitary creature who needed this outlet as a means of expression and a proof that he was alive became a creative artist with an objective clear to us now but, perhaps, dim to him then.

While Hawthorne was struggling with the deplorable problem of life, turning out his short tales with that slowness of composition peculiar to him and whipping himself to new endeavors in spite of the natural lassitude of his being—a lassitude connived at and developed by that decade or more of doing nothing in the quietude of the Salem house, his friends, particularly Horatio Bridge and Franklin Pierce, bethought themselves of the shy writer's predicament. The idea of giving Hawthorne a push forward seemed reasonable enough and they cast about for a means to this laudable end. It is doubtful that Hawthorne demanded any aid. His meager income kept him barely afloat and he knew that he would have to relinquish the Old Manse in the near future, for the heir to that ancient estate was already in the offing and clamoring for the house. The first inclination that beset Hawthorne was a removal to Salem and yet he feared this return It would not mean too much of a relapse into his former obscurity for he possessed a wife and child now and a certain modicum of fame and yet it meant a return to a curiously unloved community. Still, something must be done. He could not exist as a writer—primarily a hack-writer—because his own lethargy thwarted in him the possibilities of the necessary unceasing flow and production of the adaptable hack. He needed an anchor to windward.

Then James Polk was elected President of the United States. This was the political change that Hawthorne's friends desired and they took immediate advantage of it. The writer was to be hoisted into another political post. That patronage which had cast him out once was to take him in again. There were meetings to which various Senators were inveigled (Bridge being a moving spirit) and possible appointments were discussed. The idea of a Consulate floated in the air. The Legation at China was put forward. A clerkship in the Charlestown Navy Yard actually materialized but was refused by Hawthorne. Finally the friends concentered on Salem. The Post Office was broached first but various antagonistic influences kept Hawthorne from it. Letters were written and personal calls were made and arguments were put forth and, finally, on March 23, 1846, Nathaniel Hawthorne received his appointment as surveyor of the Salem Custom House. After a few years of release and comparative calm he was forced back into the drudgery of utilitarian life.

Even before the appointment reached him Hawthorne had removed to Salem with his family settling down in the Herbert Street house where he remained for some time. It was there, with the ghosts of his own lonely youth about him, that he wrote the introduction to the "Mosses

From an Old Manse, that gentle description of the haven where he had been initiated into the calm satisfactions of married life. Curiously enough, he does not seem to have looked back with any great regret at those years when he was his own master but rather to have entered upon his duties as surveyor with some degree of enthusiasm. Those inborn Puritan urges which demanded a life of practical usefulness and suggested that scribbling sketches was no more than the wasting of one's heritage rose to the surface of his nature again. He was periodically troubled by these apparent doubts of the usefulness of the writer's fancy. Luckily enough, these misgivings were rather feeble in comparison to the creative urge that gave sustenance to Hawthorne's mind. Indeed, his Puritanical inhibitions were curiously attenuated in him. They existed as dark deposits in the blood and they shaped his mind to some extent but, for the most part, he could see them in a coldly detached manner, could turn them over and over, so to speak, and meditate upon their curious impulses. He was, after all, a Puritan who had eaten of the lotos and who was, therefore, lethargic from sleepy syrops that coursed through his slow-moving blood and who could recline in a trance of the utilitarian, religious, and sociological faculties while his aesthetic intelligence remained awake and observant. From this trance he saw life unsteadily and by piecemeal, but what he did see he saw with a surprising clarity. Now and again the sharp summons of Duty (as that wry-faced goddess was named in New England) reached his ears but it was only when his purse was empty and he had reached the end of his rope.

The great days of Salem as a sea-port had long passed and Hawthorne's duties in the Custom House were not too onerous. He has told the story himself in that excellent and slightly spiteful introduction to *"The Scarlet Letter"* and it is hardly necessary to do more than glance at these years. At first, as usual with him, he was pleased with the novelty of his position; but as the months crept along and the creative instinct that had flowed so freely at the Old Manse became choked and dammed he experienced again that curious suffocated sensation which was the reaction from uncongenial toil. Sitting in the time-discolored building and observing the dry lot of old pensioners who made the Custom House more a club than a hive of business, plodding through the routine of the day or nosing through the yellowed files of ancient records in the deserted rooms above him, strolling back to the Herbert Street House and later to a home of his own on Chestnut Street and still later to a dwelling on Mall Street which was shared by Madame Hawthorne (now well along in years) and his two sisters, he squandered three seemingly eventless years. Yet vast albeit imperceptible changes were creeping over him and recoloring or rather deepening the already obvious coloring of his somber temperament. Although the shabby facts of daily life impinged drearily on his days it is perceptible now (with the aid of the far perspective of time) that his creative instinct was stretching to its full stature. Perhaps the instinctive rebound from the down-at-heels port and the tobacco-chewing mortals who crossed and recrossed his dreaming vista gave a strange and paradoxical strength to the inner self that was the essential Hawthorne. A great dusky orchid with petals stained by the sad hues of an old New England twilight of the soul was already growing out of the dark soil of the Salem port.

It is unbelievable that the burghers of Salem did not pause and stare after the Hawthorne of this period, for he must have been an extraordinary figure even in a physical sense. He had a massive head and a broad chest and he walked with a great stride. Although his silence may have been oppressive there was a still daemon that sat behind this veil of wordlessness and looked out with a sharp penetrativeness at the world that surged by so sluggishly. He was a strange lion in captivity. He could not see with the sweet clarity of Emerson, for instance, but his instincts spoke to him constantly and he escaped from his unlovely cage by a swift flight into the empyrean of his imagination. His shyness now had resolved itself into a deliberate preference for solitude although he mingled with some frequency with certain companions at the Custom House and in the taverns. At least, these somewhat illiterate personages could not pick his mind or peer into his inner self. He could maintain his intellectual solitude among them, a thing he could not hope to do if he attempted social incursions on "the" Salem of the day. When Hawthorne, after a three years' tenure of office,, was dislodged from the Custom House through the chicanery of certain individuals a charge of "loafing round with hard drinkers" was brought against him. There was possibly some semblance of fact for this accusation although it was obviously a straw desperately grasped at by those small-town politicians to serve their malicious and personal end. Hawthorne obviously drank (he mentions liquor time and again in his note-books and letters) but so did everybody else in New England. Longfellow, for instance, had the finest cellar of wine in Cambridge. Hawthorne, however, was never an inordinate tippler. If he had been he could never have done the work that he did.

The three years in the Salem Custom House, therefore, (until the final period of vexed political imbroglio) were dull and quiet. During the summer of 1846 another child, Julian, was born, and Hawthorne now had two children to observe and journalize about. When the family moved into its third Salem residence in a little more than a year, the house on Mall Street, Madame Hawthorne and her two daughters came along, too, and the recluse mother was given a suite to herself quite separate from the rest of the family. There she sat growing weaker as time made its inroads upon her. Hawthorne went out but seldom in the evening although he had become an officer of the Salem Lyceum and sometimes attended lectures there. In November, 1847, he began writing and the result within a year included such productions as *"The Snow Image," "The Great Stone Face," "Ethan Brand,"* and the remainder of the new tales and sketches that were to make up, with some older retrieved matter, his last volume of short pieces of fancy. He found it difficult to compose. It was like wrenching a tooth forth to get an idea out of his head. As a matter of fact he had exhausted himself as a short story writer, and, at the same time, that dark orchid was steadily growing in his mind. In *"Endicott and the Red Cross,"* one of the historical sketches in *"Twice-Told Tales,"* had appeared the following description of one of the characters in the crowd: "There was likewise a young woman, with no mean share of beauty, whose doom it was to wear the letter A on the breast of her gown, in the eyes of all the world and her own children. And even her own children knew what that initial signified. Sporting with her infamy, the lost and desperate creature had embroidered the fatal token in scarlet cloth, with golden thread and the nicest art of needle-work; so that the capital A might have been thought to mean Admirable, or anything rather than Adulteress." This personage had sunk into Hawthorne's consciousness and his somber imagination, subconsciously at first, perhaps, began to weave the thin veils of romance about it. It was this subject that was tugging at him during the last year or so of his incumbency of the Custom House and when the underhanded political attack reached its head and Hawthorne was cast forth for a second time from the meager bosom of a thankless country, he was, at last, free to begin work upon what was to be his masterpiece. Sophia had put aside a portion of her household expenses each week and this miserable sum, together with a few belated payments from magazines and even a sum made up by friends, carried the much-harassed author through. Hawthorne was forty-five years old in 1849 when he set actively to work on *"The Scarlet Letter,"* the book that was to be the great turning-point in his life.

He was not to labor at this work with any degree of case or liberation of mind. In the first place, he sat in the Mall Street house and wrote against time, against the ominous specter of disaster, and without too much hope for the future. Then, while he was in the midst of his creation, Madame Hawthorne became ill and died. The old lady had gone to join her sailor husband after long years of Hindoo-like solitude and the matriarchal shadow that had cast its somber outline over forty years of Hawthorne's life was removed for all time. The illness and death of his mother created an abrupt hiatus in the progress of *"The Scarlet Letter,"* but, after the last dolorous ceremonies were completed, Hawthorne fled again to the dusky refuge of his theme. Sickness beset the Mall Street house and Hawthorne himself suffered from an intolerable earache. Still the work went on. The more worldly Elizabeth Peabody came to the rescue and wrought some order out of the jangled ill-luck of the ménage. Hawthorne, however, stuck doggedly to his task. He was not sure of himself but he persisted, for the daemon of creation stood at his elbow and whipped him on with a ferocity that it had never exhibited before.

In the early winter of 1849 the bustling Boston publisher, James T. Fields, who had taken over Hawthorne's volumes of short tales from the bankrupt firm of Wiley and Putnam, appeared on the scene. He came with a burst of enthusiasm and a heartening faith in the Salem writer. The story of the encounter (a momentous one in Hawthorne's career) has been outlined often enough before. Fields found the writer hovering over a stove in his icy study. Hawthorne was in a most despondent frame of mind but Fields strove to cheer him up by persisting that it was time for publication. "Nonsense," gloomed Hawthorne. "What heart have I to write anything, when my publishers have been so many years trying to sell a small edition of the *'Twice Told Tales'*?" Fields overrode all of Hawthorne's selfbelittlements, his doubts as to a publisher risking money on him, even his intimation that he had written something. There was a bureau in the study and Fields accused Hawthorne of having a manuscript concealed in it. The despondent writer appeared surprised but shook his head, and Fields, knowing that his train would start for Boston soon, rose to go. As the publisher hurried down the stairs he was called back by Hawthorne who thrust a rolled manuscript into his hand, saying: "How, in Heaven's name, did you know this thing was there? As you have found me out, take what I have written, and tell me, after you get home and have time to read it, if it is good for anything. It is either very good or very bad,-I don't know which." On his way to Boston, Fields read the manuscript which proved to be the germ of "The Scarlet Letter."

The entire personality of the Hawthorne of this period is implicit in the story. He is uncertain of his own powers. He is shy. He is easily discouraged. He is naturally somber. All of these traits are quickened and strengthened by years of solitude that have deprived Hawthorne of the power of estimating himself in comparison with other beings.

Once encouraged, however, Hawthorne returned to his labors, revised his manuscript, and, at the astute suggestion of Fields, enlarged it to novel length. *"The Scarlet Letter"* had been originally conceived as a longish short story to be included in a projected volume that was to be titled *"Old Time Legends: together with Sketches, Experimental and Ideal."* Now that it was to occupy a single volume by itself Hawthorne found scope for all of his powers and for all of the nuances of the dark theme that so absorbed him. By February 3, 1850, the final touches were put to the script and in April it was issued from the press in an edition of five thousand copies that were immediately sold out. A new printing was instantly under way. The long years of mere local fame were at an end for Hawthorne and he now stepped (or, rather, was pushed) into the full limelight, such as it was, of the era. *"The Scarlet Letter"* created a furore and the shy blinking recluse (much to his amazement and rather frightened delight) found himself treading an international stage.

"The Scarlet Utter" is the completest epitome of Hawthorne's genius. It contained all the urges that had made his short tales unique and nothing that he was to do after it revealed any facets that were not implicit in the curious handling of the tragedy of the Reverend Arthur Dimmesdale and Hester Prynne. Out of this single book the spiritual nature of a man may be deduced with a surprising degree of amplification. Scant attention has been paid in this study to the peculiarities of Hawthorne's short tales and sketches but the arbitrary dismissal of that work was made with a purpose. There is nothing of importance that may be said about the short tales—in so far as an aesthetic and philosophical attitude may be predicated—that may not be indicated in a consideration of *"The Scarlet Letter."* The man who was to write this novel was adumbrated (dimly and insufficiently enough at times, it must be confessed) in the brief compositions of *"Mosses From an Old Manse"* and *"Twice Told Tales."* In *"The Scarlet Letter"* the reader of Hawthorne has the first clear fusion of all the writer's virtues as well as those various vices of conception and handling that render his work, in spite of its peculiar excellence, the work of a parochial thinker and artist. Hawthorne never got clear of the entangling dusky web of old New England but he translated the taciturn and repressed passion of that extraordinary corner of the world into a clear albeit darkly stained amber. There is a glow in it but it is never a warm glow. It is a world etched in moonlight and with a thin rain-cloud across the face of that moon, hovering above the tall pine trees and the white spires of many churches.

"The Scarlet Letter," at a first and cursory glance, is the history of a triangle set down in a Prynne, she who wears that badge of shame, the scarlet letter A, embroidered on the bosom of her gown; and the husband is old Roger Chillingworth, the self-appointed physician to Dimmesdale. But a closer reading of the book brings forth the fact that this is a triangle after the event, so to speak. The sin has been committed and Hawthorne is concerned only with the results of that sin, with its mark—growing more and more terrible as time passes—on the two men. His problem, then, is what effect will the consciousness of sin have on these people when one of them is a sensitive and neurotic creature who has concealed his participation in the sin, while another has suffered from the public obloquy of revelation, and a third is an old man eaten up with the jealous madness of revenge. Hester, betrayed by the birth of her illegitimate child, has stood on the pillory with the terrible letter on her breast and has nothing more to face than the slow years of ridicule and the stony path of regeneration. But Dimmesdale, the accomplice in her guilt, preaches each Sunday from the pulpit while the secret consciousness of his sin eats into him. Watching him with a malevolent eye night and day is old Roger Chillingworth, the husband, who waits with a fiendish patience the ultimate resolution of the situation. Hawthorne is not concerned with the sin as a sin. That, curiously enough, was a mere starting point for him and the great passionate love that must have existed between Hester Prynne and Arthur Dimmesdale is but a shadowy specter in the far background of the book. Only once is there a striking reference to it and that is when Hester cries out: "What we did had a consecration of its own. We felt it so! We said so to each other! Hast thou forgotten it?" during her last painful interview with Dimmesdale in the forest. In this flashing instant Hawthorne springs clear of all Puritan influences. But that outbreak —which might be a theme in itself for such a book —is but an instant's flare on the somber highway of *"The Scarlet Letter."* Hawthorne, after

all, is interested only in the effect of the hidden and festering sense of guilt which is slowly consuming Dimmesdale, and, in a last analysis, he becomes the center of the book, although the real protagonist, perhaps, is no more than a little letter embroidered on a bit of cloth. The Puritan consciousness of sin, evinced before in some of Hawthorne's short tales, is the dark thread that the reader follows through the ghostly labyrinth of *"The Scarlet Letter."*

Hester's guilt is absolved through her public suffering, and her great and noble will and self-command change her very badge of shame into a symbol of a lost world rewon. Yet the problem of her happiness and her love is never resolved. Dimmesdale's problem, one feels, is solved when, at the last, he makes public confessional upon that very pillory where Hester once stood with her child in her arms and endured the mockery of the populace. Even though this confession is the herald of his death it is borne in upon the reader that the much-tortured minister enters that other world with peace in his heart. As for Chillingworth there is no end to his problem, for his attempted revenge, circumvented at the very last, by Dimmesdale's safety on the pillory from the stings and arrows of men, turns like a ravenous and disappointed hound and rends him apart. Hawthorne was never surer than in the handling of these three people and through the cold moonlight of his imagination they move as abstractions garmented in a chilled semblance of flesh.

The book is a moving series of symbols within a larger symbol from beginning to end. Hawthorne, always concerned with symbols, here brings them to their highest and most concerted pitch. Even as in the short tales he employs concrete objects to illustrate the most abstract end. The scarlet letter upon Hester's gown is an obsession that possesses a terrible life of its own. It dominates the book, gives a fitful and flaming hue to the texture of the theme, and drives its almost unbearable message into the startled mind of the reader. It is not, as some critics have asserted, overdone except in a single instance. It stands for Hawthorne's conception and, with a surprising artistry, he has grouped his characters about it and put them into the proper relation to it. The one moment in *"The Scarlet Letter"* when the symbolism seems overforced and difficult to accept is when the phenomenon of the scarlet letter appears in the heavens over the Puritan town. Even Hawthorne would not express this as a fact but intimated a doubt of his own statement. The idea of a scarlet letter burning out of the bosom of Arthur Dimmesdale like some sort of a horrible stigma is not too impossible and it forms a proper and inspired balance to the embroidered insignia on Hester's gown. Here Hawthorne, through a congenital fear of excess, perhaps, was wrong in casting a doubt upon the physical fact. It is invidious to assert that these symbols are weakened because of their obviousness, for, after all, Hawthorne's idea of reality differed in great measures from that of to-day. In *"The Scarlet Letter"* his characters were the subsidiary counters in a theme and the theme was all.

It is true that these characters are arbitrary manifestations of specific urges, that their reality is extremely thin and that they exist only in so far as their particular position in the tragedy calls for their existence. They are not made of flesh and blood so much as they are made of moonlight and abstract qualities. Little Pearl, for instance, that fantastical dancing cryptically-speaking child belonging to Hester and Dimmesdale, is no more than an animated symbol introduced to emphasize certain important moments in the limited but intense action of the book. Yet she fascinates the reader and is an indubitable part of the theme. And let it be insisted again, the theme is all. No, Hawthorne has not drawn character as character in this book although he was quite capable of creating actual personages. The reality of these characters is implicit in the reality of their emotional and mental reactions and it cannot be gainsaid that Hawthorne has so superbly endowed Hester, Dimmesdale, and Chillingworth that they plunge into the consciousness of the reader, impinge upon his brain, so to speak, and remain there fixed and unforgettable.

There is an air of unreality about the entire proceedings but it is less the result of a failure to create living personages in a recognizable milieu than it is the result of a careful aesthetic selectiveness on Hawthorne's part. His three characters—representing three sides to a theme which involves the consciousness of guilt—do not actually exist in a vacuum, but it is true that Hawthorne has subdued their background into avague picture. The Puritan town is visible but it is sketched hastily and the non. essentials are left out and it is observed, perhaps, through a thin mist. It is like the wood where Pelleas and Melisande meet. Because of this treatment the principal personages stand out in bold relief. It is as though a few characters were down front on a stage and far back of them hung a slightly faded drop-curtain on which was painted the scene of a Puritan town. The few properties, the pillory, a balcony, and such requisites, are brought forth as they are needed and then removed again. There is something Elizabethan in this although the spirit of the book is far from Elizabethan. Elizabethan, too, is the technic of the theme, the presentation, one after another, of a series of selected scenes. Hawthorne's long immersion in short sustained pieces assuredly instigated and crystallized this method of construction, this division of his book into compartments, each compartment giving a rounded picture in itself. It is a triumph of his artistry that this peculiar method of conceiving a novel does not invalidate the concerted unity of his theme. *"The Scarlet Letter"* may be a series of pictures, but each picture is so fastidiously related to the one which follows that the mosaic falls into a rounded and reasonable design.

This book, then, written over a period of doubt, death, sickness, financial embarrassment, and spiritual torture, is a clear triumph and vindication of Hawthorne's choice of literature as the objective of his life. He who had started to write because writing came easily to him now found that he had something essential to say. The far-away nebulous objective of some years before had materialized into something huge and visible. He was to go on now and produce two more excellent novels within a short space of time, the urge and the power for sustained labor being mightily strengthened in him by the surprising welcome vouchsafed *"The Scarlet Letter."* He was still far from being an integral part of the awakened New England impulse (indeed, his sustenance came from the bleak soil of the Puritan days) but that awakened New England could accept him and take as much of him as he was prepared to give.

The belated shift in Hawthorne's fortunes occasioned by the unexpected success of *"The Scarlet Letter"* had one immediate effect on his life. He could remove from Salem. It cannot be doubted but that he desired to get away from the frigid atmosphere of his native town. He had never been a part of it and though it attracted him through a cold unemotional tie of kinship, though the dust of his fathers spoke faintly to him from its soil, though the specter of his lonely youth walked its quiet streets in the twilight, he knew that now was the time to break clear and clean from it for all time. The unhappy incidents relating to his dismissal from the Custom House implicated Salem in some measure, and this probably embittered Hawthorne to a certain extent. Salem has been reproached for her aloofness toward her famous son but it must be remembered that Hawthorne never made any particular attempt to orientate himself in the contemporary life of his native town. He kept to himself with an almost fanatical rigor. Salem simply did not know him except as a taciturn, striding figure who dwelt, perhaps, in a cloudy world of his own. Hawthorne's Salem, after all, was the ghost of a

Puritan town that loomed nebulously by moonlight amongst the unlovely buildings of the actual community. So far as realities went he had little to do with them and still less affection to bestow upon them.

Therefore, when moneys from *"The Scarlet Letter"* eased his situation Hawthorne, regretfully freed from the influence of his strange mother and —to his own mind, at least—cast forth by the town of his nativity, looked about him and eventually fixed upon the Berkshire Hills in Western Massachusetts as a likely haven. In the late spring of 1850 he and his family were installed in a small story-and-a-half red brick house in Lenox. A short period of comparative calm became his portion and the quiet family life somewhat freed of financial troubles that ensued must be counted as one of the pleasantest oases in his life. He was now fortysix years old, a rather grave man who had weathered stormy periods. His health was not as good as it had been and already the disastrous claw of Time was on him. He had but fourteen years of life ahead of him.

Friends surrounded him at Lenox and the hermit was drawn forth in some measure from his dusky cave. He possessed a name and a standing now, and, though his solitary instincts held him somewhat aloof all his days, he managed to achieve a sort of social ease that had never been his portion before. At Pittsfield lived Herman Melville, already at work on his leviathan of novels, *"Moby Dick,"* and a curious friendship sprang up between him and Hawthorne. The emotional exertion seems to have been on Melville's side although it is apparent that Hawthorne responded in a friendly-enough fashion. Anyway, Melville made his frequent appearances and there were long conversations between the two men over a multitude of things including the existence of God. H'wthorne's religious affiliations were neuter. He did not attend church and he did not accept ironbound dogma. He had fought clear of that Puritan impulse. He certainly believed in a Divine

Providence and his mind was inextricably interwoven with moralistic threads of impulse. But he was not orthodox in the New England meaning of the word and it is possible that the depths of his intellectual probings contained some astounding and iconoclastic conclusions. Other friends besides Melville called at the red house, especially in the summer, and among these may be enumerated Fanny Kemble, Oliver Wendell Holmes, James Russell Lowell, James T. Fields, John O'Sullivan, Duyckinck, and Whipple. The neighbors were kind and attentive, and, to view the scene as a whole, Hawthorne found himself rather "set" as a literary figure.

Naturally all this was an incentive to further endeavor. He had broken clear of the short sketch or tale in *"The Scarlet Letter"* and the excitement of discovering a new form in which to express himself,—the novel, heightened the impetus of his creative powers. Ensconced in the rural pleasantry of Lenox he immediately cast about him for a new theme and after the idyllic summer had passed with its soothing freshening of his nature he set to work on *"The House of the Seven Gables,"* beginning it in September and finishing it in January. The book was immediately sent to Fields and as immediately published.

This new novel was a decided shift from the dark symbolism of *"The Scarlet Letter."* It was a book closer to earth, a work in which a recognizable New England was expressed, although, even here where Hawthorne strove to be as rational as possible, the faint gleam of that unearthly light that colored all of his work is perceptible. His mind moved through shadows, and, though a gentle humor might sparkle like sunlight through these shadows, it was no stronger than the pale beams piercing a New England forest of high solemn pines. Somewhere there was always silence, solitude, and twilight—the green twilight of the unstirred leaf. This detached and somber aspect of Hawthorne's genius was partly molded by his instinctive desire for solitude. He simply could not be a part of the world about him. He could hover on the edge of it and observe it with some degree of faint amusement but the idea of intellectual participation was repugnant to him. It is true that he possessed a rather inchoate idea of the need of practical labor and that he entered the somewhat dusty corners of public life with the conviction (a rather wobbly one, to be sure) that he was doing his duty; but his true heart was never in these brief flurries. He could divorce his intellectual and creative self from the every-day man and it was only this every-day man that walked the docks of Boston or Salem or sat in the Liverpool Consulate. The intellectual and creative self was lost in a lonely woodland where Time was a dream and life was but the shadow of living.

It was this curious inability to accept life at its face value or to divert his intellectual ardor to the problems of the day that restrained Hawthorne from any participation in the breaking-up of the old New England and the formulation of the new scene. Though the 1830s had ushered in another era, though it had produced a prophet in Emerson, Hawthorne was congenitally debarred from riding with the vanguard. He continued, instead, to ride his horse of the night and to sit that ghostly steed with a high degree of grace and indifference. The nearest that he could come to reality was in the modern scenes of *"The House of the Seven Gables"* and *"The Blithedale Romance,"* that was to follow so soon upon the heels of the first-named book. And these modern scenes, so suggestive of the short sketches of his earlier days, were matters of observation, the observations of a solitary man who stands by the wayside and meditates upon the characters who pass by.

"The House of the Seven Gables" is no more than a series of tales relating to one family and tied together by the common heritage of a curse. Hawthorne must have

been thinking of the legendary curse uttered against his own family by the condemned witch of long ago when he fixed upon this theme. Though the novel, to all intents and purposes, is the narrative of old Hepzibah Pyncheon's feeble attempt to preserve life in the crumbling house and to usher her brother, Clifford, back into the land of living things after his long years of imprisonment, this theme is dissipated through the insistence on the origin of the curse with its consequent picture of Puritan life. As a novel the book falls to pieces and the reader is confronted with varying ingredients that do not, by any manner of reasoning, form a unified ensemble. How different this is from the coherence of *"The Scarlet Letter,"* which, though also written in separate scenes, is tightly knit through a single dominating pulse. In this second story the reader has the tale of old Colonel Pyncheon and his usurpation of the land rightfully belonging to Maule, with the consequent curse uttered against the family by the swindled witch, for Maule is convicted of being in league with the devil. Then there is the tale of Alice Pyncheon and the hypnotic influence over her exerted by Maule's descendant. And, thirdly, to use a Biblical phrase not unknown to New Englanders, there is the modern tale of the old house inhabited by Hepzibah, her attempts to earn a livelihood by a penny-store, the return of Clifford from prison, the schemes of Judge Pyncheon to secure the secret to the treasure he imagines concealed in the house, and the removal of the curse by the marriage of Phoebe and Holgrave, the two representing the Pyncheon and Maule families respectively.

All of this is loosely tied together and the reader's interest in it is compelled through a series of delicately conceived pictures and every-day scenes. Such minor figures as Uncle Venner and little Ned Higgins stand out in more life-like quality than Clifford or Holgrave. One thing Hawthorne does do that is of prime importance, a thing that opened the door to following generations of novelists,—

he permeates his modern story with what Henry James would call "the sense of the past." Indeed, Hawthorne, so identified with the past in New England, so wrapped up in it, so to speak, might be expected to do just this thing and in *"The House of the Seven Gables"* he did it with an admirable delicacy and subtle sense of values. The Past, that curious groping chimera invisible to the ëye but felt as a stark presence, prowls through the ancient sevengabled house and makes the dwelling its own. It subdues the atmosphere to its peculiar emanations. It fastens itself upon the intelligence and subconscious gestures of the beings who inhabit the house. It merges with their spirits and becomes a part of them. There is something unearthly about this, something that translates the personages of the narrative into sensibilities trembling on the verge of an unseen world. As the mournful and bitter consciousness of the slowly-devouring sense of sin dominated *"The Scarlet Letter"* so does the shadowy and impalpable sense of the past invade and permeate *"The House of the Seven Gables."*

The characters themselves are nearer the frank realities of living than the few figures who walk so like ghosts through *"The Scarlet Letter."* Hepzibah Pyncheon is a triumph of portraiture. She is the withered and retired old maid blinking furiously in the light of day and long ago diverted from the practical problem of living. No one knew better than Hawthorne the curious fright of solitary people suddenly thrust into the maelstrom of contemporary existence, for he possessed three women in his own family who were somewhat tempered by a drastic abnegation of the world. It would be a gross exaggeration to insist upon a likeness between Hepzibah and Madame Hawthorne, for instance, and yet is it not possible that the novelist could better plumb the depths of Hepzibah because of his knowledge of his own mother? Certainly Hepzibah is drawn with a confident strength of characterization that is not to be found in any of the other people who circle about the seven-gabled house. Phoebe is the typical "good little maid," full of sunlight and cheeriness, that Hawthorne uses again and again to set off the darker hues of his more somber women. She stands to Hepzibah as Priscilla stands to Zenobia in *"The Blithedale Romance"* or as Hilda stands to Miriam in *"The Marble Faun."* These young girls are not cut actually from the same piece of cloth, for as characters they are well differentiated. Their likeness is implicit in the fact that they are all young New England girls essentially "good" and that all of them perform the function of foils to more somber and stronger-willed women who are made unusual through remarkable traits. Judge Pyncheon is not as convincing as either Hepzibah or Phoebe, and this is curious in that Judge Pyncheon was undoubtedly drawn from life. The explanation of this unreality seems to lie in the fact that Hawthorne's model was a man against whom he had a grievance (he was one of the men who played his part in ousting Hawthorne from the Salem Custom House) and that, therefore, there was a deal of vinegar mixed with the novelist's ink. The Judge becomes a rather stagy villain with a few Dickensian attributes. His pompous hypocrisy is emphasized to the detriment of reality. The other characters, Clifford and Holgrave, are thin and ineffectual figures realized only in so far as they perform certain functions in the working-out of the theme.

Certain attributes render *"The House of the Seven Gables"* Hawthorne's most representative book, the work best revealing his peculiar approach to life and letters. It was not without a rare selfunderstanding that he preferred this novel to his other achievements. In the first place, it is crammed with those small and carefully-conceived vignettes of observation that form so large a part of Hawthorne's instinctive art. A village street or a garden or a passing boy buying gingerbread figures or an old man meditating on the poor-house, these things found in Hawthorne a ready and sympathetic observer. They were the small phenomena of a New England town that he might see from the road-side and put down with a gentle humor and somewhat fastidious reserve in his note-books. No writer has bettered this particular style of writing in the long history of New England letters. It is limited, of course, limited as New England is limited to a certain "feel," and Hawthorne never got beyond this parochialism. Even when he was writing about England, as in *"Our Old Home,"* or about Italy, as in *"The Marble Faun,"* it was still the parochial New Englander writing, a New Englander, to be sure; on tour but still a man with the limited horizon of the born Salemite. Within his peculiar limits he rarefied and burnished his material to a point of high excellence, and, by the compelling astuteness of his aesthetic proclivities, lifted it to a plane that before him had not existed in New England, and which, relatively, could bear comparison with the best examples of English genre writing. *"The House of the Seven Gables"* is, therefore, an important book in the history of Hawthorne's intellectual career. It does not touch that bitterly unified peak of *"The Scarlet Letter"* but it is more revelatory of the writer's talent, more the "sort" of book for which he was equipped. It was not a book over which Hawthorne and Sophia might weep (as they did over *"The Scarlet Letter"* which must have been a great release for the novelist's welled-up and inhibited passion) but it was one that they could relish in the doing as a most satisfactory enunciation of Hawthorne's intelligence, sensitivity to local values, and twilit artistry.

The completion of *"The House of the Seven Gables"* found Hawthorne ready for the green solace of country peace. He was tired out now and it was time to draw in sail a bit and let the spring and summer be a sea of flowers and pastimes upon which to drift with his children until his drained resources again filled up. In May his third child, Rose, was born. The red house rang to the laughter of small people and Hawthorne fashioned toy boats and kites, went fishing and flower-gathering, and even strove (unsuccessfully, it appears) to teach his son and daughter how to swim. It was all idyllic, a far removal from the vexatious months in Salem. Hawthorne, freed in some measure from the intolerable vicissitudes of fortune in a corner of the world that had little to give the purely imaginative, found himself in comparative peace. It is true that he had the livelihood of his family to consider. He could not lecture as Emerson did or manage a college department as Longfellow but he could write and, though writing might seem a rather pusillanimous method of earning a living to a hard-shell New Englander, he made the most of his gift. By early summer his fingers itched for the quill-pen again and in six weeks in June and July he drafted *"A Wonder-Book for Boys and Girls."* His four months playtime came to an end.

The surprising ease with which he wrote this volume of ancient myths retold is adequate testimonial to his pleasure in the task. Hawthorne, it is very apparent, loved children. There was a gentle and simple side to his nature and it found its fullest release in his reactions toward little ones. He was a companion to his own offspring and he enjoyed nothing better than to journalize about them, to set down their remarks, to describe their various gestures. It is here, perhaps, that the fact might be noted that Hawthorne was not the dour pessimist that some commentators have suggested. He was morbid because he was unsure of his own abilities and he was restrained and silent because of long years of solitude and an inability to adjust himself to the social free-for-all of the day. But there is no reason to believe that he was particularly dour in the bosom of his family and he gave ample evidence of a sense of humor that sparkles like young sunlight through his books. It is true that he was naturally attracted to somber themes but it is equally true that he detached himself from these themes in a manner that few born New Englanders colored by ancient tradition could do. He stood beside his dusky creations and was not an integral part of them. It was so with life. He stood always at the side of life and never entered into it with that completeness of submersion that marked some of his companions in letters. Though he might be one in a group he never partook of the group spirit.

After he had completed *"A Wonder-Book for Boys and Girls,"* (and there is nothing to say about that work or its sequel, *"Tanglewood Tales,"* except that it is written with a sunny freshness and a gentle New Englandism that quite translates the pagan myths into innocent fables) he had the fullest opportunity to enjoy life with his son, for Sophia and the two daughters, Una and Rose, went East for a three-weeks' visit with the Peabody family. Hawthorne was left alone with Julian and the old negro cook and the result was a journal of some length describing the adventures of the masculine household. This inveterate habit of journalizing about the most inconsequential things was an integral part of Hawthorne's nature. Of course, in the New England of the 1840s and 50s the diary and day-book played a much more important part in life than it does to-day when mankind is too busy to set down the peccadilloes and scattered thoughts. It was quite the habit to keep a journal. Nearly all of the literary figures did. Hawthorne, however, was peculiarly susceptible to journalizing, for like most solitary men he could not dissipate his countless thoughts and observations in conversations. There was always a great residue left over for the pages of the note-book. It was the perfect refuge of the shy man.

As the autumn of 1851 advanced a restlessness pervaded Hawthorne. He had never stayed very long in any place except for the desolate years of his youth in Salem and now he felt again the call to transplant himself. The red house at Lenox had served its purpose. The weather was growing inclement. It was time to turn east again where most of his friends (or, rather, friendly acquaintances) were situated. Toward the last of November, then, he packed his family goods and removed to the dismal town of West Newton. This was but a temporary refuge for Hawthorne intended to buy a house, and West Newton, where he was put up by the Peabodys', was as good a spot as any from which to reconnoiter the surrounding territory. He would not go back to Salem for he had conceived a sort of mild hatred of the place and the family ties were broken. Madame Hawthorne was dead. His sister, Louisa, was still living in Salem with relatives, but Elizabeth was installed with a farmer's family on the coast not far from Salem, where she lived out her lonely existence over a period of thirty years.

Naturally Hawthorne was revolving a new book in his mind. West Newton was near Brook Farm and this may have accelerated the idea of *"The Blithedale Romance,"* although it is impossible not to believe that this book was in his consciousness before he came east. After *"A Wonder-Book for Girls and Boys"* he had arranged a volume of tales, *"The Snow Image, and Other Twice-Told Tales,"* but, except for a few of these stories, this matter had been dredged from old periodicals. Therefore, it did not represent any part of the growth and progress that was going on at this time. He was still concerned with extended work for the double success of *"The Scarlet Letter"* and *"The House of the Seven Gables"* had been an exhilarating factor in convincing him that the novel, after all, was his particular forte. He needed little encouragement to sit down to *"The Blithedale Romance,"* and this was his occupation during the winter at West Newton. It is possible that he took a few walks over to Brook Farm in order to refresh his mind regarding certain aspects of the community where he had marked time before his marriage. But these walks were hardly necessary. His mind contained all that he needed of Brook Farm for *"The Blithedale Romance,"* after all, was not a specific picture of anything that had happened but a story that needed a retired scene for its peculiar enhancement. The book was issued in May, 1852, and it proved to be neither so good as *"The Scarlet Letter"* nor so atmospherically compelling as *"The House of the Seven Gables."*

Yet it possessed one attribute which cannot be discovered in either of the two previous novels. It was a book written more in sunlight. The light of day floods it to a greater extent than may be discovered in *"The Scarlet Letter,"* where life is observed through a gray Puritan twilight, or *"The House of the Seven Gables,"* where the vague chimaera of the Past stalks invisibly through the shifting scenes. Hawthorne, in *"The Blithedale Romance,"* strove to be as rational as he could. He attempted reality with none of those vague overtones that are so integral a portion of his creative personality. However, he was not a realist and never could be one. Though he might observe with a discerning eye and set down small facts with an artistic punctiliousness his comprehension of reality was obfuscated by an indecisive romanticism that wavered between two worlds. The prime objective of *"The Blithedale Romance"* was to present the self-destruction of a typical New England reformer through his selfish fanaticism toward his own theory of philanthropism. Hollingsworth was not a characterization which could engage Hawthorne's imaginative sympathies with any high degree of sympathy or emotional reaction and this is felt in a reading of the book. He is real enough but one senses only a half-interested author behind his creation. Worst of all, this man, who is the real protagonist of the novel, is surrounded by the material of another type of book altogether, the relations between Zenobia and Priscilla, the mesmerism and Veiled Lady appanages, and the generally fantastic qualities that probably appealed much more to Hawthorne than the social experiment of Brook Farm or the philanthropic fanaticism of Hollingsworth. Because of this bad mingling of elements the book is immeasurably weakened and it comes as a distinct anticlimax to *"The Scarlet Letter"* and *"The House of the Seven Gables."*

Yet there is much to hold the reader here. That peculiar charm which Hawthorne diffused over his work is always present. There are several stronglywrought scenes, the chief one being that of the suicide of Zenobia, a tragedy suggested by Hawthorne's own activities some years before at Concord in rescuing the body of a suicide-girl. And there are certain characterizations that insist upon seeping into the reader's mind. Hollingsworth himself may be no more than an incomplete portrait but surely in Miles Coverdale there is more than a hint of Hawthorne himself. As to Zenobia, it is futile to inquire as to whether or not she is based upon Margaret Fuller. Certain of her attributes would suggest as much. She is, in effect, that large, dark, handsome woman with a secret past who charmed the imagination of Hawthorne so often and who appeared in such completeness and complexity in *"The Marble Faun"* as Miriam. It was in such types as this that Hawthorne's innate romanticism was given its fullest vent.

As usual, *"The Blithedale Romance"* is set in a pocket of time, so to speak, and removed from the rest of the world. The small group of characters play out their drama aided and abetted with a few subsidiary personages. They are unrelated to the great mass of existence. Hawthorne always isolated his characters in this way and fashioned the scenes wherethrough they walked into subdued backgrounds. The reader, therefore, who expects any sort of adequate approximation of the socialistic experiment of Brook Farm in this novel will be disappointed for it is not there at all. He will find a semi-romantic tale of two sisters interwoven with the emotional devastation that Hollingsworth, the reformer, leaves in his trail. And he will find a deal of Hawthorne's moral energy and indignation against an over-zealous and rabid instinct for the betterment of mankind. These major trends, together with the usual pertinent vignettes of life, make up the book. It is not a great book as *"The Scarlet Letter"* certainly is or an amazingly good book as *"The House of the Seven*

Gables" is, but it is an adequate book and it is full of a sunlight and humor that neither one of the earlier novels contained.

With *"The Blithedale Romance"* Hawthorne's active years as a writer came to an end. He had turned out three novels in as many years and it was, perhaps, time to halt. He was getting weary and his health was not as excellent as it had been although on the surface he gave no immediate signs of a debilitated constitution. While he was laboring at this last novel he had purchased The Wayside at Concord from Bronson Alcott and early in June the family removed to it from West Newton. There he started to work on a new series of retold myths to be called *"Tanglewood Tales."* Early in the summer his sister, Louisa, was drowned when she leaped from a burning steamer in the Hudson River. For a time Hawthorne was desolate. Grief always oppressed him and drove him back into his cave of loneliness there to brood upon the horrors of circumstances. But he was drawn forth from this by the advent of a political campaign, the result of which was to cause the greatest change of all in his life. His old friend, Franklin Pierce, now General Pierce of Mexican War fame, became a candidate for President of the United States and Hawthorne was approached to write the campaign biography of the hero.

Hawthorne was a child so far as politics went. He was reactionary in his inclinations, his blood running too cold to urge him into such foreign matters as liberalism and progress. It was not so much that he disapproved of progress as that he was congenitally incapable of working up any enthusiasm over it. He suspected change as do most men who live very much in the past. The idea, for instance, of becoming an active Abolitionist would have been anathema to him. He was content, in large measure, to see the world drift along provided his particular environment did not suffer any sea-change into something foreign and strange.

Now Pierce was pretty much of a reactionary but it is doubtful that Hawthorne took this to mind very much when he agreed to do the campaign biography. The thing that counted, after all, was friendship and Pierce had been his warm friend over a period of many years. It made no difference that the great majority of literary men were anti-Pierce. Partylines were but tiny things after all where friendship was concerned. Hawthorne put away his unfinished *"Tanglewood Tales"* and did the best that he could do with the rather undistinguished life of his friend.

The product was unimportant but apparently it did its little share, for Pierce was elected President and was accordingly grateful to Hawthorne. The novelist, of course, knew when he wrote the book that if Pierce was elected he (Hawthorne) would probably receive some plum of an appointment. Indeed, it was because of this probable reward that Hawthorne expressed some unwillingness to put forth his effort. He desired it to be understood that his incursion into political writing was occasioned by friendship and not for a possible reward. However, the reward was to come. After the campaign biography was finished Hawthorne turned back to the uncompleted script of *"Tanglewood Tales,"* finished it, and dispatched it to his publisher. The winter crept along and life went on quietly at The Wayside. In the early spring, Mrs. Peabody, Sophia's mother, died and a touch of sadness limited the simple pleasures of the household. President Pierce nominated Hawthorne to the Consulate at Liverpool and on March 26, 1853, the nomination was confirmed by Congress. At first, Hawthorne, still rankling at the thought of being rewarded for an act of friendship, was disposed to refuse the proffered honor but his publisher, Fields, a man of great common sense, convinced him that his duty to his family forbade any such refusal. It is to be suspected that Hawthorne did not need any strong arguments, for a peculiar vein of practicality often revealed itself in his thinking. He was not a practical man but he believed that he ought to be one and he made decided efforts to achieve that status, a status so praised in old New England.

This appointment marked the practical end of Hawthorne's career as a literary man in New England. He was still to write one of his most important novels but that was to be done in England after a long Italian sojourn and never again was he to do anything memorable in the quiet harborage of a New England home. He had lived through the great day of his corner of the world, that era stretching from 1830 to the late 50s which had brought to birth all the great New England figures, and he had hardly been touched by it. Yet it had prepared him an audience and it had made possible his very existence. He was to leave New England now with regret for the quietude of The Wayside (for he was, at best, a Wayside man) but with some anticipation of the foreign scene. There was not, it may be suspected, much intellectual ardor urging him toward Europe. He was too old for that. A man on the verge of fifty years is not looking for new intellectual angles or for reorientation in the scheme of things. But he was curious about Europe, especially England, and possibly he imagined that he might find a stimulus of sorts in the antiquity of the Old Country. Then, too, he possessed an obvious wanderlust. He had never lived very long in one place and though his wanderings had hitherto, with a few negligible exceptions, been confined to New England a restlessness constantly stirred within him. It must be remembered that a long line of seafaring Hathornes had preceded him, that these men had sailed distant seas and seen strange sights. Some of that old magic may have lingered in the blood of the rather tired middle-aged novelist who boarded the steamship "Niagara," Captain Leach commanding, on a sunshiny day in the latter part of June, 1853. Surrounded by his wife and three children and numberless boxes and receptacles he must have stood on the deck looking back a little bewildered at Bunker Hill.

Americans had gone to Europe before and Americans have gone since but it is doubtful if any figure quite comparable to Nathaniel Hawthorne has ever turned a mildly speculative eye upon the English scene. He was, in effect, a walking epitome of Puritan urges which were softened and rendered malleable by a congenital aesthetic consciousness. This man, standing on the verge of fifty years, with a typical New England wife of dilettante propensities and three small children, a recognized force in his own particular milieu, was curiously inhibited in his belated voyage of discovery to the Old World. He possessed neither the youthful zest of a Longfellow who had preceded him nor the analytic doggedness of a Henry James who was to follow him. He was, as they say in New England, "set" in his prejudices and matured capabilities of receptivity. It was quite impossible for him to strike an impartial attitude or to put himself in the other fellow's place or to plumb the deep well of English culture or to adjust his mentality to the daily phenomena of a scene that was both tantalizingly like and irritatingly unlike some few aspects of New England. The England of the late 1850s was a stage of industrial domination in many ways. It was the mid-Victorian era of smugness and squirearchy and Prince Albert and dull rectitude and the novels of Anthony Trollope. The laxness of the earlier era had been stifled by the righteous tidal wave of Victorian morals. The Queen had come fully into her own, and, with her darling Albert by her side, stood as the Guardian Angel of the Home. Life—at least in theory-was all roast-beef and goodness. Hawthorne undoubtedly sensed the "feel" of English life but he was incapable of orientating himself in it or drawing any lessons from it. In spite of his position in Liverpool as the representative of a foreign government and therefore a cog in the commercial wheel of the dirty city his four years in the Consulate never found him very far from the rôle of a tourist. He was on the outside always.

The Liverpool Consulate he found very similar to the Salem Custom House. It was the same old story of dreary details with dreary people in a dreary office. There was one outstanding difference, however, and that was when the clerk each afternoon brought in the neat rouleaux of gold and silver and copper which were Hawthorne's perquisites for the day. It was for this rather than for the glory of the Republic that the novelist—now stifled into silence for a number of years—endured his dull task. He saw before him the opportunity for financial freedom from material worries and in that freedom the prospect of greater literary endeavors. At the same time he must have suspected that his creative powers were weakening, that the three novels he had drawn forth from a reservoir that was deep rather than wide had nearly exhausted him, and that his health was steadily diminishing within his still sturdy form. The shadow of time was on him already although he had touched but half a century of years. Passing from Rock Park across the Mersey to Liverpool it is possible that he dreamed at times of the blessed freedom of the pen although we may be sure that he did not look back with too fond an eye on those comparatively free days at the Old Manse and in Lenox. He did not find a spiritual release in England but, at the same time, he exhibited but little nostalgia for New England. Rather was his dream of Italy and sunlit days unalloyed with tasks and obligations. Perhaps he did not realize that his greatest obligation was the obligation of his birth and that he would have to carry *that* wherever he traveled. His love for New England was a cold love and it was impossible for him, at his age and with his fixed outlook, to work up any great enthusiasm over any other land. He was on the outside of everything except himself and he was very much inside of himelf. It was both his curse and the secret of his genius. Man of solitude as he was, he had ossified into the eternal observer, the creature who looks fixedly but who does not partake. He saw England, then, as a foreign scene, as a spectacle into which he could merge by no manner of means. It was as though he had wandered upon a huge stage during a play and was mingling rather helplessly and critically among the actors.

Yet he had his social moments. He ventured upon dinners and visits and trips and even made a few speeches, discovering to his own bloodless satisfaction that he could get through a harangue without breaking down. At the same time he was possibly more at home with the piratical-looking sailors who crowded the Consulate and the swindling Americans who ran to him for aid which they rarely repaid. His few friends, notably Henry Bright and Francis Bennoch, sponsored him to some degree and led him into social bypaths that, perhaps, he never would have ventured upon by himself. He had ample opportunity, therefore, to embark upon a close study of mid-Victorian life, to elucidate it to himself, and to compare it with the New England scheme of living. It is true that his voluminous note-books continued to grow during this period, that he set down the various scenes and characters with whom he came into contact; still, there was no high degree of analysis perceptible. He saw all these things, saw them with a disconcertingly acute eye at times and set them down with a fine freedom of utterance, but he hardly profited by them. It was impossible for him to make a cosmopolite of himself; to the last he would remain a provincial figure wandered out of his New England milieu, a little restive occasionally at what he considered foreign barbarisms, a little villagy in his acceptance of the color and thunder of those great cities that heretofore had been no more to him than figments out of books. He was uneasy before the spectacle of Europe although his uneasiness was repressed by a certain gracefulness of demeanor, a dark and silent grace, to be sure. He could not drink in color and sound with an eager and romantic expectancy as Longfellow had done years before and neither could he race from notability to notability with letters of introduction as that more successful and urban-minded poet did.

Hawthorne may not have been more doubtful of himself than long fellow but he was certainly less volatile. The strong hand of custom drew him back into the twilight of his solitude and from that shadowy thicket he peered out at the world.

During Hawthorne's tenure of office he traveled through various portions of England, the Isle of Man, Wales, the Lake Country, London, and what he observed was put down carefully in his note-books. He could appreciate and understand the shifting vistas of landscape and ancient edifices but he could not realize that deeply-rooted sense of the Past which quickened about him wherever he went. Superficially he comprehended the ancient foundations of England but he was not excited by them. They brought him no message and inspired no pulse in him to faster beating. He was coldly observant of this as he was of the contemporary flurry of mid-Victorian life about him for the same reason,—namely, that he had congealed within, that he was irretrievably molded for better or for worse by the opportunities and vicissitudes of his fifty years of life in New England, a life passed in villages and amidst rural scenes. Until he came to England the largest city with which he had been in any way familiar was Boston and the Boston of the 1840s was in no sense of the word a metropolis. It was an overgrown town with all of the impulses of a town. Hawthorne had never been able to lift himself beyond the boundaries of the New England town, although his unquestionable genius had plumbed the depths of that particular Puritan nature that had made the New England town possible. His knowledge of the great world was narrow and one-sided and flawed by parochial impulses but this limitation did not invalidate his probings into the New England soul with its omnipresent consciousness of sin. He was a portion, although a detached portion, of the Puritan tradition and when he adjusted himself to it he could work miracles with his pen. But he was not, distinctly not, a portion of the Victorian scene (as a good Victorian he never would have dismissed Hester Prynne's sin so easily) and, therefore, he could not adjust himself to it. He could do no more than stand by, praise a little, blame a little, and wish—in the depths of his nature—that he were somewhere else. England miserably failed to reanimate his creative powers. Or, to put it another way, he miserably failed to take advantage of the English scene, a thing that is curious in a New Englander when we realize that he did strive to profit by the Italian scene in "The Marble Faun."

During the years he lived in England, Hawthorne also failed to take advantage of the opportunity to meet the prime literary figures of the day. He never talked with Thackeray, Dickens, Trollope, Tennyson, Swinburne, Arnold, or George Eliot. It is possible that he had no curiosity about them, that he felt them to be outside of his orbit. It is also possible that his years of solitude had hardened a certain sense of inferiority in him and that he felt he had nothing to give to these figures so to the fore. A sense of his village origins, of his social uncouthness, of his dispirited appearance in public, these things, too, may have had something to do with it. He satisfied himself with secondary figures, paying calls on old Leigh Hunt and that mid-Victorian fount of treacle, Martin Tupper, and meeting at dinner-parties Charles Reade and Douglas Jerrold and the Brownings. Richard Monckton Milnes, Lord Houghton, was one of the few English writers who strove to put himself out for Hawthorne but the American was so gloomy in receiving Milnes' well-meant effort that the Englishman thought he was disliked by his taciturn companion. It is quite possible that Hawthorne would have disapproved of some of the famous English figures he did not meet. Swinburne was but a boy in his early twenties and had published nothing, although he was somewhat of a phoenix at Balliol. It is safe to say that Hawthorne would never have liked Swinburne's early poetry. Thackeray might have appeared too cynical and Dickens too vulgar.

As for George Eliot, had she not been guilty of certain iconoclasms in domestic life? Trollope, however, might have pleased Hawthorne and it is regrettable that these two men, one of them the peculiar representative of the old New England tradition and the other the expositor of mid-Victorianism in fiction, did not meet and discourse about life and letters. As it was, Hawthorne's only close connection with English literary life was his imbroglio with Delia Bacon, an affair in which he lost a thousand dollars by backing the lady's book on the Bacon-Shakespeare theory and the lady's friendship as well by his lukewarm preface to the book.

In October, 1855, Sophia Hawthorne sailed to Lisbon where she remained as a guest of the O'Sullivans until June, 1856. Hawthorne, left with his son, led a fairly quiet life but after Sophia's return with her two daughters he began to bethink himself about his place and its monetary prospects. His emoluments had already been cut down by an act of Congress and, long before this, Hawthorne had become completely fed up with his job. Liverpool, to him, was a dirty hole. His restlessness was on him again, that restlessness which had taken him from Salem to Boston to Brook Farm to Concord to Salem to Lenox to West Newton to Concord to Liverpool. It was time to pack his household effects and remove elsewhere. Four years seems to have been Hawthorne's limit for holding any position and this, after all, is quite as long as any born writer should keep his creative gifts in subjection to his need for material aggrandisement. In the autumn of 1856, therefore, when James Buchanan was elected President and the weak Pierce was blessedly removed from office, Hawthorne decided to resign his place as Consul at Liverpool and to depart via France to Italy. He had already laid aside quite a sum of money for him and he could afford to look toward the immediate future with some degree of complacency and ambition. In a literary sense he had nothing to show for these four years except his note-books and journals out of which he was to subsequently dredge the essays that made up the volume called "Our Old Home," but it is certain that the idea of writing a new book was ticking somewhere in the back of his brain. He did not know what it was to be about, and, perhaps, he dimly imagined that Italy would supply the seed for it. Then, again, there is reason to believe that he had an English romance in mind. Anyway he looked forward to the Latin south with some degree of anticipation. It was to be a carefree time and he was to be master of himself and his days.

He did not look back at England with any regret as he set forth early in January, 1858, for the Continent. He had not been too unhappy in the "tight little isle" but neither had he been unduly worked up over the Victorian scene. His vague and tentative inroads on the intellectual life of England had been disappointing so far as he was concerned but this was, after all, his own fault. He had dodged the real intellectual life, fought shy of its social obligations, and failed to encounter those personalities who might best of all have represented intelligent mid-Victorian England to him. Instead of the larger figures he had been content with a third-rate poet like Milnes or a second-rate novelist like Reade or a journalist like Jerrold or a purveyor of pap like Tupper. Part of his abstinence from the intellectual scene was his own inveterate shyness, the result of his long years of solitude. He didn't like people to take an interest in him as an extraordinary figure and that, after all, was the only reason why any intelligent Englishman should take an interest in this quaint New Englander. "It is ungracious, even hoggish," he wrote in his note-book, "not to be gratified with the interest they expressed in me; but then it is really a bore, and one does not know what to do or say. I felt like the hippopotamus, or—to use a more modest illustration—like some strange insect imprisoned under a tumbler, with a dozen eyes watching whatever I did." It is exactly this "one does not know what to do or say" phrase that explains a part of Hawthorne's awkwardness in public. It was because of this that the well-meaning Milnes misunderstood him. That bewildered gentleman must have felt as though he were leading about a bear with a sore nose. Hawthorne's experiences in England, then, were onesided because of his own one-sidedness. He could not slide into the intellectual current. He could observe, but as everything is not on the surface in life he was bound, because of his method of observation, to misapprehend many things. It was a man who had not actually been a part of English life in spite of his four years' residence who hurried through Paris southward to Rome.

Rome! The Eternal City! *Mater Triumphalis!* We may imagine Hawthorne (and his wife in particular) scurrying south through Paris, through Lyons, through Marseilles, across the winedark sea of Ulysses, with pauses at Genoa and Leghorn and *Civita Vecchia*, to the City of the Seven Hills, thrilled with the prospect of historical and artistic and blithe Latin intimacies. We may imagine this but the actual picture of Hawthorne's venture upon Rome is something else altogether. What we do see is a sneezing, influenza-ridden gentleman in his mid-fifties huddled before an ineffectual fire ungratefully deciding that "Old Rome lies like a dead and mostly decayed corpse, retaining here and there a trace of the noble shape it was, but with a sort of fungus growth upon it, and no life but of the worms that creep in and out." And another sneeze nearly demolishes the feeble pretense of a fire!

It was in the midst of a cold, sleety rainstorm that the Hawthornes reached Rome and for some time thereafter the arctic weather retained its throttling hold on the joyous southern city of ruins, carnivals, and popes. The fountains of the Piazza were frozen and dirty little urchins were sliding on the ice. It was the dirt in Rome that made the first impression on Hawthorne. As he perambulated through the streets he looked down oftener than he looked up. Sophia might fly into rhapsodies over the Coliseum, St. Peter's, the Forum, and a hundred and one other sights but the observing realist in Hawthorne, unlifted by tourist-gush, saw a swarming unwashed humanity crowding through narrow, unclean thoroughfares. While the ruins were not exactly heaps of heathen rocks to him we may be sure that he did not find in them those lofty sermons in stones that the sensitive and idealistic observer is supposed to discover in Rome. He revered antiquity but this was an antiquity that was a stranger to his peculiar cast of mind. He needed an abrupt adjustment to it before he let himself go with any degree of emotion. Settled down in lodgings in the *Via Porta Pinciana* (where he remained for three months) he strove, therefore, in a rather coldly critical frame of mind, to adjust his New England temperature to the Roman scene.

He saw everything, of course. During this first tenure in the Holy City he probably tramped hundreds of miles, pausing before numberless ruins, exploring scores of broad streets and narrow alleys, dragging his way through leagues of picture galleries, peering into dozens of churches. He was the dogged sightseer determined to see all that there was to see and to give Rome its chance, as it were, to make what impressions it might on his securely-set temperament. Sophia must have kindled the urge of curiosity in him to some extent for she was the rather lush dilettante, ultra-sensitive to the appeal of pictures and properly impressed by antiquities. Dabbling in drawing herself and blessed with an untrained taste in such aesthetic emanations she performed the function of an excellent foil to Hawthorne's deadened aesthetic sensitivity before the Italian masterpieces. He was a stranger in a strange land and he knew it. England, after all, had been England, the mother-country from which his own blood had originally come and where the language was his own; Italy was something outlandishly new, a land with no points of contact for him, no reminders of his own past, and practically nothing to meet his half-formulated desires. Hawthorne could not meet on a common-ground with the Italian temperament. In England he could carp at the natives for he possessed some sort of vantage point from which to observe them; they were, after all, animals rather similar to himself. Italy, however, could be viewed without the critical malice of one who "belongs." He could stand before the Roman scene supremely untouched, as a man stands before a puppet-show, and like it or not, approve or disapprove, much as he pleased. This must have given him a sense of solitary freedom more perfect than he had ever experienced either in New England or old England. He was in no sense of the word a part of the picture and this very sensation of being so unrelated to his environment thrust him into more amiable social relations with the American-English colony in Rome than he had ever ventured on before.

Two dominating aspects of the Roman scene forced themselves sharply into his consciousness and he must have given them a great deal of thought. They were religion and art. Although Hawthorne had fought shy of church-going all his life it was perceptible in his life, his letters, and his books that the Puritan consciousness had deeply invaded his intelligence and his spirit. He had reached maturity in a land of unadorned churches, where religion was a matter of exposition and rigorous abnegation of gauds and liturgies and colored shows. Yet the spectacle of the Roman Catholic Church with its bells, its censers of curling aromatic smoke, its chanting priests and monks, its wandering friars, its gorgeous vestments and sacramental vessels, its mystery of the mass, its inspired pictures, and its reassuring doctrines of papal infallibility and the blessed absolution of the confessional, reached subtly into the aesthetic mysticism of his nature. He realized that Protestants were all choked up, so to speak, and with no emotional outlet for their inhibited natures.

It was only in witch-burnings and repressed hysterics and dry expositions of doctrine and gloomy meditations which stifled the quivering soul that the Puritans might give vent to the subterranean passions that shook them inwardly. But the Roman Catholic Church was different. It offered a series of brightly-hued safety-valves for the emotions of mankind. The laden soul might fling itself upon Mother Church and find appeasement there. It might come forth from the confessional cleansed in spirit and free in mind. It was this realization that occasioned that daring expedient (at least for Hawthorne) in "The Marble Faun" of having Hilda lift the weight of guilty knowledge from her soul in the confessional booth. Hawthorne's sensitivity toward the Roman Catholic Church was the direct result of his brooding observation. He comprehended better than most of his New England contemporaries how much the solitary man perplexed with the incubus of sin might relieve himself through the soothing ministrations of the confessor. It was a long way for a man brought up in the old Puritan tradition to go, but Hawthorne, at least, achieved a broken glimpse of that deep mystic foundation upon which the invulnerable strength of the Roman Catholic Church is based.

He was less certain about art, for he did not really comprehend the purpose of art. Technique as such and the value of the picture in itself for what it was meant little to him. After he grew to understand in some measure the mysteries of the church his pedestrian attitude before pictures was tempered. He could rise to the occasion with some degree of aesthetic comprehension. He saw obliquely, to be sure, and his glimpses were but fragmentary. Still, in the end, he realized in some measure the immeasurable phenomena of art. However, he was really too old to suffer a sea-change from what he was into anything different. He had been under Puritan influences too long and his course had been somewhat shaped before his birth. It is the peculiar failing of the Puritan temperament to be quite unable to understand the importance of technique in any work or to realize the value of a thing in itself for its sheer beauty. There must always be a purpose behind the object, a moral somewhere implied. Hawthorne ran true to form when he was before pictures or sculpture and the works that pleased him most were those that suggested a moral or that were rather sentimentally disposed. He did not express any predilection for pure art or expatiate on the supreme cleverness of technique, a rather peculiar failure on the part of a man who took so much pains with his own prose. It must be remembered, however, that his prose was nearly always a means to an end which betrayed a moral. The moral was not always a clean-cut New England moral but Hawthorne was in vague rebellion against the iron-bound doctrines of his own community. In no clearer or more ridiculous manner were Hawthorne's shortcomings as an appreciator of art to be found than in his attitude toward nude sculpture. "Man is no longer a naked animal," he expostulated, "his clothes are as natural to him as his skin, and sculptors have no more right to undress him than to flay him." This is the complete height of absurdity. The hard-shell Baptists could go no further.

The circle into which Hawthorne was flung while in Rome was, in the main, an artistic one. Import. ant among these Roman friends was William Wetmore Story, the sculptor and intimate friend of Robert Browning, whose statue of Cleopatra plays a minor part in *"The Marble Faun."* Passing from studio to studio and observing his acquaintances at work Hawthorne picked up a lot of the jargon of professional artists. He appears to have been a little sunnier in disposition now, more willing to mingle with people at gatherings, and rather satisfied with Rome. It is true that he knew no Italians and that he made no noticeable attempts to probe the intricacies of the Italian mind. Contemporary Rome, dirty, colorful, sinful, martial, boiled about him, but he always thought of the capital as a city of the past. For him it was a huge *Salle Carrée* lined with the broken monuments of vanished eras. In spite of his acquaintances and his own sensitivity he remained a tourist to the last, a provincial who had strayed far from his proper environment, and it was in this spirit that he trudged through the streets of Rome. He does not appear to have been concerned at all with the political phenomena of the day although he mentioned several times the red-trousered French soldiers who roystered through the byways. He was, in effect, Uncle Jonathan abroad, and yet he lacked the vulgarity of that type. He was too sensitive, too reserved, too much the master of his own feelings, to be the average American abroad. But he was an American and a New Englander and it was with the inborn reactions of such a type that he faced the free amoral life of Rome.

The typical American brings his own country with him wherever he goes, and, to a certain extent, this is what Hawthorne did, although he never attempted to impose his country on the scene about him. Hawthorne knew that he was an American (or rather a New Englander; his patriotism really extended no further than that corner of the Re. public) but he also knew that he was in a world wherein he could take no part and which cared very little about him. It was a little wistfully, therefore, that he observed this old world that was so strange and new to him. He knew that he could never be a part of it, that he could never take it in all its complexity and shifting values. He did not try, then, to understand the contemporary scene, its art, its letters, its language, its personality, but satisfied himself with the world which he created for himself out of old ruins, objective contacts, and the conversations of acquaintances. His note-books became crammed with descriptions of churches, palaces, picture galleries, streets, people, and chance words. The zest of an alien people induced a renascence of the creative urge within him and he found materials to his hand in the Roman scene. The idea of a romance (and for a long time he had felt guilty because of his abysmal silence) plucked at the back of his mind. The idea evolved slowly as he plodded about the streets of Rome gaping at faded pictures in musty churches and the blank walls of old palaces. He had never before written about anything but New England and the type of mind that he understood so clearly, and he had always been in the midst of New England when he had written about it. What should he do now in barbarous Rome where everybody talked about art and the masked people raced through the streets flinging flowers (and sometimes lime) at one another during the pagan Carnival and married ladies drove forth in the *Corso* with their cecisbeos on one side and their husbands on the other and dirty monks strode through the unswept thoroughfares and church bells rang day and night and leering fauns peeped out of museum galleries? His long rest from creative writing had refreshened his brain and the reservoir from which he had drawn *"The Scarlet Letter," "The House of the Seven Gables"* and *"The Blithedale Romance"* was filling up again. It was filling up with new and jangled things. Although he could not be a part of the Roman scene neither could he wholly escape it. He conceived his idea for a romance, therefore, that should circumscribe all that he had seen in his three months of wandering over the surface of Rome.

It was with this nebulous scheme of a romance boiling in his mind that Hawthorne, together with his wife and children, departed in May, 1858, from Rome to seek a cooler summer in the more northern city of Florence. During the months of June and July he lived very near the Robert Brownings, who were installed in their famous *Casa Guidi*. Near him, also, was Hiram Powers, the American sculptor whose Greek Slave had been so admired by an American public hungry for culture and art provided they were not too esoteric. Powers was not too esoteric and he filled the bill. Behind the thin mask of his artistic instinct loomed a "handy Yankee" full of "smart" mechanical ideas. He could turn out marble buttons from an iron apparatus he had invented as easily as he could turn out a marble Venus. A confirmed egotist crammed with dogmatic convictions, he interested Hawthorne, who listened to him calmly enough but nearly always spiced Powers' ululations with the proverbial grains of salt. Another cross Hawthorne had to bear was the spiritualistic inclinations of Elizabeth Barrett Browning, that frail poetess who was to pass away within so few years from this time. Sophia lent herself all too readily to these manifestations. There was to be much more of this when the Hawthornes moved to the Villa Montaüto on the hill of Bellosguardo about a mile from Florence, in August. Before this removal, however, Hawthorne had done his duty by Florence in the tourist sense of the word, tramping all over it and setting down the usual notations. There was the Duomo to see, the Baptistery, the Palazzo Vecchio, the Cathedral, the Uffizzi Gallery, and the Pitti Palace. He did not see the ghost of Savonarola. And there was the Venus di Medici. Hawthorne was plainly moved by this famous statue. "I felt a kind of tenderness for her," he noted, "an affection not as if she were one woman, but all womanhood in one." Averting his eyes from Titian's Venus, "reclining on a couch, naked and lustful," he concluded his day's observations with: "The Venus di Medici has a dimple in her chin."

Although Florence was extremely hot during these months and the children strove to cool off by devouring numberless cherries and apricots—their youthful appetites not being up to figs—Hawthorne seems to have thoroughly enjoyed himself. He was arriving at the point where he could look a picture in the eye without wincing even if it were lightly clad, and notes for the new novel were dripping from the nub of his quill. Life was leisurely in Florence, a warm, luxurious existence untinged by the helter-skelter of Rome. It was possible to think, to meditate, to walk slowly, to let one's dreams crystallize. The newness of his environment had worn off somewhat and Hawthorne, although he was still pretty much the curious tourist, did not feel that it was so absolutely necessary to trudge about constantly seeking nascent aspects of Italian life. The Feast of St. John came along and he had the dubious pleasure of again observing natives in carnival spirits although this time, unlike the Romans, they went without masks and confetti. He saw the Grand Duke during this festival and, according to Sophia, that unfortunate nobleman "looked like a monkey with an evil disposition." It was all a period of blissful poking about, frequent conversations—especially with the domineering Hiram Powers, and intellectual adjustment toward the new work shaping itself so rapidly in Hawthorne's mind. He sat before his bottles of pale golden wine and smiled frequently.

But the heat continued without abatement. The stuccoed walls of the city and the flat pavements caught the burning flood and flung it against the faces of the pedestrians. The young ostler across the way stripped himself to the waist and lounged in the street, his torso gleaming like a marble from the Uffizzi. Hawthorne, although he loved the tropic heat on his body, realized that it was time to get away to the country, to find some hill where the wind blew, and, at the same time, to find a haven for writing the first sketch of *"The Marble Faun,"* which now had formulated itself sufficiently in his mind. Presently a delicately-built anaemic young man whose every vein bespoke unadulterated blue blood called at the Casa della Bella and conversed with Hawthorne on weighty matters. He was the Count of Montaüto, an impoverished scion of an old Florentine family, and the result of his conversation with Hawthorne occasioned the renting of the Villa Montaüto at Bellosguardo. It was with some enthusiasm that the Hawthorne family removed in August from the stifling city to the villa on the hill. Young Julian danced and shouted before the iron gates. For forty scudi a month Hawthorne had hired a castle with forty rooms, a *podere* of grapes and figs extending to a dozen acres, and an historic tower that was haunted. What more could any novelist desire as a scene for a new romance?

Here the family settled until October and here the first draft of *"The Marble Faun"* was written. The location was ideal. Each member of the family had three or four rooms to himself or herself and there were at least twenty chambers left for communal occupation. After sunset the comet of Donati streamed across the sky and remained, a blazing phenomenon, until near morning. From the haunted tower the owls floated forth on ghostly wings after dark, their mournful hooting sounding eerily from the battlements. The tables were piled high with bursting figs and purple grapes. In the evening the family mounted to the top of the tower and reposed in darkness gazing off across the valley of the Arno to the distant hills where the raging Italian thunder-storms made a mystery in the night. Above them the great starry wheel revolved. Hawthorne had come a long way for this. He had crossed the patching desert of repression and fought his way through the swamp of despond. He had walked dubiously in a twilight of oblivion and he had sat, a stranger, among the tobacco-chewers of the Republic and waited with an uncommon patience for what time might bring forth. It was a great journey for a taciturn and solitary New Englander.

There was but little to hold Hawthorne from his self-imposed task. In a neighboring villa dwelt the Brownings, and Sophia, entirely bitten by the spiritualistic idea, may have introduced an alien element into the daily life of the novelist. Then, too, Florence was but fifteen minutes away and there were frequent trips to the city. On the whole, however, it was an exceedingly quiet period, a lull, so to speak, in the months of dashing hither and thither. A few visitors came, but not many. Hawthorne again had his life to himself. It is possible that he saw signs and portents in Donati's comet, prophecies "importing changes of times and states," and it is also possible that he felt the old sadness of Italy, that sadness that comes from observation of quiet countrysides in the sunset, of an ancient life founded upon a still more ancient way of living. But, on the whole, for him, he was contented. It was from the Villa Montaüto that he wrote to a friend: "It is pleasant to feel at last that I am really away from America—a satisfaction that I never really enjoyed as long as I stayed in Liverpool, where it seemed to be that the quintessence of nasal and hand-shaking Yankeedom was gradually filtered and sublimated through my consulate, on the way outward and homeward. I first got acquainted with my own countrymen there. At Rome, too, it was not much better. But here in Florence, and in the summertime, and in this secluded villa, I have escaped out of all my old tracks, and am really remote." It was remoteness, really, that he sought, remoteness from the small peccadilloes and actualities of a practical living, remoteness from a false and superficial social scene, remoteness from problems and dogmas and duties and obligations. On the quiet hill-slope of Bellosguardo he found it. If he could have stayed there for five or six years the entire history of his after-life might have been changed. He could not do this, however. His children were in that formative state that was to shape them for all time and he wanted them to be Americans, perhaps better Americans than he had been. It was necessary to turn his eyes backward to that bleak northern terrain which had been his own sustenance during his early years. In the meantime, however, he could apply himself with a high degree of diligence to his new romance.

"The Marble Faun," upon which he labored a few hours each day, had received its original inception in April, 1858, when Hawthorne had visited the sculpture gallery in the Capitol at Rome. "We went afterwards into the sculpture gallery," he noted in his journal, "where I looked at the Faun of Praxiteles, and was sensible of a peculiar charm in it; a sylvan beauty and homeliness, friendly and and

wild at once. The lengthened but not preposterous ears, and the little tail which we infer, have an exquisite effect, and make the spectator smile in his very heart. This race of fauns was the most delightful of all that antiquity imagined. It seems to me that a story, with all sorts of fun and pathos in it, might be contrived on the idea of their species having become intermingled with the human race; a family with the faun blood in them having prolonged itself from the classic era till our own days. The tail might have disappeared, by dint of constant intermarriage with ordinary mortals; but the pretty hairy ears should occasionally reappear in members of the family; and the moral instincts and intellectual characteristics of the faun might be most picturesquely brought out, without detriment to the human interest of the story. Fancy his combination in the person of a young lady!" However, Hawthorne, brooding over the idea, did not "fancy" this combination so far as a young lady was concerned. Various elements entered into the theme as he mulled it over in his mind, a handsome young Jewess whom he had seen at a dinner in England, the aristocratic young Count of Montaüto who had rented the villa to him, the villa itself with its haunted tower, the scores of descriptive passages of Rome he had set down in his note-books, a tower in the Via Portoghese with an everlasting light burning before the Virgin's shrine, the blessed consolation of the Roman Catholic confessional, the artistic jargon he had picked up in the studios, the pictures and sculptures he had seen, the tragic story of Beatrice Cenci, a dead monk from whose nostrils streamed blood in the church of the Capuchins, a buffalo-calf grazing in the Via Latina, the Carnival with its masks and mummeries. All of these things floated about in his consciousness and gradually they began to assume a coherent ensemble.

The theme about which these colored particles of a Latin world floated and then adhered was not to be a mere tale with "all sorts of fun and pathos in it."

Hawthorne's ancient Puritan obsession came to the front and shaped his material for him and *"The Marble Faun"* became another study in sin and conscience. The idea of a happy innocent creature without a human soul committing a crime and then through self-torture evolving a soul with all the divine obligations of spiritual essence eventually became the basis of his novel. Whether or not the first draft—which may have been no more than a full sketch or synopsis—contained all the implications included in the later version written in England is unknown, but Hawthorne must have had his main theme well in mind while he sat in the pleasant Villa Montaüto and scribbled away at his new creation.

He had done no creative work for six years and it must have been with some degree of gusto that he sat down to his task. It was with this labor that he passed the hot summer months on his hill-slope of Bellosguardo. No more acute betrayal of his congenital New Englandism was possible than this spectacle of an aesthetic personality fresh from the turmoil of Rome and soothed by the quietude of the hills about Florence bending all of his intellectual and imaginative powers toward the solution of a stark moral problem. The essential man had not been changed by a changed life. His surface values may have taken on new colors but the impenetrable twilight of the soul that cut him off so sharply from other men and translated him into a sort of veiled mystery was too much the man himself to endure any changes. Emptied of that cloudy content he would have been a hollow figure. He sat, therefore, as he had sat in the haunted chamber under the eaves in Salem or in the mossy seclusion of the Old Manse and created his characters for a specific function, a problem of the soul that had nothing to do with the Italian scene. And when his problem was solved his characters would blow out on thin air as all his others had vanished.

October came and with it came colder winds from the Apennines. Hawthorne knew that it was time to leave his pleasant villa and journey southward, He packed his manuscripts and note-books away, therefore, and, together with Sophia, Julian, Una, and Rose, moved leisurely toward Rome, pausing for ten days at Siena, where William Wetmore Story acted as host. Once in Rome the family settled in an apartment on the Piazza Poli and Hawthorne decided to remain there for six months and finish his book. However, Fate intervened and although Hawthorne remained in Rome for the winter he did little work. His daughter, Una, while out sketching in the Palace of the Caesars with her governess, Ada Shepard, contracted Roman fever and for four months her life hung in the balance. This was a time of dark and repressed suffering for Hawthorne, and, coming so close upon the idyllic days at Villa Montaüto, it must have impressed upon the sensitive-natured man again the fatalistic vagaries of uncertain life. He was a man who concealed the wounds of fortune as much as possible and this very repression undoubtedly intensified the anguish he endured in crises such as this of his daughter's illness. Never of a sanguine temperament he was prone to accept the dark side of things and to adjust himself almost automatically to the worst that fortune might have to offer. It was the attitude of the confirmed addict to solitude, of the man who cannot relieve himself through outward gestures and a spontaneous flood of sorrow. Such a man is dammed up inside; his tears will not flow, there are no words for him to speak. He hugs his grief to his secret bosom and makes no attempt to rise above it, to stun it with the triumphant sanguinity of religious expectation. Hawthorne was no Doctor Pangloss. He was a man who instinctively made up his mind to face the imminent possibility of his daughter's death in an alien land rather than waver wretchedly between hope and fear.

He moved in a pocket of darkness during these days. The unfinished book was laid away and forgotten for the time being, and as the dark and doleful winter spread its desolate grayness over Rome, Hawthorne wandered through his days like a lost man in a trance. At first there were cards in the evening, games at which the children laughed and chattered while Hawthorne strove valiantly to summon up a smile from the depths of that nature which was but on a bowing acquaintance with laughter. One day the doctor, Franco, came from the sick-room and spoke seriously and privately with Hawthorne and his wife, and the children sensed from the immediate chill in the air that the hopes were against Una's recovery. That evening they sat down to cards as usual. The game was whist and it was started in a dead silence. One hand was played. Hawthorne laid down his cards. "We won't play any more," he said. He had reached the limit of his endurance, and, like a lonely and wounded animal, could stand casual contacts no longer.

The winter crept on leaden feet and Hawthorne dumbly awaited the worst. Then came the crisis of the illness and Una, after hours of doubt, turned the corner safely toward life and a wan liveliness permeated the household. A long and tedious convalescence ensued, a convalescence that proceeded without untoward relapses and Hawthorne, with a mighty weight lifted from his nature, stepped once more into life, stepped tentatively and shyly as usual. Horatio Bridge came to Rome and there were pleasant moments between the old friends. Then, too, shortly after this, Franklin Pierce arrived in the Holy City and Hawthorne had an opportunity to test his regard for the man who had been President of the Republic and his intimate as well. He found him as faithful and responsive as ever to the old relationship. "I do not love him one whit the less for having been President." noted Hawthorne, following a curious line of reasoning, "nor for having done me the greatest good in his power; a fact that speaks eloquently in his favor, and perhaps says a little for myself. If he had been merely a benefactor, perhaps I might not have borne it so well; but each did his best for the other as friend for friend." An independent man sensitive to the nuances of relationships is speaking here.

With early spring came the Carnival and Hawthorne, now that Una could take a feeble part in the festivities, entered more fully into the spirit of the *festa* than he had done the year before. He rode in a carriage up and down the Corso and flung flowers and confetti at the shouting and boisterous masked figures. Each flower that he flung, each handful of colored shreds of paper was one of the winter's cares tossed into the masked face of destiny. While he was in the act of playfulness he could realize the zest of this carefree abandonment but the moment that he leaned back in his carriage and became the brooding observer he saw the absurdity of it all. He was not shaped for these games and he knew it. He was a gray-haired New Englander of fifty-five years and the chill eastwind of Salem was in his bones. There was no Merry Mount where he might dance about a pagan May-pole.

He now began to bethink himself about a return to America. There were his children to think of, two daughters to educate and a son to be sent to Cambridge. He did not want them to be denationalized and he realized that they were passing through formative periods that would shape them mentally and morally for all time. New England, therefore, beckoned in the distance. In May the family set out traveling via Marseilles, Avignon, Geneva, and Paris to London. His immediate purpose was to set sail for America, but these plans were disrupted for various causes, the more important being financial, and Hawthorne decided to remain for another year in England, to finish his romance and have it published there, and then to return to The Wayside, Concord. His Italian days were over but the memory of them was fresh in his mind and he was to make the most of them in his new romance. The color and magic, none of which had been very close to his heart, were dissipated in the gray weather of London and it is possible that he began to feel a little more at home as he wandered for a few weeks through the narrow streets of the English capital and then retired to the country, first to Whitby and then to Redcar, and concentrated upon his last novel.

At Redcar Hawthorne wrote every morning until the dinner-hour, which was at half-past one, and after the meal he would take his son walking with him along the sands facing the German ocean. It was a solitary place, just the sort of cul-de-sac from activity that best suited Hawthorne when he was at work on any extended composition, and a certain picturesque quality enhanced the lonely features of the little community. The drizzling rain came down frequently and obscured the dark mass of the town. Then there was the dull red sunset sky to furnish a background for Redcar. It was quiet, deserted, almost desolate, the typical tiny resort "out of season." There were days of the dull progression of labor and there were no interruptions. By October, however, the weather became too chilly and boisterous and the Hawthornes removed to Leamington. On November 8, 1859, Hawthorne completed *"The Marble Faun"* but he stayed on at Leamington until March of 1860. *"The Marble Faun"* was immediately sent to Smith, Elder and Company, and late in February, 1860, was issued under title of "Transformation." Some weeks later the book was published in America bearing Hawthorne's chosen title, *"The Marble Faun: A Romance of Monte Beni."* In the meantime Hawthorne and his family went to Bath for a vacation and from there to London, where he was entertained as much as he would permit himself to be entertained by such personages as Lord Dufferin and Richard Monckton Milnes. During this period he began to receive many adverse notices of *"The Marble Faun,"* (it is as well to call this book by its commonly-known title instead of "Transformation"), the English press deprecating what it regarded as an inconclusive ending. Hawthorne, always inclined to have but small faith in himself, went about muttering, "It is a failure." As a matter of fact *"The Marble Faun"* is both a failure and a success.

It is impossible to escape the conviction that two Hawthornes, the old one and a new one, are struggling in the pages of *"The Marble Faun."* The old Hawthorne wins, as we should expect him to do in a man so "set" in nature and matured to an iron point of view, wins handsomely but at some expense to the unity of his art. The new Hawthorne, perhaps no more than a shadowy figure, strove indecisively to employ the European scene and European characteristics for the purposes of a theme that only the old Hawthorne could properly outline and mold to a coherent purpose. The commingling of the two Hawthornes was so unequal that it might be symbolized in a man striding along accompanied by a thin shadow. The shadow falls on Italy but the man walks through New England. Heretofore Hawthorne had been faithful to the locale of his nativity. *"The Scarlet Letter"* was a shadow of his own spiritual past. Both *"The House of the Seven Gables"* and *"The Blithedale Romance"* were the direct result of an observation of and a brooding over the New England scene as he knew it and as he could detach himself from it. But in *"The Marble Faun"* he strove to circumscribe a foreign scene, to animate that scene with urges kindred to it. In so far as he strove to do this he failed lamentably. There is nothing of Europe in *"The Marble Faun."* Donatello may be a faun but he is not the faun of Praxiteles. He is rather a quaint New England faun who would be more at home peering out through the thin trunks of white birch trees, and, when a soul is vouchsafed him, he attains it through suffering, and the soul is colored with the moralistic passions of Puritan conceptions. As for Miriam, she, again, is an at. tempt to create that strong, dark type of rebellious woman first put forward in Hester Prynne and then modernized to a certain extent in Zenobia. These women have been sophisticated by sin and it is never the sin in itself that holds Hawthorne's interest. He is intent only on the spiritual results of that sin. We know Hester's sin but only through the necessity of Hawthorne's situation. In the cases of Zenobia and Miriam their sins are cloudy indications and it is exceedingly doubtful that Hawthorne himself knew what they had done.

This superb indifference on Hawthorne's part to either the past or the future of his principal characters is an outstanding aspect of his intellectual and emotional attack in his books. It is brought out most clearly in *"The Marble Faun."* Hawthorne's absorption in the quartet of starkly differentiated personages who play out the drama is intensive only while the puppets are in actual play. Donatello's youth is frozen into the marble of Praxiteles and his future is whatever the reader desires to make of it. Miriam's past is a matter of semitragic hints flung out carelessly. What her crime was, what the influence of the sinister monk (who stepped out of Gothic romance to serve Hawthorne's purpose) on her, are secrets and, though the novelist, perhaps, had a vague identification of her with Beatrice Cenci, we may be sure that he did not know what crime she had committed. After all, such knowledge was hardly necessary for Hawthorne's purpose and though various friends rebelled at his mistiness he confined himself steadfastly to the purpose he had in hand. He was artist enough not to dissipate the unity of his central theme, although he was not artist enough, except in "The Scarlet Letter," to maintain that unity in his actual arrangement of incidents. "The Marble Faun" is a loosely written book in which the action is frequently clogged. It lapses, gathers itself together again with an effort, rises to a sure peak, and then drops weakly. This is repeated time and again. But though this is so Hawthorne never releases his characters from their contemporaneity. They are isolated specimens under the strong microscope of Hawthorne's mind and from whence they came or whither they go is a matter of indifference to the gentle scientist of souls. They are caught in a state of being and it is that state of being with its consequent reactions to life which absorbs the curiosity of the novelist.

Donatello's love for Miriam, his committal of a crime for her sake, the ravages of the crime on his gentle faun-like nature, and his spiritual birth and regeneration through that crime, are the threads which are woven into the central theme of the story. Subsidiary to this is the study of Hilda's soul, her purity and the dark blot of guilty knowledge of Donatello's and Miriam's crime which destroys her peace and faith, and the eventual release from that bondage through the Roman Catholic confessional. Barely indicated under all this is Kenyon's love for Hilda. He, after all, is little more than an interested observer, a Miles Coverdale, Hawthorne himself. The situation so conceived is worked out with a minimum of characters (always a marked feature of Hawthorne's selective and thrifty mind) although the whole of Rome is set off as a background for the action. This theme is the theme of a New Englander and it is alien to the blood-currents of the Italian scene. It is as un-European in its development and dénouement as "Rappaccini's Daughter." The moral values involved all sprang from the soil of New England and the scene might very well have been laid in Boston. Yet the elaborate decoration of the theme reveals certain European influences, influences that Hawthorne never would have revealed if it had not been for his years abroad. Especially is this so in those portions of the book concerned with art and aesthetic questions. Hawthorne displayed here a sluggishly eager desire to enlarge his own artistic perspective and there is even an occasional hint of a far-away comprehension of the philosophical implications of art in life. It is but a thin light on the horizon but it is sufficient to awaken the thought that if Hawthorne had ventured on Europe sooner (at the age and with the opportunities of Longfellow, say) he might have been an important link between an awakened aesthetic consciousness and the naturalistic ardor of the New England mind. Greater, perhaps, than this vaguely aspiring interest in art (the interest of a rather old man who realizes deep inside of himself that he can hardly go very far) is the surprising revelation of Hawthorne's instinctive reaction to the Roman Catholic Church. When he takes his pretty little New England heretic into the confessional-box and brings her forth still a heretic but cleansed in spirit, newly washed, as it were, in the sparkling bath of innocence, he shows how amazingly far he has traveled from Gallows Hill, Salem. This incident, together with Hester Prynne's unexpected avowal of her faith in the consecration of her sin with Dimmesdale, forms a brief but flaring revelation of the potential aesthetic proclivities of the man, proclivities that break away cleanly from a drab but intense New England heritage.

Of the Roman scene itself as interpreted in "The Marble Faun" little more may be said than that it sometimes heightens the reader's interest and nearly always weakens the technical structure. Hawthorne's Rome was the Rome of the guide-books and he was almost ridiculously zealous in putting down everything that he saw. Galleries, churches, and streets are dragged in and interest in them is sustained only through that mellow light which the novelist throws across his paragraphs. Though the various facets of Roman life are drawn with clarity and dexterity it is obvious always that these facets are observed from a unique and falsifying angle. This is not Rome as it was but Rome as one man saw it. It is Rome seen through the vaguely sad eyes of a New Englander. The sun shines brightly enough, the maskers fling their confetti with abandonment at Carnival time, and a certain actuality is made manifest; still, all this is seen through a faint mist, a mist that rose from the Salem marshes. Perhaps the very anguish of his quartet of figures adds something to this doleful aspect of the Holy City, this retracing of an old pattern with a quill dipped in the lonely essence of New England parochialism. None of the four personages, not even Donatello, belong to the Roman scene. They are aliens wandering through a huge barbaric stage, lost people not even striving to orientate themselves to an existence that is supposedly a very part of their physical or mental being. They do not fit in as do the characters in *"The Scarlet Letter," "The House of the Seven Gables,"* and *"The Blithedale Romance."* In those earlier books the environment was a part of the characters, a portion of their being, but in *"The Marble Faun"* Rome is never anything but a purely arbitrary stage for Miriam, Hilda, Donatello, and Kenyon. They walk through it but their thoughts and minds (except in the solitary case of Hilda and the confessional) are not touched by it. Their griefs are their own and their attitude toward those griefs is wholly untouched by the faint pagan memorials hovering in the air about them.

These four people who occupy the scene in *"The Marble Faun"* are curious creations in so far as the reality of characterization goes. Not one of them is real in a four-square meaning of the word. Miriam is romance incarnate, romance dwelt upon by an essentially repressed nature. Hilda is another type of that New England maiden, pure and trusting, made familiar to his readers by Hawthorne in the Phoebe of *"The House of the Seven Gables"* and the Priscilla of *"The Blithedale Romance."* She is drawn to greater purpose than either of her previous sisters but she is still a type. It would be unjust (as has been intimated before) to assert that Hilda, Phoebe, and Priscilla were all cut from the same piece of cloth, for there is an obvious differentiation between them. But the differentiation is purely to fit them to the exigencies of the particular theme which Hawthorne had in mind. Indeed, this is true of all of Hawthorne's characters except those smaller subsidiary vignettes such as Uncle Venner or Old Moody which were the result of observation retouched to magic by imagination.

He was concerned mainly with the implications of his theme and he cast about to find certain puppets to properly exploit it. He was concerned with these figures only while they were serving his specific purpose. Viewed from this angle it is obvious that Hawthorne was not a realist at all. But, at the same time, his inveterate observation of the human animal wrought an inclination for naturalism in him, and, therefore, these personages created on so unreal a basis were developed with some degree of reality.

With *"The Marble Faun"* Hawthorne concluded his sustained labors as a creative artist. He was fifty-six years old, tired in mind and spirit, although he was not fully conscious of this weariness, and his powers of creation and concentration were grievously diminished. He had what might be called four major works to represent him to the world and it is to be suspected that he was not particularly complacent about any of them. Yet those works served to place him definitely and for all time in the proud-minded hierarchy of New England writers. His attitude had been one of isolation from the very first, and because of this, his work revealed an essential uniqueness that was not duplicated by any of his contemporaries. He had explored the consequences of sin, ignoring the causes, and in doing this he had expressed better the essential New England spirit than any of the more placid moralists who surrounded him. He knew that conscience was a hidden and terrible thing, and he made o conscience a protagonist that was without parallel in the history of the letters of the Republic. And he clothed his creations in an atmosphere that was peculiarly his own, an atmosphere partially induced by an agreeable and unforced prose and partially colored by the mist-like sadness of a solitary and introspective nature. He was an Ethan Brand of the soul searching not for the Unforgivable Sin but for the immitigable consequences of sin. He was never to destroy himself as Ethan Brand did, for the fires that moved him were subterranean fires and the deeper portion of his knowledge was subconscious and not as plain to him as it to us to-day. There were moments when he moved through the world of the intellect as a man in a lethargy and we must believe that he was never quite conscious of the depth of the springs from which he drank so fastidiously. We must believe also that he never—even unconsciously —achieved the eventual depth of those springs and that if his environment had vouchsafed a fairer and more compelling surface he might have placed "The Scarlet Letter" as a point from which to advance. As it was, "The Scarlet Letter" became the high point of his achievement. He did nothing better in intensive and unified creation although he touched more naturalistic moments in "The House of the Seven Gables."

"The Marble Faun," as excellent as it is (and it must be remembered that one or two of Hawthorne's finest moments are in this romance), belongs on a lower level than either "The Scarlet Letter" or "The House of the Seven Gables." He strove most plainly for a greater work, for his greatest work of all, but the two Hawthornes that became entangled in the pages of the Italian novel nullified his ambitious effort. He had reached that point of time where he could no longer leap very far beyond himself. The shadowy Hawthorne, born from an unceasing observation of the Roman scene with all its multicolored surfaces, was too weak a creature to do more than indicate certain inclinations. The real Hawthorne, the taciturn and solitary New Englander with his sharp eye turned against time and the yeast of a semi-dissipated Puritanism fermenting within him, was still strong enough to dominate his material. But it was the strength of a forced exertion. It depleted whatever residue remained in the man, and, though he was now to go back to New England, he was no Antaeus. Though his feet were to tread familiar lanes and though he was to hear old voices and experience the atmosphere that had shaped him from maturity he could not regain new strength. He was a tired man and the world was changing, after all. There was war and rumors of war in the air. The prophecy of Donati's comet, that blazing crystalline phenomenon that had flared above the quiet hillslope at Bellosguardo, was about to come to pass. When in June, 1860, Hawthorne, accompanied by his family, set forth from Liverpool for Boston, he must have suspected that his work in this world was practically ended. The year 1860 was to draw a sharp line between two periods of the mind and Hawthorne assuredly did not belong on the hither side of it. He belonged, body and soul, to the old New England and he was not a man who adjusted himself to new conditions easily.

Through a countryside shriveled by heat and dotted with dusty herbage the Hawthornes drove in the station wagon to The Wayside, Concord. Around them they saw the familiar white clapboard houses, the small churches perching like roosters on their miniature eminences, the meandering stone walls, the color and scent and feel of the New England summer. After seven years of willing exile Hawthorne had unwillingly returned to the land of his birth. His heart was not in this return although an inborn pragmatism convinced him that only in return could he still remain himself. He was, after all, a man of duties and obligations although an aesthetic daemon dominated him at times and suggested an escape from this weighty heritage. He did not possess the virility for a complete escape and it was only in a series of tentative gestures, half-expressed desires, and instinctive manifestations that he could express his vague dissatisfaction with the lot apportioned him by the genius of his being. He looked back at Europe not with a nostalgia but with a cold regret. He was too old to actually reveal a passionate dissaffection for the familiar scene but there is no doubt that the comparison of this meager rural existence with the more buoyant and colored spectacle of Rome aroused a perceptible unrest in him. At the same time there was an unmistakable relief in reaching home, in settling back into an old familiar groove, of being himself in a corner of the world that knew him and did not expect him to be anything but himself. He could outreach his solitary instincts only by an effort of the will and this effort occasioned an uneasiness in him that disturbed his peculiar equilibrium. There was no need for efforts of this sort in Concord, where he was amongst old acquaintances, a riper Emerson, a calmer Thoreau, a less volatile Channing. Time had moved along with all of them but except for this they were essentially the same. Hawthorne himself had known none of them so well that he would have to adjust the broken threads of communication. He had but to slip back into his old scene and remount his horse of the night.

It was a feverish atmosphere into which he inducted his growing children. Julian was packed off to Mr. Frank Sanborn's school and Mr. Sanborn was a gentleman of stout abolitionist tendencies who had been involved with John Brown. Indeed, there were abolitionists all around Hawthorne. There was talk of war and threats of war, expostulations, fiery denunciations, schemes for freeing the negroes, plans and counterplans, loud and constant argumentation. Hawthorne listened to as much of it as came his way with a sort of unconcerned boredom. During this first summer of his return to Concord he did not mix intimately with his friends but remained in the rural solitude of The Wayside primarily concerned with certain additions to the old house. Carpenters came and there was a screaming of saws and a whistling of planes. A tower was reared over the building that had once belonged to the peripatetic philosopher and in it Hawthorne arranged his study. Why did he want a tower after all these years? Did he think that he could raise himself somewhat from the New England scene, that from such a vantage-point he could gaze down on the dusty lanes along which the cows moved and Mr. Emerson strolled? Was there a subtle satisfaction in lifting himself even this tiny bit above the soil that had taken the bones of his dark preceding generations? The real reason, it is to be suspected, was a sharp and almost nostalgic memory of the haunted tower on the hill-slope at Bellosguardo, the tower of the Villa Montaüto where he had passed so carefree and comfortable a summer. His Concord tower could not overlook the Valley of the Arno and there were no sun-smitten Apennines to gleam in the distance. Neither was the fiery wonder of Donati's comet to flare above him during the long summer evenings. But there would be a suggestion of height and removal from the world, a place where he could sit like a wise old sage and stare down at Time, a refuge from voices and doorbells and visitors. The tower was a substitution for that haunted chamber under the eaves on Herbert Street in Salem. At the end he desired to return to the loneliness and remoteness of his youth.

He could not escape from the imminent war in this tower. No tower would be high enough for that. The autumn and winter crept along and Hawthorne strove vainly to hide himself from the uneasy bruit of the day. It beat about him, however, and increased that lassitude of being which had permeated his tired frame. He discovered that it was an effort to write, that his powers of concentration were grievously impaired. Still he stuck to his task and passed his mornings in the tower striving to arrange the inchoate romance that kept mercilessly tapping at his intelligence. He was trying to tie together into a single theme two subjects which had haunted him for a long time, that of the elixir of life and that of the Bloody Footprint which he had seen in Smithell's Hall in England. His powers of coördination, however, were weakened and he made small headway with the proposed task. In the meantime the secession movement developed, the Union was split apart by gigantic agitation and in the spring of 1861 the first guns roared. Hawthorne could not but take in all this. He had never been a nationalist in the true sense of the word. To him patriotism had meant sectionalism. He was a New Englander first of all and an

American after that. His reactions to slavery were slight. There was not a particle of sentimentality in his being and it was impossible for him to enter into the fiery demonstrations of the Massachusetts abolitionists. If there was to be a war it merely simmered down to a choice between two evils and it is possible that in the back of his mind he rather approved the idea of a little republic to be fashioned out of the New England States. The Union, as such, did not mean much to him and this attitude set him apart from his many familiars in the New England scene. They could not understand his coldness in the face of passion, his abstinence from the embroiled factions of the day. It must be remembered that he had never been in the thick of the argumentation that had so aroused the country. He had been in Europe dreaming of art during those feverish seven years of preparation for a cataclysm that was to split apart half the world. Even if he had never been abroad, however, it is doubtful that Hawthorne would have entered strenuously into the quarrels of the time. He was a born reactionary, a statement that has been made before, and he was less concerned with the fluctuations of the world about him than he was with the tinier ripples in his own mind.

This peculiar blindness to circumstances is nothing unusual in a solitary man. When Hawthorne's youth had been formulated in Salem he had been forced into a lonely existence which took no cognizance of the small phenomena of his native town. He was the constant observer, standing apart from life and its multifarious manifestations and seeing them as matters of shifting surfaces. He was to be the same in his attitude toward the phenomena of the greater world that comprehended the United States. While Hawthorne was not exactly like a turtle drawing his head into his shell at the slightest approach of unusual circumstances he was pretty near that type of creature. Old-fashioned in politics, ignorant of sociological! problems, concerned not at all with national economies, he went his quiet way with neither rancor nor unrest. When the blow fell and war was declared and Concord became a hurried martial scene he automatically adopted the viewpoint of the North although there was, perhaps, just as much reason to take a Southern view of things. The truth was that he was not on either side, but that he traveled half-heartedly with his own Commonwealth. The splitting apart of the Union did not seem to him so terrible a thing and we must guess that he possessed no conception of nationalism or any prophetic insight as to the future. His lassitude before the momentous situation in which his country found herself may have been aggravated by his physical condition, which, after all, was that of an old man enfeebled in body and enthusiasms. Life might roar by but he desired a quiet haven after years of gloomy effort. It was of such a haven that he dreamed and if the Union must be ripped apart to provide it for him he could see no reason why this should not happen.

As the summer of 1861 crept along his bodily frame became weaker and his anxious family realized that Hawthorne was approaching a precarious condition. He was old and grey; his flesh had fallen away; his mind did not function with the clarity that had been peculiar to it in bygone years. Now and then he forced a flash of life out of himself, even going so far as to assert that he was glad war had come as it had aroused a consciousness of his country within him. But he meant by this country his own corner of America and he went on to assert that the Republic had never been one people since the Constitution was formed. As the news of disastrous battles drifted back to Concord he became more and more desolate and alienated from the human contacts about him. In July, 1861, he went to Pride's Crossing for a vacation with his son, Julian, and managed to take some faint pleasure in the change. But he was tired, woefully tired, and the seal of his fate was in his face. His old world was falling to pieces about him and, perhaps, he began to realize that he belonged to a generation which was falling to pieces with that world. It was the quiet, rural New England of previous decades that had given him such nurture as it could and not this excited, war-inflamed terrain where the drums beat and the sons of his acquaintances went forth to do battle with other Americans. What *could* become of the dream of the ghostly house of the seven gables in such a world as this where everything fine and old was falling into a dolorous abyss that might be explored only through the ventures of sad memory? He did not understand it all and he was a trifle bewildered by the rapid shifts of fortune. It was in a seething world that he strove to sit down quietly in his tower and sketch out a romance that had nothing to do with the world as it was, a romance that was uncalled for inasmuch as the audience for it had suffered a sea-change into something fierce and forbidding and alien to his peculiar temperament.

The literary labors of these years were doleful endeavors. Hawthorne simply could not release the romance that he knew was somewhere within him. It was there all right, a definite subject, but it would not come forth. Back in 1858 he had sketched a romance, *"The Ancestral Foot-Step,"* but he had done nothing with it, had laid it aside before his Italian residence, and then *"The Marble Faun"* had seethed up in his mind and that had occupied him until his return to America. Once installed in Concord, however, and with the added adjunct to solitude—his tower—he had returned to this theme and he made a more or less half-hearted attempt to tie it up with another plan that had occurred to him. The result was an abortive and hastily finished romance entitled *"Septimius Felton,"* which remained unpublished until some years after Hawthorne's death. There is nothing that can be said about this work for it is only representative of Hawthorne in so far as it indicates how far he had fallen from his former clarity. When Hawthorne bought The Wayside he wrote to a friend: "I know nothing of the history of the house, except Thoreau's telling me that it was inhabited a generation or two ago by a man who believed he should never die." It was this man Hawthorne resuscitated as Septimius Felton and it was The Wayside itself he used as the scene. It was like him to take the thing that was nearest home, the thing that he had observed most clearly, for his book. Hawthorne became dissatisfied with "Septimius Felton" long before he had finished it and the final chapters were flung together hurriedly and in an almost ironical manner. It was put away but the theme was not forgotten. As Hawthorne drew nearer and nearer to death he meditated more and more about the elixir of life and immortality in the flesh.

His uneasy mind turned back again to the "bloody footprint" episode and he determined to make that the dominating motif of the romance and not the theme of immortality. Once more he set to work and the chapters that ensued were published some time after his death under the title of *"Dr. Grimshawe's Secret."* Here, again, he experienced that humiliating knowledge that the work would not do. Another bundle of manuscript was laid away. These tentative endeavors (and *"Dr. Grimshawe's Secret"* was not to be the last) testify with a sad eloquence to the state of Hawthorne's mind. He was a lost soul running after a shining light that constantly eluded him. He could no longer recapture the essence of his fancy and mold it to the purpose that his intelligence divined. Tired, for the time being, of the mental struggle he laid his theme away (still troubled by the immortality motif, however, and determined to do something with it) and began to dredge descriptive papers on English towns and scenes from his note-books and diaries. These articles appeared in The Atlantic Monthly and in 1863 they were published in a single volume by Ticknor and Fields under the title of *"Our Old Home."* It is revelatory of Hawthorne's peculiar attitude toward the passions of his time to note that he insisted on dedicating this book to his old friend, Franklin Pierce.

Now Pierce, a reactionary and unpopular ex-President, was in high disfavor in the North and Hawthorne's few friends tried to impress upon him the danger of so dedicating a book. It was the very height of the war-time fever and a disgruntled and dogged North, suffering from unexpected vicissitudes and moody with the realization of a long and terrific struggle, was in no state of mind to receive pleasantly a book bearing Franklin Pierce's name upon its forehead. Hawthorne ignored all protests, however. To Fields he wrote: ". . . I find that it would be a piece of poltroonery in me to withdraw either the dedication or the dedicatory letter . . . I cannot, merely on account of pecuniary profit or literary reputation, go back from what I have deliberately felt and thought it right to do; and if I were to tear out the dedication, I should never look at the volume again without remorse and shame . . ." *"Our Old Home"* came out, therefore, with Franklin Pierce's name in the dedication. No clearer picture of the doggedness of Hawthorne's friendship and his courageous conviction may be found in the annals of the novelist's life.

"Our Old Home" was received well enough in this country, although it aroused some antagonism in England, where a few of the animadversions on the English scene stirred up inflammable tempers. There is little enough to say about these essays. Hawthorne wrote them primarily for the cash they would bring in during their publication in The Atlantic Monthly and while they are done with his usual grace there is nothing unusual or unique about them. They are no better or no worse than the usual type of travel-essay which exhibits the personal reactions of a man to an unfamiliar environment. Hawthorne could not do anything else than have a comparison between the States and England in mind as he wrote, for that was his only standard. He did not enter deeply enough into the

English scene to depict or analyze it with any great degree of authority but he did see the surfaces of that world with a peculiar clarity and he made the most of what he saw in his essays.

It was after this brief foray into the field of the essay that he turned back to the romance which still continued to churn in his mind. He could neither get rid of it nor write it and this occasioned a curious sensation of frustration in him which was heightened by his now acute realization of his failing strength. The immortality theme became the dominating influence and dark angel of his last months of creative work and he strove valiantly but weakly to encompass the romance that was obviously too much for him. At the very threshold of the new version of the book which he called *"The Dolliver Romance"* he was assailed by a strange reluctance. "I linger at the threshold," he stated, "and have a perception of very disagreeable phantoms to be encountered if I enter." His subconscious self undoubtedly knew that it was too late, that the hour was too far advanced, that the scribbled chapters were but an indefinite gesture to be broken off in thin air. Foolishly enough, Hawthorne agreed to permit the serial publication of *"The Dolliver Romance"* in The Atlantic Monthly before he had gone very far with the book, but his promise was premature. He lived to finish but three chapters and the function of those chapters was to repose upon his coffin as a symbol of the creative thread snapped short.

He had reached the end of his literary life without knowing it (or with a determination to hide the knowledge from himself and his family) and there was little more he could do than ruminate over the past and bewail the present. Behind The Wayside was a small hill affectionately dubbed the Mount of Vision. There, among the pines and sweetfern, he walked, a halting, emaciated figure, and what he saw in the quiet twilight was his own secret. He saw, perhaps, a smashed world falling in fragments about him, an old world that was sweet and slow-moving and scented with country flowers and peopled with thin ghosts. Out of the débris of this world another world was to arise, a loud shouting, hurried, materialistic world where industry was the chief objective. He was not to be a part of that new world, however. He was to go with the ancient quiet and the gallant South and the village-era of New England. As he strolled along the path on the Mount of Vision he saw no clouds of fire and a bright angel in them; he saw nothing but a* perplexing and shifting scene that would not accept him and which he could not accept. He had run his race in his own way and he had never had close companions in that race. The New England that he knew and loved with the still passionate love of a moody son for a recluse mother was a specter. It had been a specter right along in so far as he was concerned; but he, himself, had partaken of the qualities of a specter. He had lived in the past more valiantly than he had lived in the future. He had shaped his world out of cloudy visions and stealthily moving phantoms. Life was a far-heard echo of sounds to him.

All of this had been the natural heritage of his inborn solitude. In the quiet chamber on Herbert Street, Salem, on the icy surface of Lake Sebago at midnight, in the piney forests about Brunswick, in the hermitage of the Old Manse, in the little red brick house at Lenox, even in the Custom House at Salem and the Consulate at Liverpool and the apartment in Rome and the Villa Montaüto at Bellosguardo, he had walked like a ghost among men, not a part of the vital world about him but an unaffected observer, the Eternal Observer, the man in a trance. He had striven half-heartedly to fight clear of this dusky dominion of solitude and he had lost his fight. He probably rejoiced in the defeat. Only that part of him that possessed an uneasy New England realization of the duties implicit in the practicalities of living, of a utilitarian arrangement of his days, aroused him to indecisive forays into the world of living men.

He could take stock of himself now if he desired and perhaps he did ruminate to some extent upon the laborious road of his career as he strolled backward and forward on the Mount of Vision. It is to be suspected that he did not regard himself as a success. After all, he was not leaving much to his family—a bare subsistence, perhaps, and his faith in his own works was shaken and uncertain. "I have been a happy man, and yet I do not remember any one moment of such happy conspiring circumstances that I could have rung a joy-bell at it." This he wrote to a friend during these last days and the statement may be taken as an epitome of his life. How close in spirit this moody declaration is to Edgar Allan Poe "The Happiest Day, the Happiest Hour." The best that he had known was a limited peace. Thin, pale, weak, troubled in mind as he was, he yet managed to retain some playfulness of demeanor in the bosom of his immediate family. The days came and went and the newspapers bruited the accounts of bloody battles in the south and New England steadily faded into an aspect that was not at all the New England of *"The House of the Seven Gables."* Hawthorne laid his quills and his papers away. They had been his stout companions for more than thirty years and now he had no use for them any more. Perhaps as he put them away he begrudged those wasted seasons in the employment of the government that was now smashing his world to bits. In any case, he was done.

Hawthorne's movements during the Civil War were limited. In March, 1862, he went to Washington with William Ticknor and they both obtained a lively impression of the capitol in war-time array. The novelist saw General McClellan, Harper's Ferry, Fortress Monroe, and the battle-field of Manassas. These things brought the war very close to him. Most important of all, he saw Abraham Lincoln and he viewed the war leader in his usual detached fashion. It is to be doubted that he saw any particular genius in the tall, shambling figure who stood before him garmented in a rusty black frock-coat and unbrushed pantaloons. It was not Hawthorne's habit to romanticize people. His eye was too active and too inquiring and his critical sense—so far as individuals were concerned—roved over the surface and did not trip very far beneath it. When he returned from this trip he wrote an article for The Atlantic Monthly, "Chiefly About War Matters," that was so unsympathetic as to arouse the fears of the editors as to its reception by the public. Hawthorne simply could not get into the war. To him it was a monstrosity spawned by an unnecessary ideal for Union. He was absolutely out of the national spirit as it revealed itself in the North and he made no attempts to adjust himself to any patriotic demands. His self-possession and coolness were admirable during a period dominated by feverish and unthinking urges but these laudable traits were not the result of wisdom. They were the result of a strange disinterestedness. He simply didn't care and that was all there was to it. Not even Abraham Lincoln could make his blood flow a whit the faster.

During this summer of 1862 he went to Gouldsboro, Maine, with his son, Julian, and appears to have had a fairly peaceful and contented time. They went out rowing every day, fished for flounders, swam, cooked chowder on the beach, walked through the pastures and picked berries, and otherwise disported themselves in a gentle way. Hawthorne would sit beneath the shadow of a huge rock and smoke for hours as he gazed off across the quiet landscape to the sea. It was the last peaceful interim he was to know in his life. He was conscious of it and made the most of it. Across this sea, beside which he had been born, lay England and Italy and he undoubtedly thought wistfully about those countries and the seven years he had passed there. In the early autumn he returned to Concord and settled once more into the retired life of the reticent author. During the winter his daughter, Una, fell ill again and Hawthorne was once more harassed and perturbed by sickness in the home. Una recovered, however, but not so Hawthorne, who, upset by this illness, slid more rapidly than ever into his final decline.

During the spring and summer of 1863 he gave indications of no specific ailment but grew thinner, more pallid, and more emaciated day by day. He stayed in the house most of the time but would occasionally walk forth with a slow and feeble step and stand gazing off across the fields with a world of wistfulness in his eyes. He was looking his last at the New England scene, looking his last now with the acute realization that he would not look much longer, that his abilities had forsaken him, and that he was so constituted that he would not outlast his ability so very long. During the summer he had an aggravated attack of nose-bleeding, it remained with him for twenty-four hours, and this further debilitated the sapped body of the man. In September he made a short visit to Rockport with Una but it did not improve his condition. He faltered on into the winter and his state, for the first time, became rather alarming. Sophia and the children could no longer close their eyes and hope for the best. Sophia wrote: ". . . he is very nervous and delicate; he cannot bear anything, and he must be handled like the airiest Venetian glass . . ." It was a good image for at the last Hawthorne was very like a piece of "the airiest Venetian glass." He turned his thoughts rather plaintively to England, writing: "If I could but go to England now, I think the sea-voyage and the 'Old Home' might set me all right." It was a forlorn thought and he must have realized it as he wrote it.

In March a decision was made to send him on a brief trip with Pierce and Ticknor, the idea being that the change would invigorate his flagging spirits. It was a mistaken idea and the tragedy that befell the travelers hastened Hawthorne's death.

Pierce discovered at the last minute that he could not accompany the party and Hawthorne set off alone with his faithful friend and publisher, Ticknor. They traveled as far as New York, where they put up at the Astor House for a week. The weather was exceedingly bad, a series of storms raging, and the semi-formulated idea of pushing on as far as Cuba where bright sunlight and warmth might restore Hawthorne was abandoned. In the meantime a cold which Ticknor had contracted grew steadily worse. Still, all his care was for his friend. They went on to Philadelphia, and, during a lull in one of the spring storms, decided to take advantage of the sunlight by riding in Fairmount Park. It grew cold as they rode and Ticknor, removing his overcoat, insisted in wrapping it about Hawthorne. The next day Ticknor felt that his cold was aggravated, the day after that he took to his bed, the third day physicians were summoned and diagnosed the case as one of congestion of the lungs, and on the fourth day Ticknor died, leaving his invalid friend alone in a strange city with a corpse and its countless concomitant details. It was a terrific blow to Hawthorne. He returned home pale and haggard and trembling in every limb, his strength completely sapped and his vitality at a dismally low ebb.

The irony of death had been completely experienced by Hawthorne in this tragedy and he could not remove the horrid lesson from his tired and sensitive mind. Ticknor's face was before him always; those last few days in the bitter spring-storms, the cruel fact of the stronger taken and the weaker left to bear the burden of desolation, these things blazed themselves on Hawthorne's tired brain. They were an epitome of life to him and he could no longer fight against the depression which they intensified. He went to the funeral (as he had gone a short while before to the funeral of Thoreau) and the look of the grave was marked in his face. Sophia ministered to him tenderly, the children were quiet and attentive, his few friends rallied about him, but he remained in a trance-like state of desolation. He could barely walk now and the spectacle of the man was heart-breaking.

His family knew that he would die immediately unless he were taken from Concord, unless his flagging mind could fasten on new scenes and people. Pierce was called and it was agreed that Hawthorne was to go on an excursion with him through northern New England. After all, that was his native territory and there he might find some few and pathetic reminders of those happier hours that he had known in his solitary youth. Hawthorne acquiesced in the plan but he knew that it was his last journey and one from which he would never return. During these last days before the hour of his departure he was taking, a mute farewell of Sophia and the children, turning back in memory to the white-clad girl who had greeted him for the first time in the Peabody parlor in Salem. It was all so long ago and far away, so gently suffused with the tender romance of ancient things, so wrapped up in his memory as a precious object is wrapped in lavender-scented tissues and put away in a bureaudrawer.

On the eleventh of May, 1864, Hawthorne traveled to Boston, where he was met by Pierce and they took the evening train to Concord, New Hampshire. The weather was bad and Hawthorne was extremely feeble. Therefore, they rested at Concord, the ex-President administering carefully to his friend, until the following Monday when they resumed travel stopping at Franklin, Laconia, and Center Harbor, and eventually reaching Plymouth on the 18th at six o'clock in the evening, where they put up at the Pemigewasset House. It was an impossible pilgrimage upon which they were bound and both men must have realized it, a pilgrimage as impossible as the search for the philosopher's stone or the elixir of life. They were seeking life for a man who was already dead.

That night Hawthorne had a little tea and toast in his room (a chamber adjacent to Pierce's quarters) and then slept for an hour upon the sofa. He was weary and went to bed soon after he roused himself from this short slumber. Pierce remained up for an hour or two (the door between the two rooms was open) and tiptoed about keeping a watchful eye upon his friend. Hawthorne did not seem to be particularly restless in his sleep although he moved somewhat time and again. Between one and two o'clock Pierce crept into the room and stood beside Hawthorne's bed studying the worn face of the sleeping man. His eyes were closed and his posture was natural. Again, between three and four o'clock, Pierce returned to the room and was surprised to note that Hawthorne had not changed his position in any respect. He placed his hand upon the sleeper's forehead. Hawthorne was dead.

2

Hawthorne and the Universal Reformers

—Gorman Beauchamp

Writing to Thomas Caryle in 1840, Emerson reported that "We are a little wild here with numberless projects of social reform. Not a reading man but has a draft of a new Community . . . One man renounces the use of animal food; another of coin; . . . and another of the State; and on the whole we have a commendable share of reason and hope" (Correspondence, I, 334-35). Emerson engaged no doubt in some hyperbole here, not only as to the number but the nature of his countrymen's reformist projects. Few were the sort of detailed drafts for the complete reorganization of society such as Charles Fourier produced contemporaneously in France or Robert Owen in England—the sort of imaginative reconstructions that we call utopias. And compared with the enormous outpouring in the last half of the nineteenth century, the first half of the century generated far fewer utopian fictions; furthermore, according to Joel Nydahl, "the main thrust of American utopian fiction during the first half of the nineteenth century was anti-progressive"—offering, that is, primarily negative visions of America's prospects and possibilities (274). In this sense, then, Emerson's era produced little memorable utopian literature, fictive or otherwise; it was, however, an era fermentative with the utopian impulse, rife with plans, projects, schemes and visions for reforming the world. "The present age," Emerson claimed elsewhere, "will be marked by its harvest of projects for the reform of domestic, civil, literary, and ecclesiastical institutions" (Works, I, 269).

Indeed, 1840 witnessed the convocation in Boston's Chardon Street Chapel of the Convention of Friends of Universal Reform, an assemblage—to cite Emerson once more—of "madmen, madwomen, men with beards, Dunkers, Muggletonians, Come-outers, Groaners, Agrarians, Seventh-Day Baptists, Quakers, Abolitionists, Calvinists, Unitarians, and Philosophers . . . [all come] to chide, or pray, or preach, or protest" (Works, X, 374). Thoreau, viewing this melioristic mania with the wryly skeptical eye that shades Walden, avowed: "If anything all a man . . . if he have a pain in his bowels even, he forthwith sets about reforming—the world" (53). Much pain must have afflicted many bowels in the decades of the 40s and 50s, for, as James Russell Lowell declared, "every possible form of intellectual and physical dyspepsia brought forth its gospel. Everybody has a mission (with a capital M) to attend to everybody-else's business" (Works, I, 362). The Friends of Universal Reform clearly were afoot.

Hawthorne was no friend of the Friends of Universal Reform, nor, indeed, of sweeping reform of any sort. Of all the significant intellectual figures of this time and place, he was probably the most conservative, certainly the most skeptical of the efficacy of human effort to effect its conscious design. In his 1852 campaign biography of Franklin Pierce, Hawthorne claimed categorically: "There is no instance, in all history, of the human will and intellect having perfected any great moral reform by methods which it adapted to that end" (Works, XII, 417).[1] Ten years later in "Chiefly About War Matters," that curious, provocative account of his trip to the battlefields of Virginia, he reiterated this view: "No human effort, on a grand scale, has ever yet resulted according to the purpose of its projectors . . . We miss the good we sought, and do the good we little cared for" (Works, XII, 332). Construed literally, such statements would entail a fatalism severe enough to satisfy the most orthodox Muslim. Hawthorne was, however, no rigorous philosopher of history, and one could most charitably construe such sweeping generalizations as the somewhat overwrought response to the meddlesome and misguided attempts of the Universal Reformers to impose simplistic rationalistic theories on the intractable complexity of life. Put another way, Hawthorne may be suggesting, in these skeptical pronouncements, what Marx in The Eighteenth Brumaire called "the irony of history"—the fact that historical actions frequently have unintended consequences, consequences often in complete contradiction to the purposes of the actors. Thus, in Hawthorne's view, ironically a Northern victory in the Civil War would prove of greater benefit, morally, to the South: "whether we intend it so or no, they have a greater stake in our success than we can possibly have. For ourselves, the balance of advantages between defeat and triumph may admit of question. For them, all truly valuable things are dependent on our complete success; for thence would come the regeneration of a people, removal of a foul scruff that has overgrown their life . . ." (331). Even so pernicious a policy as Archbishop Laud's religious persecution had the paradoxical result of promoting the cause of liberty by driving the Puritans to the New World: "Liberty would have had no cradle," Hawthorne asserted, "and the world would have been hindered in its march, perhaps for centuries, but for the timely aid of the Archbishop." Truly, then, as he put it in one of his most memorable formulations, "Man's accidents are God's purposes" (Works, XII, 332).

What Hawthorne saw as "the intricate and unintelligible machinery of Providence" at work in the world, the divine hand directing events supraliminally and even in opposition to declared human purpose, led him, then, to an almost mystical quietism regarding political reform. Take, for instance, the Abolitionist agitation that dominated the 1850's, unquestionably the most important reform movement of the decade. Hawthorne opposed the policies of the radical Abolitionist—the John Browns and William Lloyd Garrisons and Harriet Beecher Stowes—not because he favored the maintenance of slavery, but because he "look[ed] upon slavery as one of those evils which divine providence does not leave to be remedied by human contrivances, but which, in its own good time, by some means impossible to be anticipated, but of the simplest and easiest operation, when all its uses shall have been fulfilled, it causes to vanish like a dream" (Life of Pierce, Works, XII, 417). Even after the Civil War had begun and its outcome was apparent, Hawthorne still argued to his sister-in-law Elizabeth Peabody, herself an ardent abolitionist, that the war could "only effect by a horrible convulsion the self-same end that might and would have been brought about by a gradual and peaceful change" (Letters, Works, Cent. Ed. XVIII, 590).[2] While it is possible, of course, that slavery might have disappeared gradually and peacefully, over time, the proposition nevertheless enmeshes Hawthorne in contradiction: even if the War were an evil—one of man's "accidents"—it must nevertheless be viewed, on the Providential premise, as God's purpose. The concept of providence, that is, commits the proponent to the proposition that whatever is, is right: that how things happen must be how they were divinely ordained to happen. That God's vessel for ending slavery in America was Abraham Lincoln not Franklin Pierce, convulsion and civil war not compromise and evolution His modus operandi, ought, it seems, have suggested itself to Hawthorne. While one cannot be expected to anticipate the course of "the intricate and unintelligible machinery of Providence," still one should at least be able to discern it, if at all, post facto.

The concept of Providence generally—and certainly as Hawthorne invokes it—serves to validate a worldview that exalts tradition and inherited institutions over innovation and the exercise of unaided human reason as a guide to action. So meager is the personal stock of any man's experience and knowledge that to set it against the accumulated wisdom of the ages, as distilled into custom and tradition, constitutes a sort of intellectual hubris, foolish if not dangerous. Given this predisposition, Hawthorne, not surprisingly, viewed with utmost skepticism the attempts of Universal Reformers to remake the world according to their various rationalistic theories. "If mankind were all intellect," he wrote in The English Notebooks, "they would be constantly changing so that one age would be entirely unlike another" (45). The continuity of history, the persistence over centuries of the same beliefs and patterns of behavior, is explicable only on the premise that human nature is a constant, essentially unalterable—a view that entails a pessimistic assessment of mankind's ability to alter radically, by conscious design, itself or its institutions. Witnessing a troop of soldiers, Hawthorne mused: "Set men face to face, with weapons in their hands, and they are as ready to slaughter one another now, after playing at peace and good will so many years, as in the rudest ages, that never heard of peace societies" ("War Matters," Works, XII, 388-89). This view—so surprisingly like Freud's, for instance, in his exchange of letters with Einstein in Why War?—is meant as a descriptive statement, not a normative judgment: a realistic acknowledgment of the enduring psychic substructure of the human race. "The great conservative," Hawthorne declared, "is the human heart which remains the same in all ages" (English Notebooks, 45).

The Universal Reformers, deluded in believing that they could alter substantially either the heart or condition of humanity, intrigued Hawthorne throughout his career. As early as 1835 he sketched in his notebooks the plot for a tale (never actually written) of a messianic reformer who, on the point of converting many to his extreme doctrines, is discovered to be a lunatic escaped from a madhouse; and in his last published work, Our Old Home, he contemplates a tunnel under the Thames that he thinks would make a good dungeon for this sort: "How would every successive age rejoice in so secure a habitation for its reformers . . . [who seek] to burn up our whole system of society, under the pretense of purifying it from its abuses! Away with him into the Tunnel . . .!" (Works, VII, 296). In the three decades between these two examples and in various forms, Hawthorne reverted to the motif of the maniacal reformer doing his worst attempting to do good. The best known and artistically most satisfying version of this cautionary scenario is probably "The Birthmark," with the reformer cast as a scientist (Aylmer) intent on ridding his wife of the one flaw, a small hand-like birthmark on his cheek, that—to him—mars her otherwise perfect beauty. Certain that his knowledge can yield a creation superior to God's own, he vaunts that he will "triumph" in correcting "What nature left imperfect in her fairest work!" (Works, Cent. Ed., X, 41). The operation is a success, but the patient dies: the birthmark, that is, the emblem of Georgiana's humanity, reaches so deep into her being that its removal amounts to murder. While this tale—like all those that have established Hawthorne's reputation as one of the world's great writers—is too complex, too aswirl with countercurrents, to yield an unambiguous moral, still it takes no great leap of imagination to see Aylmer as the only slightly "displaced" utopian reformer, what Robert Heilman, in his classic study of the story, calls "a romantic perfectibilitarian . . . [who] in his presumption . . . proposes to establish heaven on earth" (587). Though blinded by his hubris to human limitation, Aylmer is drawn with considerable sympathy for the nobility of his aspiration. Hawthorne seldom showed so much sympathy, however, for this type. In "Rappaccini's Daughter," Hawthorne's other take on a maniacal scientist, he again presents the misguided idealist destroying what he seeks to improve, through his unwillingness to accept the natural, normal limits of human existence. The Universal Reformer is here figured as a perverted Prospero, a wicked magician employing his supernal arts in the cause of an unholy (and wholly illogical) perfectibilism. Likewise Hawthorne's tales of the New England Puritans—whose purpose, of course, was the utopian goal of founding, in John Winthrop's famous phrase, a City on a Hill, a New Jerusalem—evince a skepticism toward their fanatical zeal to redeem the world, with the whipping-post and brand when necessary. "The May-Pole of Merry Mount," "Endicott and the Red Cross," "The Gentle Boy" all present the Puritans as rigid, self-righteous, persecutorial in imposing their vision of truth upon the world; "The Man of Adamant," thin and clumsy as fiction, nevertheless reveals most unambiguously Hawthorne's antipathy toward the type who will sacrifice the fullness and complexity of life for the narrow rigidity of ideological purity: for Hawthorne, the very definition of the reformer. Of this type he charged: "You look at matters with an awful squint, which distorts everything within your line of vision; and it is queer, though natural, that you think everybody squints except yourselves" (Letters, Works, Cent. Ed., XVIII, 89).

It was not so much the content of reformist ideology as the psychology of the reforming ideologue that interested Hawthorne, so that he tended to locate his crypto-reformist tales not in contemporary times confronted with specific contemporary problems, but rather in abstract and vaguely distant times and places (the Padua of "Rappaccini's Daughter" has no more reality than, say, the Paris of Poe's detective tales) or in the world of pure allegory, as in "The Hall of Fantasy," "The Celestial Railroad," or

"Earth's Holocaust"; and to project the reformer's schemes in metaphoric and symbolic terms rather than literally. This displacement of the reformer's purpose in time and space allows Hawthorne to concentrate on the universal character of the reformer, sub specie aeternitatis, not on the specifics of the reform—a strategy in keeping with the general allegorizing imperative of Hawthorne's creative imagination. The major exception to such a strategy would seem to be The Blithedale Romance, with its contemporary setting and interplay of some of the pressing social issues of the day. Here, it is often claimed, Hawthorne revealed most explicitly, with the least indirection, his attitude toward utopia and utopian reformers. But that, as Hamlet says, would be scanned.

Blithedale, of course, is Hawthorne's fictionalized version of Brook Farm, the experiment in communitarianism located in Roxbury, near Boston. Much of the enduring fame of Brook Farm results no doubt from Hawthorne's having been one of its first inhabitants and his having memorialized his experience in fiction. Given the generally skeptical turn of Hawthorne's mind and particularly his skepticism of—even antipathy toward—the reformist mentality, it surprises to find him engaging in an enterprise whose founder, George Ripley, declared to be a harbinger of the millennium: humanity, the constitution of Brook Farm proclaimed, "is at length prepared to enter into that universal order toward which it has perpetually moved" (qtd. in Frothingham, 179). Although Hawthorne left Brook Farm before it was reorganized on strictly Fourierist principles, still its utopian aspirations were apparent from the outset. Speculation abounds on what led the introverted, intensely private, and skeptically conservative Hawthorne to cast his lot with the Universal Reformers, but the simplest and perhaps quite sufficient answer is economic: he could support himself there, he thought, and still find time to pursue his writing career. The venture did not work out for Hawthorne personally—he left after less than a year—nor, ultimately, for Brook Farm itself, which lasted for only six or seven years. Still, it provided him with the sort of first hand experience that could have enabled him to construct a trenchant analysis of utopian communitarianism in action. Such, however, proved not to be the case. In The Blithedale Romance, the reality of Brook Farm recedes into a hazy, insubstantial background, little more than a stage set for a melodrama of clashing personalities who have no real commitment to the experiment that they are ostensibly engaged in. Henry James long ago noted that the ground of Blithedale slips from under our feet as we read: "we get too much out of reality . . . I should have liked to see the story concern itself more with the little community in which its scenes are laid." The complaints that Hawthorne had slandered his former compatriots were misdirected, James declared: "Indeed, the brethren of Brook Farm should have held themselves slighted rather than misrepresented," for he "treated their institution mainly as a perch for starting upon an imaginative flight" (108).

What James judges a minor aesthetic flaw in a generally successful work, George Eliot more sweepingly condemns as both an intellectual and moral failure of the novel's total conception. Blithedale, as a socialist community, serves merely "as a scaffolding": the ideal animating the experiment "has so little business in [the plot] that it never grows into an organic part of the story . . . [I]t is really not made responsible for anything, good, bad, or indifferent. It forms a circumference of circumstances, which neither mould the characters, nor influence the destinies, of the individuals . . . forms, in short, not an essential part of the picture, but an enormous fancy border, not very suitable for the purpose for which it was designed." Having taken up the challenge "to dramatize his experience and observation of Communist life," Eliot concludes, it was incumbent on Hawthorne to follow through on his premise in a consequential way; this he fails to do, substituting scenery for substance (263-64).[3]

In fairness to Hawthorne it should be noted that in his Preface he explicitly abjures any intent to render a realistic account of Brook Farm: the author's "whole treatment of the affair," he insists, "is altogether incidental to the purpose of the Romance; nor does he put forward the slightest pretention to illustrate a theory, or elicit a conclusion, favorable or otherwise, in respect to Socialism." Anticipating, perhaps, the James-Eliot sort of objection, Hawthorne acknowledges that his use of a socialist community served only to establish a theater removed from ordinary life "where the creatures of his brain may play out their phantasmagorical antics"—a strategy defended by appeal to the generic character of the romance, with its release from "every-day Probability" and its evocation of an atmosphere of fairy tale or daydream (Works, Cent. Ed., III, 1). With so much conceded by the author, what cogency remains in the critics' strictures?

The problem with his rationale appears when Hawthorne claims: "Furthermore, the scene was in good keeping with the personages whom he desired to introduce." This is simply not so: that is, the three central characters—Coverdale (the narrator), Zenobia, and Hollingsworth—are not in the least "in keeping with" the communitarian spirit supposedly uniting the inhabitants of Blithedale. Coverdale, a rich young dandy and would-be artist, is far too arch, too cynical, too aware that he is engaged in what Emerson called a perpetual picnic of shepherds and shepherdesses, "an Age of Reason in a patty-pan" (Works, X, 364) to pass for a utopian of any sort; indeed, in his skepticism about human nature, Coverdale sounds very like his author, who, it is sometimes suggested, was offering here a masochistic self-portrait. In any event, he provides for Coverdale sentiments we know to be entirely his own: "we may be very sure . . . that the good we aim at will not be attained. People never do get just the good they seek. If it come at all, it is something else, which they never dreamed of, and did not particularly want" (75). Coverdale, then, might well have gone on to write The Life of Franklin Pierce, but he can never convince us that he had any serious desire to reform the world—or even to farm communally.

Zenobia (much the most fascinating character in the book) does have a portion of the fanatical reformer's furious zeal, but a zeal in no way channeled into the life of Blithedale. She is presented as a proto-feminist, angry, frustrated, fulminating against the oppression of women and the narrowness of the meager opportunities afforded them; but Blithedale offers no alternative gender roles—the women are quite traditionally domestic—nor is Zenobia ever shown trying to institute any. Her philippics could as well have been delivered in a Beacon Hill drawing room, which, truth to tell, would better suit her luxurious and luxury-loving personality. No more than Coverdale does Zenobia belong, intellectually or temperamentally, in a utopian commune. Furthermore, Hawthorne reveals that Zenobia's true motive for coming to Blithedale is the quite un-feminist one of trying to catch a husband—Hollingsworth, to be exact. Indeed, even her feminism is exposed as an expression of purely personal frustration, a sublimation of unfulfilled sexual passion. Women, claims Hawthorne-as-Coverdale, "are not natural reformers, but become such by the pressure of exceptional misfortune. I could measure Zenobia's inward trouble, by the animosity with which she now took up the general quarrel of woman against man" (121). If not altogether a pretense, Zenobia's forcefully articulated feminism appears finally as only a defense mechanism disguising her true feelings—and, in any event, evaporates before her desire to become Mrs. Hollingsworth. "Can it be, Zenobia," cries Coverdale at one point, "that you ever really numbered yourself with our little band of earnest, thoughtful, philanthropic laborers?" (164). The answer is no; but the answer would also be no, if the question were directed at Coverdale himself.

Or at Hollingsworth. Of all the characters in The Blithedale Romance, he has the true personality of the Universal Reformer—as Hawthorne conceived it: radical, monomaniacal, ruthless. Had he been presented as the guiding spirit of Blithedale, Hawthorne could have merged the radical reformer and the utopian reform in a single encompassing experiment, demonstrating how personality and program re-enforced each other. The situation, that is—given Hawthorne's anti-millennarian animus—had all the makings of the great American dystopia. Hawthorne, however, depicts Hollingsworth not as a supporter of Blithedale's socialist experiment, but actually as its subverter. He is an agitator for some vaguely presented panacea of penal reform and joins Blithedale only in hopes of using it as a means for furthering his own ends. To Coverdale's urging that he enter into the spirit of the place, Hollingsworth remains impervious, even hostile. "I begin to discern," Coverdale confesses, "that he had come among us, actuated by no real sympathy with our feelings and our hopes" (54-55). That puts the matter rather mildly, for, as Robert Elliott sums up, "Hollingsworth is contemptuous of the project from the beginning, seeing it as a miserably frivolous thing compared to his own scheme for reforming criminals" (73-74). With Hollingsworth alienated from Blithedale and its ideals and with the injection of his advocacy of a conflicting agenda of activism, Hawthorne dissociates the reformer from the reform, the personality type that is drawn to utopia from the utopia to which, one would have thought, it would naturally be drawn. "A radical incoherence," Elliott correctly claims, "exists at the heart of The Blithedale Romance" (79).

The result is a dual failure in The Blithedale Romance: first, the failure to make Blithedale real, an idea-in-action exerting discernable influence on the lives of the characters inhabiting it; second, the failure to effect the obvious ideological union between Hollingsworth, Hawthorne's archetype of the Universal Reformer, and the attempt at radical social reform that Hawthorne saw firsthand at Brook Farm. A result of these failures is that utopia never gets—not a fair hearing: one would hardly expect that from Hawthorne—but a serious hearing. What could have been a profound political novel—perhaps even on a par with The Possessed or The Charterhouse at Parma—becomes instead an exercise in evasive Gothic mystification, so that one can but agree with Irving Howe that "by any serious reckoning The Blithedale Romance must be called a remarkable failure by a very remarkable writer" (174).[4]

I want to suggest that, despite its contemporaneity, the setting of Hawthorne's romance has about it the same distanced abstractness as the setting of his earlier tales—and, perhaps, for the same reasons, though with less fortunate results. Clearly, crucial to the purpose of his story is the exposure of the true nature of the Universal Reformer, whose benevolence is all coldly theoretical, never personal and practical. Although Hawthorne squandered the opportunity to realize this figure in a realistic and socially significant context, he nevertheless provides in his blacksmith-turned-philanthropist the most extensive anatomy anywhere in his opus of the psychology of the reformer. Some years earlier Coleridge had written: "I have never known a trader in philanthropy who was not wrong in heart somewhere or other. Individuals so distinguished are usually . . . men not benevolent or beneficent to individuals, but almost hostile to them" (qtd. in Abel, 186). This provides an exact description of Hollingsworth—or, indeed, of any of Hawthorne's philanthropists: like the one in "The Christmas Banquet . . who had become so deeply sensible of the calamities of thousands and millions of his fellow creatures ... that he had no heart to do what little good lay immediately within his power" (Works, Cent. Ed., X, 303). In characterizing Hollingsworth, Hawthorne hammers this theme relentlessly: his only friend, Coverdale relates,

> was the cold, spectral monster which he has himself conjured up, and on which he was wasting all the warmth of his heart, and of which, at last—as these men of a mighty purpose so invariably do—he had grown to be the bond-slave. It was his philanthropic theory! . . . Sad, indeed, but by no means unusual. He had taught his benevolence to pour its warm tide exclusively through one channel; so that there was nothing to spare for other great manifestations of love to man, nor scarcely for the nutriment of individual attachments, unless they could minister, in some way, to the terrible egotism which he mistook for an angel of God. (55)

This terrible egotism leads him to exploit others—particularly Zenobia and the pitiful ice-maiden Priscilla—to further his monomaniacally embraced ideal: fruitlessly, as it proves, for Coverdale, embittered by the damage he has done, forces him to confess that he has reformed not a single criminal.

> The moral which presents itself to my reflections, as drawn from Hollingsworth's character and errors, is simply this:—that, admitting what is called Philanthropy . . . to be often useful by its energetic impulse to society at large, it is perilous to the individual whose ruling passion, in one exclusive channel, it thus becomes. It ruins, or is fearfully apt to ruin, the heart . . . (243)

The ruined heart, reflecting the loss of human sympathy, figures in "Ethan Brand" as a metaphor for the Unpardonable Sin, the forfeiture of one's hold "on the magnetic chain of humanity." Brand, too, begins as a philanthropic idealist, but the hypertrophy of his intellect results in an atrophy of his heart—which "had withered—had hardened—had perished! It had ceased to partake of the universal throb" (Works, Cent. Ed., XI, 98-99). When, in despair, Brand leaps into the flaming lime furnace, his heart is revealed to have turned to marble—the symbolic equivalent of what Hollingsworth's reformist mania had done to him. If Blithedale is Hawthorne's most ambitious attempt to depict the type of the Universal Reformer, "Earth's Holocaust"—one of the most complex and successful of his allegorical satires—presents the spectacle of Universal Reform itself. Quite literally, universal reform: for, in it, all the "evils" that have plagued human history are consigned to the flames of a great bonfire of the vanities. One of Hawthorne's pure allegories, it has none of that shifting interplay between the real and the fantastic that marks his great stories—"Young Goodman Brown," say, or "My Kinsman, Major Molineux." Rather "Earth's Holocaust" is unalloyed fantasy, playful in manner but wholly serious in intent—and patently didactic. Allegorical satire, as a genre, with its palpable intent to instruct, exerts little appeal to modernist readers who want unresolved tensions and teasing ambiguities in their tales, and less to the post-modernists who embrace only uncertainty: so that, as a type, "Earth's Holocaust" seems old-fashioned and literal, univocal. However, as Hyatt Waggoner suggests, we may often go to these works "to find out the meanings Hawthorne intended to express in his fiction. In the sketches belief is generally in control, the phantoms that haunt the mind mostly absent.... `Earth's Holocaust,' for instance, tells us what Hawthorne must have intended to say on his theme of social reform in Blithedale" (27). Without subscribing wholly to this instrumental way of reading the allegories, I would agree that belief rather than imagination, in the deepest sense, informs them. In any event, "Earth's Holocaust" provides Hawthorne's clearest credo on the subject of utopian reform.

The allegory has two "voices" that run throughout: a naivé young narrator, initially enthusiastic, but increasingly alarmed at the escalating virulence of reform; and his older, wiser companion who offers skeptical, often wryly understated judgments on the consequences of the frenzy. In addition there is a babble of other voices, arguing the merits of each new consignment to the fire—with the more radical voice always carrying the day. Hawthorne's strategy is to begin with what his readers, nineteenth century American democrats, would universally concur ought to be swept out of existence—the vestiges of hereditary monarchy and aristocratic privilege—and, by increments of destruction and a Pyrrohnist logic, to arrive finally at the inevitable tossing-on meant to horrify these same readers the most—the Bible itself: for what was the Bible but the symbol of traditional authority that checked the will of man himself and for which "the inhabitants of the earth had grown too enlightened? Therefore, as the final sacrifice of human error, what else remained, to be thrown upon the embers of that awful pile, except the Book, which, though a celestial revelation to past ages, was but a voice from a lower sphere, as regarded the present race of man? It was done!" (Works, Cent. Ed., X, 400). Between the baubles of aristocracy and the Bible, an array of the world's evils is conflagrated: liquor, of course, and tea and coffee and tobacco—"Everything rich and racy—all the spice of life!", complained one old gentleman—female modesty, armies and all the weapons of war, the instruments of punishment and then the idea of punishment itself, marriage, money, property, the state, literature and philosophy, and all organized religions. This is Universal Reform with a vengeance, a catalogue lacking only fur coats, Styrofoam cups and veal chops to satisfy even the most demanding philanthropist of this, our own demandingly philanthropic age.

The allegory, Waggoner states, "invites, indeed almost demands, the kind of explication best offered by historical scholarship, for it is a satirical comment on many of the most important trends and historical events of Hawthorne's age" (19). One recognizes throughout echoes of many of the contemporary melioristic or millenarian voices of the times—satirically distorted, of course, but recognizable. To take a single instance, the burning of the books follows from arguments against the burden of tradition and for the sufficiency of nature as a guide that are easily identified with the Transcendentalists: "Is not Nature better than a book?—is not the human heart deeper than any philosophy?—is not life replete with more instruction than past observers have found possible to write down in maxims?" (398). These are of course the Romantic, anti-traditionalist sentiments found, for instance, in Emerson's "The American Scholar": admirable—or at least innocuous—sentiments in themselves, they serve as the premise for a reductio ad absurdum that leads ultimately in Hawthorne's fantasy to the burning of all books: "Now we shall get rid of the weight of dead men's thought, which has hitherto pressed so heavily on the living intellect . . . The chief benefit to be expected from this conflagration of past literature, undoubtedly is, that writers will henceforth be compelled to light their lamps at the sun or stars" (396). The American rejection of the past and faith in its intellectual independence are thus presented as contributory to a destructive mania.

Hawthorne's strategy involves creating a context in which ideas, individually well-meant and supportable, are condemned by association—or, perhaps, by acceleration: a sort of whirlpool effect in which each reform sucks the next into the fire behind it, until only desolation and a pile of ashes remain. At one point the old observer comments: "Believe me, the fire will not be allowed to settle down, without the addition of fuel that will startle many persons, who have lent a willing hand thus far" (399). Correspondingly, Hawthorne's strategy presupposes that each reader, who has lent a willing ear thus far, will mentally call a halt, at some point in the allegory, to the orgy of reform, will draw the line somewhere between what should be burned and what spared. Some will agree that the gallows must go, but prisons too? Some will reject this or that form of government or perhaps some feature of all governments, but how many will endorse anarchy? No one, presumably, is expected to go all the way in endorsing the reformist pyromania: but where to stop—or, more importantly, why stop? Hawthorne, that is, anticipates the dynamics of the leftward imperative of modem politics, the drive toward ever more radical solutions to social ills and the consequent contempt felt by the more extreme for the less extreme: the Jacobins for the Girondists, the socialist for the liberal, the Marxist for the socialist, the Stalinist for the Trotskyite, the anarchist for them all. Once one begins down the slippery slope of radical reform, Hawthorne suggests, there is no secure purchase until one reaches bottom. "Unless we set fire to the earth itself," laments the once true-believing narrator, "I know not that we can carry reform to any further point" (399).

The implicit inference from the allegory—and the conclusion that I think Hawthorne himself drew—is that radical reform should not be under-taken at all. Consequently, even the initial reform—the destruction of monarchical/aristocratic structures, which, as I noted earlier, nineteenth century American democrats could be expected to endorse—is called into question, subtly but unmistakably. First, Hawthorne allows an exponent of the old order to have his say:

> This fire is consuming all that marked your advance from barbarism, or that could have prevented your relapse thither. We—the men of the privileged orders—were those who kept alive, from age to age, the old chivalrous spirit; the gentle and generous thought; the higher, the purer, the more

> refined and delicate life! . . . In abolishing the majestic distinctions of rank, society loses not only its grace, but its steadfastness—. (383-84)

The egalitarian spirit no doubt rejects such objection as the worst sort of special pleading—and it keeps not a single crown or coat-of-arms from being consigned to the fire—but Hawthorne encapsulates here the argument for aristocracy that prevailed in European culture at least since the Renaissance, the locus classicus of which is probably Ulysses' speech on degree in Troilus and Cressida, and that still found vigorous expression in, for instance, the words of Samuel Johnson, one of Hawthorne's intellectual heroes. In Boswell's Life, Dr. Johnson declares: "Sir, I am a friend of subordination, as most conducive to the happiness of society . . . Were all distinctions abolished, the strongest would no longer acquiesce, but would endeavor to obtain a superiority by . . . strength . . . As subordination is very necessary for society . . . mankind, that is to say, all civilized nations, have settled it upon a plain invariable principle . . . Were we all upon an equality, we should have no other enjoyment than mere animal pleasure" (I, 442). To what degree Hawthorne shared such sentiments is debatable, but certainly he agreed with Dr. Johnson that remedies for life's ills must be palliative not radical, for "Radical changes, or changes en masse, would very probably make things worse than they are" (Sewell, 313). When the narrator exults that all the aristocratic nonsense has been swept away, the wise old figure replies, "And in good time—if no worse nonsense come in its place" (384). Hawthorne no doubt had in mind the example of the French Revolution, which yielded, along with the Declaration of the Rights of Man, the term terrorism; but his old sage may be accorded even a degree of prescience: in the worst year of political repression under the last Russian czar, known to history as "Bloody Nicholas," far fewer political prisoners were executed than in any year of Stalin's purges, as Robert Conquest reminds us, when the body count ran into the tens of thousands (285-88). At all events, Hawthorne, ever suspicious of any radical rupture in the social fabric, presents the overthrow of the ancien regime as the first step in that imagined process of reform that leads inexorably to the earth's holocaust. He seems to draw the line, then, right at the beginning, counseling the bearing of those collective ills we have rather than flying to others that we know not of.

Yet it is finally not so much the danger as the impossibility of utopian reform that Hawthorne stresses. In his essay on Hard Times, Shaw states, "whereas formerly men said to the victims of society who ventured to complain, 'Go and reform yourself before you pretend to reform society,' it now has to admit that until Society is reformed, no man can reform himself except in the most insignificantly small ways" (334). Hawthorne clearly belongs to that earlier age, for he believed that the source of evil was not institutions but individual human hearts and that no amount of social tinkering would avail against the heart's impurities. He ends "Earth's Holocaust" with a coda in which the old wise man offers the disillusioned narrator "a strange assurance"—that "there is far less both of good and evil, in the effect of this bonfire, than the world might be willing to believe" (401). Tomorrow, he promises, will be very much like yesterday. Then, to overstate his point, Hawthorne introduces a dark stranger—clearly Satan—to have his say:

> There is one thing that those wisacres have forgotten to throw into the fire, and without which all the rest of the conflagration is just nothing at all . . . the human heart itself! . . . And unless they hit upon some method of purifying that foul cavern, forth from it will re-issue all the shapes of wrong and misery—the same old shapes, or worse ones—which they have taken such a vast deal of trouble

> to consume to ashes . . . Oh, take my word for it, it will be the same old world yet! (403)

Hearing this, the narrator draws the allegory's moral: "Purify that inner sphere; and the many shapes of evil that haunt the outward, will turn to shadowy phantoms. and vanish of their own accord. But, if we go no deeper than the Intellect, and strive, with merely that feeble instrument, to discern and rectify what is wrong, our whole accomplishment will be a dream" (404). Universal Reform, Hawthorne thus contends, will be achieved, if at all, only heart by heart, never by the sort of top down restructuring of society envisioned in utopias. The picture of Hawthorne's conservative attitude toward reform that I have drawn here, while accurate, is nevertheless monochromatic and not quite the whole truth. Scattered throughout his works one finds the occasional more forgiving estimate of the idealism that animates the reformer. I will close, then, with perhaps his most generous characterization, this from another of his allegories "The Hall of Fantasy." There are, first, the usual reservations:

> It would be endless to describe the herd of real or self-styled reformers that peopled this place of refuge. They were the representatives of an unquiet period, when mankind is seeking to cast off the whole tissue of ancient custom, like a tattered garment. Many of them had got possession of some crystal fragment of truth, the brightness of which so dazzled them, that they could see nothing else in the wide universe.

And yet, he continues,

> The heart of the stanchest [sic] conservative, unless he abjured his fellowship with man, could hardly have helped throbbing in sympathy with the spirit that pervaded these innumerable theorists. It was

good for the man of unquickened heart to listen even to their folly. Far down, beyond the fathom of the intellect, the soul acknowledged that all these varying and conflicting developments of humanity were united in one sentiment. Be the individual theory as wild as fancy could make it, still the wiser spirit would recognize the struggle of the race after a better and purer life, than had yet been realized on earth. My faith revived, even while I rejected all their schemes. (Works, Cent. Ed., XI, 180-181)

NOTES

1. For Hawthorne's attitude toward "reform," see Doubleday ("Hawthorne's Criticism"), Turner, Hall, Abel, Van Cromphaut, and Ziff. More tangential, but also relevant see Johnson, Reynolds, and Newberry (206-17). And for the attitude of some of the "reformers" toward Hawthorne, see Moore (128-129).

2. For Hawthorne's ambiguous position on abolition and the Civil War, see Mellow (409-10), Flint, and Yellin ("Hawthorne and the American National Sin" and "Hawthorne and the Slavery Question").

3. Although the review was unsigned, it has been convincingly attributed to Eliot by Rust.

4. Most recent commentary on The Blithedale Romance takes a more positive view of that work than the one reflected here; but comparing that commentary with the bracing rigor of Eliot reaffirms that, as in art, there is no progress in criticism. Among the spate of criticism, however, for that most relevant to my focus here, see Howard, Stoehr and Berlant. A good general discussion is found in Miller (Ch. 26).

REFERENCES

Abel, Darrel. "Hawthorne's Skepticism about Social Reform." *University of Kansas City Review* 19 (1953): 181-93.

Berlant, Lauren. "Fantasies of Utopia in The Blithedale Romance." *American Literary Realism* 1 (1989): 30-62.

Boswell, James. *The Life of Samuel Johnson*. Ed. G.B. Hill. Oxford: Oxford UP, 1934.

Clark, Harry Hayden. "Hawthorne: Tradition Versus Innovation." In *Patterns of Commitment in American Literature*. Ed. Marston LaFrance. Toronto: U of Toronto P, 1967. 19-37.

Conquest, Robert. *The Great Terror: A Reassessment*. New York: Oxford UP, 1990.

Doubleday, Neal Frank. "Hawthorne's Criticism of New England Life." *College English* 2 (1941): 639-53.

——. "Hawthorne's Satirical Allegory." *College English* 3 (1942): 325-37. Eliot, George. "Contemporary Literature in America," *Westminster Review* (Oct. 1852). Rpt. in *Hawthorne: The Critical Heritage*. Ed. J. Donald Crowley. London: Routledge and K. Paul, 1970. 263-64.

Elliott, Robert C. *The Shape of Utopia: Studies in a Literary Genre*. Chicago: U of Chicago P, 1970.

Emerson, Ralph Waldo. *Complete Works*, Century Ed. 12 vols. Boston: Riverside, 1903-04.

——. *Correspondence of Thomas Carlyle and Ralph Waldo Emerson*, Vol. 1. Boston: J.R. Osgood, 1883.

Fisher, Marvin. "The Pattern of Conservation in Johnson's Rasselas and Hawthorne's Tales." *Journal of the History of Ideas* 19 (1958): 173-96.

Flint, Allen. "Hawthorne and the Slavery Crisis." *New England Quarterly* 4 (1968): 393-408.

Freud, Sigmund. "Why War?" *Collected Papers*, Vol. 5. Ed. James Strachey. London: Hogarth P, 1950. 273-87.

Frothingham, O.B. *George Ripley*. Boston: Houghton, Mifflin, 1882.

Hall, Lawrence S. *Hawthorne: Critic of Society*. New Haven: Yale UP, 1944.

Hawthorne, Nathaniel. *The English Notebooks*. Ed. Randall Stewart. New York: Russell and Russell, 1941.

——. *Works.* 22 vols. Boston: Houghton, Mifflin, 1900.

——. *Works*, Century Ed. 23 vols. Columbus: Ohio State UP, 1974.

Heilman, Robert. "Hawthorne's `The Birthmark': Science as Religion." *South Atlantic Quarterly* 48 (1949): 575-83.

Howard, David. "The Blithedale Romance and a Sense of Revolution." In *Tradition and Tolerance in Nineteenth-Century Fiction*. Ed. David Howard, John Lucas, and John Goode. New York: Barnes & Noble, 1967.55-97.

Howe, Irving. *Politics and the Novel*. New York: Meridian, 1957.

James, Henry. *Hawthorne* (1879). Rpt. Ithaca: Cornell UP, 1956.

Johnson, Claudia D. "Hawthorne and Nineteenth-Century Perfectionism." *American Literature* 44 (1973): 585-95.

Lowell, James Russell. *Works: Literary Essays*. 4 vols. Boston: Houghton. Mifflin, 1890.

Mellow, James R. *Nathaniel Hawthorne and His Times*. Boston: Houghton, Mifflin, 1980.

Miller, Edwin Haviland. *Salem Is My Dwelling Place: A Life of Nathaniel Hawthorne*. Iowa City: U of Iowa P, 1991.

Moore, Thomas R. *A Thick and Darksome Veil: The Rhetoric of Hawthorne's Sketches*, Prefaces, and Essays. Boston: Northeastern U P, 1994.

Newberry, Frederick. *Hawthorne's Divided Loyalties*. Rutherford, NJ: Fairleigh Dickinson UP, 1987.

Nydahl, Joel. "Early Fictional Futures: Utopias, 1798-1864." In *America as Utopia*. Ed. Kenneth Roemer. New York: Burt Franklin, 1981. 254-91.

Reynolds, Larry J. "The Scarlet Letter and Revolution Abroad." *American Literature* 57 (1985): 44-67.

Rust, James D. "George Eliot and The Blithedale Romance." *Boston Public Library Quarterly* 7 (1955): 207-15.

Sewell, Richard B. "Dr. Johnson, Rouseau and Reform." *The Age of Johnson: Essays Presented to Chauncey Brewster Tinker*. New Haven: Yale UP, 1949. 307-17.

Shaw, George Bernard. "Introduction to Hard Times" (1907). Rpt. in *Hard Times: Critical Edition*. Ed. Fred Kaplan and Sylvere Monod. New York: W.W. Norton, 2001.357-63.

Stoehr, Taylor. *Hawthorne's Mad Scientists*. Hamden, CN: Archon, 1978. 147-224.

Thoreau, Henry David. *Walden*. Boston: Houghton, Mifflin, 1960.

Turner, Arlin. "Hawthorne and Reform." *New England Quarterly* 15 (1942): 700-14.

Van Cromphaut, Gustaaf. "Emerson, Hawthorne and The Blithedale Romance." *Georgia Review* 25 (1971): 471-80.

Waggoner, Hyatt. *Hawthorne*. Cambridge: Harvard UP, 1963.

Yellin, Jean Fagan. "Hawthorne and the American National Sin." In *The Green American Tradition*. Ed. H. Daniel Peck. Baton Rouge: Louisiana State UP, 1989. 75-97.

——. "Hawthorne and the Slavery Question." In *A Historical Guide to Nathaniel Hawthorne*. Ed. Larry J. Reynolds. New York: Oxford UP, 2001. 135-164.

Ziff, Lazar. "The Great Conservative: Hawthorne in America." In *Literary Democracy*. New York: Viking, 1981. 108-28.

3

Letters Turned to Gold: Hawthorne, Authorship and Slavery

—Teresa A. Goddu

In her "Cuba Journal," a series of letters written home about her daily life on a Cuban coffee plantation, where she traveled for a rest cure in 1833, Sophia Peabody describes Cuba as a realm of romance imbued by moonlight. Recounting an evening when she joined King Salvador, one of the plantation's slaves and a former African king, in conversation about his "former kingdom & subjects," she writes:

> I think the splendor of that evening surpassed anything I have yet seen in Cuba. The air was soft as the down of a dove's breast and delicately perfumed with the jessamine fragrance of the coffee blossom & the moon was so dazzling that to look straight at it gave me a shooting pain through the head—like that caused by the sun's direct rays . . . It does indeed seem palpable & like an intelligent presence—Every object looked as if the heavens

> had snowed pearls & diamonds . . . Even the ordinary share in the royal profusion & magnificence of beauty which showers down, & are for the lime [en]folded and robed in loveliness as in a mantle.

The "disembodied spirit" of the moonlight, coupled with the fragrance of coffee blossoms, transforms the actual into the imaginary—simple objects into things of wealth, magnificence, and beauty, slaves into kings. Cautioned by her sister Elizabeth Peabody in an earlier letter to "drive slavery from [her] thoughts," Sophia mystifies the slave economy: she masks the power dynamic between master and slave behind polite conversation and detaches the labor of slavery, as figured by coffee, from its political and economic meanings by transforming it into a picturesque backdrop. Sophia's moonlit evening depends upon, even as it obscures, the economy of slavery.[1] The "magic moonshine" that produces Hawthorne's realm of romance in "The Custom-House" has much in common with Sophia's moonlit evening.[2] It also "spiritualize[s]" (CE 1:35) the everyday objects of domestic life, converting them into "things of intellect" (CE 1:35) and "snow-images" (CE 1:26). By translating the actual into the imaginary, Hawthorne's moonlight aestheticizes everyday life and transports it to the literary realm of romance. Like Sophia's description of Cuba, Hawthorne's formulation of romance converts a material economy into a symbolic one. Despite his efforts to obscure the relationship between these two economies, in order to establish his romance as separate from the commercial marketplace, Hawthorne recognizes their intimate relationship: he insists upon the "coal-fire" as an "essential influence in producing" the moonlight's effect (CE 1:36) and he repeatedly describes the scarlet letter as a "rag" (CE 1:31), thereby emphasizing its relation to the raw materials of the writer's trade in the 1850s—paper made of reconstituted cotton fibers (CE 1:25).[3] The traces of "gold embroidery" in the letter's "fine red cloth" figure Hawthorne's art in both aesthetic and economic terms:

the golden needlework is meant to earn him cultural as well as commercial capital, a literary reputation as well as a livelihood (CE 1:31).

Similarly, Hawthorne seeks to mystify the economics of his authorship in order to claim cultural prestige in an increasingly commodified and professionalized literary marketplace. Through the fiction of his early obscurity and the persona of the withdrawn writer, Hawthorne attempts, as Meredith McGill argues, to situate his authorship as free of the marketplace. Yet, as McGill shows, this withdrawal from the market is itself a market strategy, the way he "'renegotiates a relation to the reading public" and redeems his minor fiction "by the success of his later work."[4] Hawthorne finds his place in the literary marketplace by standing apart from it. He manipulates the literary marketplace even as he veils his commercial affiliations to it.

While a number of critics have begun to disentangle the fictions of Hawthorne's authorial self-construction from the economic realities of his authorship, I want to pay particular attention to how the slave economy operates in Hawthorne's understanding of—and place within—the literary marketplace.[5] Although Hawthorne never wrote the novel about slavery in Cuba from Sophia's journal that Mary Peabody proposed, he did fashion his authorial persona and his theory of romance in relation to a marketplace that he knew to be inextricably intertwined with the economy of slavery. Not only did Hawthorne imagine that he would "make a great many stories"[6] from Sophia's "Cuba Journal," but he sustained his authorship by taking political jobs that placed him in commercial ports—Boston, Salem, Liverpool—historically linked to the slave trade and, when his own career was unprofitable, by editing literary works that take slavery and its commerce as their theme: Journal of an African Cruiser (1845) and "Papers of an Old Dartmoor Prisoner" (1846).[7] By repositioning Hawthorne's career in relation to the commercial ports he worked within and the early texts he edited for money, I argue that Hawthorne was economically embedded within a commercial marketplace connected to the slave economy and that he formulated his authorial identity as well as his romance in relation to this economy. Hawthorne's early career—especially his edited work, Journal of an African Cruiser—makes visible his professional stake in the subject of slavery and its trade.

In order to reconstruct the economics of Hawthorne's authorship and its commercial connections to slavery, I read against Hawthorne's authorial divide between the artist and the marketplace and his opposition between the canonical status of his romances and the commercial function of his edited works. An understanding of Hawthorne's authorship as a complex market construction, both cognizant of its commercial connections and intent on mystifying them, requires tracing the affinities between his commercial and authorial professions as well as between his edited and his imaginative works. Instead of reading Hawthorne's romance through his self-proclaimed "inactivity in political affairs," I focus on his career's commercial interest in the trade in slaves.[8] Shifting our attention away from Hawthorne's political stance on slavery to his economic embeddedness within commercial networks intertwined with slavery, and situating The Scarlet Letter in relation to Hawthorne's edited works about the slave trade that directly precede it rather than his statements about slavery in The Life of Franklin Pierce (1852) and "Chiefly About War-Matters" (1862) that follow it, shows how Hawthorne's authorship and his romance are indebted to and articulated through the economy of slavery.[9] Read in these terms, Hawthorne becomes central to a broader investigation of how the trade in books is connected to the traffic in slaves in the antebellum period.

"Another Piece of Book-Manufacture": Journal of an African Cruiser

In order to trace the function of the slave economy in Hawthorne's canonical text, The Scarlet Letter, I will situate it in relation to an obscure text that haunts the margins of Hawthorne's literary canon: Journal of an African Cruiser (1845). Even after the publication of Patrick Brancaccio's 1980 article, which calls for a reassessment of the text as an "important biographical and cultural document," the Journal has received little critical attention."[10] In accepting Hawthorne's division between his editing—or "book-manufacture" as he called it—and his imaginative writings, critics have missed the Journal's significance to the formulation of Hawthorne's authorial identity and his romance.[11] When Arlin Turner states that "[a]t the Old Manse, Hawthorne edited two works [the Journal and "Papers of an Old Dartmoor Prisoner"] he might have considered drudgery, but he welcomed the occasions to be generous to friends," he not only adopts Hawthorne's denigration of editing as a type of piece-work but elides its economic imperative by turning jobs desperately done for money into a gift economy based on friendship.[12] Instead of challenging critical configurations of Hawthorne's canonical identity, Hawthorne's edited works remain segregated from it by being located in the marketplace of book-manufacture or subsumed into it and, hence, recast as a type of patronage. My reading of the Journal operates to break down these divisions and so reveal the commercial foundations of Hawthorne's authorship and his art. Instead of showing Hawthorne's editorship and authorship to be at odds, the Journal reveals how editorship becomes Hawthorne's mode of authorship.

In the mid-1840s, after Hawthorne published The Twice-Told Tales (1837, 1842) but before he had gained any margin of literary fame and when his financial situation was precarious, he edited two works: Horatio Bridge's Journal of an African Cruiser and Benjamin Frederick

Browne's "Papers of an Old Dartmoor Prisoner." Both works were published under Hawthorne's editorial name alone. Both are about slavery and its trade: Bridge's journal gives an account of a Navy cruiser policing the slave trade and U.S. commercial interests along the west coast of Africa, and Browne's papers describe his time as a privateer plundering the Caribbean and South America during the war of 1812 and as a prisoner in Barbados and then Dartmoor.[13] Both circulated in places that were crucial to the establishment of Hawthorne's canonical reputation: the Journal was published in Wiley and Putnam's Library of American Books, which sought to establish a canonical series of American literature, and "Papers of an Old Dartmoor Prisoner" was serialized in The Democratic Review (January-September 1846), where Hawthorne was a frequent contributor and where Evert Duyckinck, the major publisher and promoter of Hawthorne's work in the 1840s and the architect of Wiley and Putnam's Library, had published an article on Hawthorne's genius the previous year (April 1845).[14] While both works helped to keep Hawthorne's finances afloat by earning him money and by enabling his successful bid to become surveyor of the Salem Custom House, and while both sustained his literary reputation by keeping his name in circulation during a time when he was not producing much of his own work, I will focus here on the Journal because of Hawthorne's "very long and unbroken connection" with Horatio Bridge and because of its prominent place of publication in the Library of American Books.[15] The Journal is crucial to Hawthorne's authorship both financially and formally: besides helping to keep him financially solvent and earning him a wider reputation, it provided a venue for him to shape his authorial identity and his theory of romance.

The Journal both animates and reveals Hawthorne's authorial strategies. In his preface to The Snow-Image, Hawthorne writes to Horatio Bridge, "If anybody is responsible for my being at this day an author, it is yourself."[16] Bridge, Hawthorne's Bowdoin college classmate, not only helped Hawthorne begin his literary career by ensuring the publication of the Twice-Told Tales with his guarantee to the publisher to cover any losses, and by reviewing it in an Augusta newspaper, but also loaned Hawthorne money throughout the 1840s and tried to help Hawthorne get a political appointment. The Journal was another way for Bridge to assist Hawthorne's finances and his career: Hawthorne earned a fee of $125 and a percentage of the profits for editing the journal.[17] While Hawthorne's main stake in the book was financial, he recasts his economic interest in the form of literary patronage. Telling Bridge, "I should like well to launch you fairly on the sea of literature," Hawthorne invokes a classical image of epic adventure that the actual circumstances of Bridge's voyage as a military and economic enterprise undercut. Hawthorne later states, "A little of my professional experience will easily put it into shape . . My name shall appear as editor, in order to give it what little vogue may be derived from thence—and its own merits will do the rest."[18] Lending Bridge his editorial experience and, more importantly, the vogue of his authorial name, Hawthorne plays the role of patron rather than debtor to Bridge.

Despite his attempt to frame the Journal in terms of literary patronage rather than as an economic transaction, Hawthorne is often startlingly clear about his own profit motive: "If I mistake not," he writes to Bridge, "it will be our best plan—both as regards your glory and my profit—to publish the journal by itself rather than in a Magazine, and thus make an independent author of you at once."[19] While Hawthorne separates the aims of author and editor in this letter to Bridge—one seeks glory and the other profit—he constantly collapses the two positions both within the production of the text and in its relation to his own fiction. Within the text, editorship becomes the way

Hawthorne projects a successful mode of authorship. The complex intersection of personas within the Journal reflects the way Hawthorne mediates his authorial identity through Bridge: "My own share of it is so amalgamated with the substance of the work, that I cannot very well define what it is," he writes. At the end of the preface to the Journal, the narrator remarks that he "smiles[20] to find himself, so simply and with so little labor, acquiring a title to be enrolled among the authors of books!"[21] The "little labor" is one of "correction and amendment"—of editing—rather than a "re-arrangement on artistic principles" (v). Bridge becomes the projection of Hawthorne's authorial fantasies: to achieve the title of author without much effort. Moreover, in presenting the author as an amateur who lacks "literary practice" (v) and who makes no high claims for the "humble pretensions" (v) of his work, the writer frees himself from the restrictions and responsibilities placed upon literary authors: "He puts forth his work . . . with no higher claims than as a collection of desultory sketches, in which he felt himself nowise bound to tell all . . . but only to be accurate in what he does tell. On such terms, there is perhaps no very reprehensible audacity in undertaking the history of a voyage" (vi). Relieved of the labor of imaginative writing as well as its moral responsibilities, Hawthorne projects himself a successful author. Indeed, it is through editing, or "another piece of book-manufacture as the Journal," that Hawthorne imagines he will fashion a successful career in the 1840s. He writes: "If I am to support myself by literature, it must be by what is called drudgery, but which is incomparably less irksome, as a business, than imaginative writing."[22] Appropriating Bridge's journal as well as his persona, Hawthorne authorizes himself.

Just as editorship and authorship become complementary modes of production in the Journal, so too do they become intertwined in the production of Hawthorne's own works. While editing the Journal, he was simultaneously trying to establish his own authorship by preparing a second volume of tales, Mosses from an Old Manse (1846). The two works are frequently connected in his letters to Duyckinck and he arranged for both works to be published in the Library of American Books. Hawthorne's advice to Bridge on how to become an "independent" author reflects his own conclusions about how he might best make a living through his writing in an increasingly piratical publishing system. In the same letter that he counsels Bridge on how to shape the Journal for publication, Hawthorne complains of his own work that "the pamphlet and piratical system has so broken up all regular literature, that I am forced to work hard for small gains."[23] Finding piecemeal work in periodicals unprofitable and disturbed by the rampant literary theft of an increasingly competitive literary marketplace in the 1840s, Hawthorne decides to publish the Journal as well as his own tales in book form.[24] Moreover, by positioning himself as an editor in both works, Hawthorne allies himself with the increased power of this profession to control the (re)production of an author's work. Unable to compose new stories for Mosses, Hawthorne figures the Journal as a substitute for his imaginative work. He states in the preface to Mosses, "Save editing (an easy task) the journal of my friend of many years, the African Cruiser, I had done nothing else."[25] He offers the Journal to Duyckinck in place of Mosses writing: "I can offer you nothing of which I claim to be author; but, for some weeks past, I have been employed in arranging a Journal, kept by a friend during a recent cruise on the West Coast of Africa." He anticipates for the Journal "a considerable circulation—more than of my own book proper."[26] Once again, Hawthorne figures editing as a more commercially viable mode of authorship. While he reinscribes the differences between editorship and authorship in the preface to Mosses (editing is an "easy task" that produces circulation while invention is difficult work that adheres in a proprietary relationship), the form of the text insists on their connection: like the Journal's "desultory sketches" (vi), Mosses is described as being composed of "fitful sketches" that claim "no profundity of purpose" nor afford a "solid basis for a literary reputation" (CE 10:34). In Mosses Hawthorne is unsuccessful as a "man of letters": "[t]he treasure of intellectual gold, which I hoped to find in my secluded dwelling, had never come to light" (CE 10:34). Instead, he fashions Mosses as an edited collection made of "idle weeds and withering blossoms" intermixed with "old, faded things" "produced long ago" (CE 10:34). The secluded author of the preface to Mosses, it turns out, is quite similar to the "scribbling tourist" (vi) of the preface to the Journal: both are editors who amend and recycle their previous work. While Hawthorne cannot find a "treasure of intellectual gold" in the Old Manse, he does discover in the subject of his "book-manufacture"—the trade in slaves and other commodities on Africa's gold coast—the gold his pocketbook seeks and, in its edited form, a way to craft a successful authorial identity.

If the Journal furnishes a model for Hawthorne's authorship, it also provides the context for his understanding of the marketplace's contaminated property relations within which his authorship operated. The Journal has much to say about the slave trade and its concomitant traffic—the commercial trade along Africa's west coast. Through its description of trade between commercial vessels and slavers, its explanation of the economic system where the price of slaves rises and falls in accordance with the price of colonial products, its revelation that U.S. commercial ships are sold to become slave ships, and its recountings of New England products visible in African huts, the Journal shows slavery to be at the heart of the commercial world and intimately linked to the U.S. market economy.[27] One striking passage states: "It is quite an interesting moral question, however, how far either Old or New England can be pronounced free from the guilt and odium of the slave-trade, while, with so little indirectness, they both share its profits and contribute essential aid to its prosecution" (112). While this speculative question—typical of Hawthorne's ambivalent moralizing stance in the text—raises the issue of New England's moral position in the slave trade only to suspend it, it discloses that New England participates in the international commerce of slavery by sharing in its profits and supporting its traffic. This revelation would only reinforce Hawthorne's understanding of how the slave economy permeated all aspects of market relations that he gained from working as a custom's officer in the ports of Boston (1839-41) and Salem (1846-49) and from his family's seafaring history: many of his ancestors were sailors and the Hawthorne family estate was built in part through "maritime adventures that included a wharf, warehouses, and vessels for trade with Newfoundland, England, and the West Indies"[28]; Hawthorne's father was a sailor who voyaged to the Caribbean and South America as well as to the East Indies; and his uncle, William Manning, had an interest in a privateer, The Frolic, discussed in "Papers of an Old Dartmoor Prisoner."[29] Salem also had a lengthy history of participating in the slave trade (it was particularly active in the slave trade in the 1780s); even its legitimate trade with West Africa in the mid-nineteenth century cannot, as George Brooks argues, "be studied in isolation from the slave trade" since "[t]he two trades in fact existed in a sort of symbiotic relationship, so intertwined were the paths of commerce in West Africa in the first half of the nineteenth century."[30] A letter Hawthorne writes from the Salem Custom-House suggests the interconnectedness of Salem's illicit and legitimate trades: "The Schooner Stirling put into this harbor on Thursday, and sailed this morning. She reported herself to the boarding-officer as from Boston, and bound for Bangor; but circumstances have since led to the suspicion that she was from the West Indies, with her original cargo on board."[31] Hence, when at the end of his career in "Chiefly About War-Matters," Hawthorne situates the slave trade at the heart of the American national enterprise by describing the Mayflower as a slave ship—"in her first voyage, sent forth a brood of Pilgrims on Plymouth Rock, and, in a subsequent one, spawned slaves upon the Southern soil"—he is restating the "monstrous" relations of the marketplace that the Journal first articulates.[32]

In showing how all trade circulates in the same system, then, the Journal blurs the line between commerce and crime. The sailor, the slaver, and the pirate, it argues, all operate in a single economy: "I have often thought" the narrator of the Journal states, "that the private history of a man-of-war's crew, if truly told, would be full of high romance, varied with stirring incident, and too often darkened with deep and deadly crime . . . Many a blackguard on board has been bred in luxury; and many a good seaman has been a slaver and a pirate" (6). By identifying himself with a sailor—Bridge—and by turning Bridge's private history into a romance, Hawthorne comes to see his authorship as well as his art as participating in this trade. For Hawthorne, as the Journal first explicates, authorship becomes associated with piracy and romance with the material by-products of this trade.

One episode in the book, the history of the Mary Carver, a Salem ship whose crew is murdered and bounty plundered by African natives, underscores the material foundations of Hawthorne's romance. Intent more on protecting American trade than on stopping slavers, Bridge's squadron sets fire to several towns up and down the coast near Little Berebee as punishment for the attack on the Mary Carver. This retaliative act is defended as virtuous: "An example was of peremptory necessity; and the American vessels trading on the coast will long experience a good effect from this day's battle and destruction" (84). The gruesome episode is ironically described as a "very pretty past-time" (85)—"in all probability, few of us had ever spent a day of higher enjoyment than this, when we roamed about, with a musket in one hand and a torch in the other, devastating what had hitherto been the homes of a people" (83)—and the burning of an Edenic hamlet is rationalized as a romantic episode:

> But when man takes upon himself the office of an avenger by the sword, he is not to be perplexed with such little scrupulosities, as whether one individual or family be less guilty than the rest. Providence, it is to be presumed, will find some method of setting such matters right. In fine, when the negro patriarch's strong sable sons supported their decrepit sire homeward, with their wives, "black, but comely," bearing the glistening, satin-skinned babies on their backs, and their other little ebony responsibilities trudging in the rear, there must have been a dismal wail; for there was no ancestral tree, its foliage shrivelled with free, stretching out its desolate arms over the ashes of the three wicker dwellings. (83-84)

By turning the man who bears a musket and torch into "an avenger by the sword," this passage shifts the moral position of the attacker in order to wrap the commercial causes of this war in a robe of righteousness. Moreover, picturing the war's destruction as a blighted ruin rather than as bloodied bodies romanticizes war and renders it redeemable by providence. While the romantic racism of this passage and its moralizing use of providence prefigure Hawthorne's later statements about slavery in The Life of Franklin Pierce and "Chiefly About War-Matters," they also exemplify the ways in which he transforms the actualities of a commercial war into romance.[33] In a letter to Bridge after he has read accounts of this episode in the newspaper, Hawthorne advises: "I really do consider the shooting of these niggers a matter of very questionable propriety; and am glad, upon the whole, that you bagged no game on either of those days . . . In one point of view, these warlike occurrences are very fortunate—that is, in supplying matter for the journal. I should not wonder if that was your object in thrusting yourself into these perils. Make the most of them."[34] Hawthorne's racism, which turns Africans into "niggers" and humans into "game," enables his commercial interest since it provides him the point of view from which he can plunder this war for his own profit. For Hawthorne, romance becomes the fortunate by-product of the commercial collisions initiated by the slave trade. Indeed, as the editor of the Journal, Hawthorne profits from material that issues from the slave trade and its colonial and commercial practices in Africa. He transforms the raw materials of African slavery and colonialism—Bridge's descriptions of the slave trade and "the settlements of the various nations of Europe, along that coast" (vi)—into a romance from which he expects high circulation: "Oh, it will be an excellent book!" he exclaims to Bridge.[35] Stating in the Journal's preface that "[t]he West Coast of Africa is a fresher field for the scribbling tourist, than most other parts of the world" (vi), Hawthorne plays to the interest in travel literature in general and Liberia in particular.[36] Moreover, in counseling Bridge on how to compose his journal, he underscores the author's role as entertainer:

> I would advise you not to stick too accurately to the bare fact, either in your descriptions or narrations; else your hand will be cramped, and the result will be a want of freedom, that will deprive you of a higher truth than that which you strive to attain. Allow your fancy pretty free license, and omit no heightening touches merely because they did not chance to happen before your eyes. If they did not happen, they at least ought—which is all that concerns you. This is the secret of all entertaining travelers.[37]

Like the sailors who must be allowed "[g]reat latitude" or their "voyage cannot be expected to turn out profitably"

(115), Hawthorne counsels Bridge to give his fancy freedom in order to make the most of his materials. This passage also summarizes the theory of romance that Hawthorne later articulates in the prefaces to his novels as well as in his own composition of Bridge's text: "As he gave me pretty large license, I have re-modelled the style, where it seemed necessary, and have developed his ideas, where he failed to do it himself, and have put on occasional patches of sentimental embroidery—at the same time avoiding to tamper with his facts, or to change the tenor of his observations upon them; so that the work has not become otherwise than authentic, in my hands."[38] Hawthorne's editing of the Journal becomes a mode of writing romance: the embroidering of bare facts to depict an authentic truth. Romance, the Journal reveals, is a more liberal form of editing: the license to transform other people's property into art. The Journal figures the romancer's art as a type of privileged piracy: the romancer, like the scribbling tourist or the entertaining traveler, appropriates the allure of Africa and embroiders its actualities of bloodshed and trade in human flesh into sentimental and sensational images that will sell at home. The romancer is an editor, a man of business, who traffics in other people's property—and people as property—in order to profit from a "rich theme." Throughout his prefaces Hawthorne figures the "conventional privilege" of the romancer's latitude as a crime even as he justifies his lawlessness.[39] In his preface to The House of the Seven Gables, he defends himself from having committed a "'literary crime" by claiming that he "appropriat[es] a lot of land which had no visible owner"; and in The Marble Faun, he depicts himself as a robber with "felonious hands" who steals other artists' designs by allowing himself "a quite unwarrantable freedom."[40] In his novels' depictions of the marketplace as a realm of "blackness" and slavery as well as their construction of the romancer's art as a type of theft, Hawthorne configures his art's relationship to the contaminated property relations of the marketplace in terms the Journal first lays out.

Moreover, from his plans to edit Sophia's journals, his role as editor of Surveyor Pue's manuscript in The Scarlet Letter, his reworking of the historical figure of Judge Pyncheon in The House of the Seven Gables, his cannibalizing of his experience at Brook Farm in The Blithedale Romance and of his journals in The Marble Faun to his recycling of his periodical productions into new books in Twice-Told Tales, Mosses from an Old Manse, and The Snow-Image, Hawthorne's authorial productions rely upon the model of book-manufacture first successfully used in the Journal.[41]

Through editing the Journal, then, Hawthorne both produces a book that sells and discovers how to make himself a successful author. The Journal not only furnished Hawthorne with the direct benefit of money but also provided him the fringe benefit of acquiring the "very pretty amount of literary reputation" he originally promised to Bridge.[42] Hawthorne's name as editor supplants Bridge's authorial identity: the title page of the Journal reads "By an Officer of the U.S. Navy. Edited by Nathaniel Hawthorne." Here, Bridge occupies the anonymous position that was often Hawthorne's in the publication of his early tales. The reviewers also attributed the book to Hawthorne: The Critic notes it as "'Hawthorne's Journal of an African Cruiser"; The Spirit of the Times titles its review "Scraps from Hawthorne's Book"; The Biblical Repository simply lists the book as "by Nathaniel Hawthorne'; and The New-York Mirror describes the Journal as having been "re-written by Hawthorne." In lending Bridge the vogue of his authorial name, Hawthorne accrues notice for himself in return. The Rover states, "From what we have read of this book and from the known ability of the editor, we judge it to be a work of uncommon interest and merit," and The Southern and Western Magazine writes, "His work is edited by Nathaniel Hawthorne, one of our most exquisite and original essayists." The Journal's positive reviews—Duyckinck claims that "No American book in a long time has been so well noticed"—belie Hawthorne's later claim to have been at this time the "'obscurest man of letters in America."[43]

Hawthorne's desire to distance himself from his successful career of "book-manufacture" once his authorial reputation was firmly established with The Scarlet Letter is foreshadowed in his private unwillingness to take credit for his editorship of the Journal. As Meredith McGill argues, Hawthorne's construction of his early obscurity has to do in part with an attempt to mask "his participation in mass-cultural and feminized forms such as the eclectic magazine, the gift book, the children's book, and the women's periodical."[44] Similarly, Hawthorne's ambivalence about publishing the Journal under his name as editor has more to do with a fear that his commercial role might detract from his authorial name than with his stated desire to give Bridge full credit for the work. He writes to Bridge on May 2, 1845: "It seems they have put in my name as editor—contrary to my purpose, and much to my annoyance; not that I am troubled with any such reluctance about introducing you to the public . . . But I wished you to have all the credit of the work yourself. Well; you shall still engross all the merit, and may charge me with all the faults." Here Hawthorne walks a fine line between seeming ashamed of introducing Bridge as an author and of appropriating that role himself. He resolves the tension by insisting that Bridge receive the authorial "credit"—"all the merit"—and that he, as editor, be "charged" with the book's faults. Hawthorne's financial language implies an opposition between the financial "credit" he earns through his editorship and the debt his authorship may potentially accrue by being "charged" with its faults. His note to Duyckinck on the same day underscores his ambivalence about taking on the public role of editor: "It would have pleased me better to have the Journal come before the public without my name; not that I am anywise ashamed to be known as the Editor, but because I wish the author to have the whole credit of the book. However, it must be as you and Mr. Wiley think best. Is it absolutely essential? Well; be it so—but I am very sorry." Hawthorne's insistence upon giving "'the author" the "whole credit of the book" masks his discomfort in being named editor The letter underscores the importance of giving authors full credit, even as it reveals how publishers retain control over how authorship is ultimately credited: Hawthorne quickly succumbs to Duyckinck's and Wiley's decision to circulate his authorial name in this way. When Hawthorne asks whether the use of his name is essential, he already knows the answer: in originally offering Bridge the vogue of his authorial name and in telling Bridge that Duyckinck will want his "American series to be led by some already popular names," he is well aware of how the Journal trades on his authorial name.[45]

While Hawthorne feared that his editorship of the Journal would devalue his authorship, the Journal's publication as the first number in the Library of American Books circulated his name within a prestigious cultural space. Under the editorship of Evert Duyckinck, the Library of American Books (1845-47) sought to encourage native authorship by publishing American authors at a time when it was cheaper to reprint foreign editions. As the name of its sister series, the Library of Choice Reading, suggests, the Library of American Books proposed to publish the best books in the best form and at the cheapest price. The Democratic Review notes that "in the face of the popular theory that the only books that will sell are the very entertaining and the very useful," Wiley and Putnam "have commenced the publication of a library, neat and tasteful in its mechanical execution, reasonable in its price, claiming support chiefly on the ground of literary merit, and, best of all, composed of the writings of native authors." The tastefulness of the books' material production—their "graceful and readable character" and their "elegant" style—reinforced their literary merit, as it allowed readers to "once more enjoy the luxury of 'Books which are Books.'" Anticipating James T. Fields' packaging of books in fine leather in the 1850s, Duyckinck's series began the process of turning American authors from commodities of the book trade into the cultural elite. Circulating on the title page of the inaugural book in the series, Hawthorne's name benefited from the recognition and cultural prestige the Library conferred.[46]

Moreover, the publication of Mosses from an OM Manse in the same series of American books reveals the ways in which Hawthorne's authorial and editorial identities mutually reinforced each other. The advertising circular at the back of the Journal for the Library of American Books lists the yet to be titled Mosses under the heading "in preparation": "A New Book. By Nathaniel Hawthorne" (xii). Circulating in the same places—The Library of American Books as well as The Democratic Review, which published Hawthorne's tales as well as lengthy excerpts of the Journal, and a flattering review of Hawthorne's authorship by Duyckinck—Hawthorne's edited and imaginative works mutually created his authorial reputation.[47] In its production as well as its circulation, then, the Journal demonstrates the necessity of reading Hawthorne's canonical and commercial works in conjunction.

If Hawthorne's self-portrait as an author in the secluded fairy-land of the moss-grown Old Manse, rather than his role as editor who trades in the subject of slavery, dominates the critical understanding of Hawthorne's authorial identity, the Journal illuminates the ways in which Hawthorne's early career successfully invested in the subject and capital of slavery in order to build his cultural capital and to manufacture his authorship. Just as Hawthorne's image of himself as a secluded artist in the Old Manse is contradicted by his editing the Journal in its study, so too does the Journal underscore the material foundations of Hawthorne's romance and the commercial basis of his canonical reputation. With the publication of The Scarlet Letter and the establishment of his "successful" authorship, Hawthorne no longer had time for editing other people's work: his interest in publishing a second edition of the Journal waned and he turned down a request in 1853 to edit the memoirs of a notorious slave trader, Captain Canot, due to other commitments.[48] Yet, while the publication of The Scarlet Letter created Hawthorne as a canonical author, it has much in common with his commercial book-manufacture. Despite the aim of "The Custom-House" to establish the author and his romance as separate from the commercial sphere, they remain, as they were in the Journal, connected to the marketplace and its questionable traffic.

Sailors and Slaves: Hawthorne in "The Custom-House"

With the publication of The Scarlet Letter, Hawthorne had, as Duyckinck wrote, "at last a palpable hit." While his conversion to successful author appeared to happen overnight, his "great prolonged early period," as Nina Baym calls it, belies the suddenness of The Scarlet Letter's success.[49] By situating The Scarlet Letter at the end of his early period—as another piece of book manufacture—rather than at the beginning of his major phase, Hawthorne's authorship in "The Custom-House" appears as an extension of his editorial persona in the Journal: Hawthorne not only presents himself "in [his] true position as editor, or very little more" (CE 1:4) of Surveyor Pue's manuscript and of his own posthumous papers as a decapitated Surveyor, but the preface also retains references to the novel's original conception as an edited collection of tales. Moreover, his description of how he composed Surveyor Pue' s text echoes his editing of Bridge's journal: as with the Journal, Hawthorne so amalgamates his own writing with Pue's "dozen sheets of footscap" and allows himself so much "license" that he can only claim an "authenticity of the outline" (CE 1:33). Pue "authorize[s]"

Hawthorne's story without confining it within strict limits (CE 1:32). Like Bridge, Pue provides the "groundwork of a tale" without insisting on authorial rights or claiming the profits: "do this, and the profit shall be all your own!" he says (CE 1:33). As with Bridge, Hawthorne recasts his debt to Pue—this time in terms of "filial duty" rather than literary patronage (CE 1:33). In doing so, he transforms his commercial interest in the text into paternal inheritance. While the thrust of "The Custom-House" is to construct Hawthorne's authorship as free of the marketplace that produces it—to establish him as a "gentleman who writes from beyond the grave" (CE 1:44)—its edited form underscores his authorship's commercial connections. Hawthorne may invoke Mosses throughout "The Custom-House" in order to project a division between his identities as secluded artist and as Surveyor of the Revenue, but he continues to figure his authorship and his art through the Journal's commercial terms. Indeed, it is from the commercial papers of the Custom-House—not the intellectual wealth of the Old Manse—that Hawthorne discovers how to turn his "letters . . . to gold" (CE 1:37).

The Journal haunts The Scarlet Letter as well as "The Custom-House." In both, Hawthorne configures the marketplace in terms the Journal lays out as a realm of slavery as well as crime. "The Custom-House" follows the Journal in figuring the marketplace in the specific terms of a maritime/mercantile culture. Despite its "decaying trade" (CE 1:6), Salem is a port where vessels from Africa or South America arrive regularly with hides or other cargo, where merchandise is often "smuggled ashore" (CE 1:15), and where "smart young clerk[s]" get a "taste of traffic as a wolf-cub does of blood" when sending out "adventures in [their] master's ship[s]" (CE 1:6). Naming the key merchants of Salem's West African trade—Kimball, Pingree, Hunt, Upton (CE 1:44)—"The Custom-House" underscores the Journal's claim that "[mitre vessels come to the coast of Africa from Salem than from any other port in the United States" (110) and signals Salem's imbrication within a broader trade tied to slavery.[50] Within The Scarlet Letter—and Hawthorne's romances more generally—"blackness" becomes the sign of a market economy that turns people into property and traffics in questionable merchandise.[51] From Chillingsworth, who with his face "sooty with . . . smoke" practices his "black art" (CE 1:127) on Dimmesdale and entices Hester "into a bond that will prove the ruin of [her] soul" (CE 1:77) to Hawthorne's "dark" woman, Hester, who stands in the marketplace before a public who would "put the brand of a hot iron" (CE 1:51) on her forehead and who is bound by a chain of "iron links" (CE 1:80), Hawthorne sees the author and his art as operating within a commercial market economy figured in relation to slavery. The "Black Man's book," which Hester signs "with [her] own blood" (CE 1:117), represents the book trade as a realm of contracts and bonds rather than of privilege and license. Working in a business, described in his letters as the devil's trade, Hawthorne characterizes the author in The Scarlet Letter not as a secluded artist but as a commodified object who must sell his soul to the trade.[52]

Hawthorne's authorial anxiety about circulating within and becoming enslaved by this market economy is mediated through two identities tied to the maritime/mercantile trade: the sailor and the slave. Like the slave, the author is property to be traded in the marketplace; however, like the sailor, the author can traffic in the commodities issuing from the slave trade in order to make a profit. Claiming to have given up all artistic ambition in his job as Surveyor of the Revenue, Hawthorne figures his authorial identity in the commercial terms of shipping:

> No longer seeking nor caring that my name should be blazoned abroad on title pages, I smiled to think that it had now another kind of vogue. The Custom-

> House marker imprinted it, with a stencil and black paint, on pepper-bags, and baskets of anatto, and cigar-boxes, and bales of all kinds of dutiable merchandise, in testimony that these commodities had paid the impost, and gone regularly through the office. Borne on such queer vehicle of fame, a knowledge of my existence, so far as a name conveys it, was carried where it had never been before, and, I hope, will never go again. (CE 1:27)

Here Hawthorne's literary and commercial capital circulate in the same system: his authorial name, "blazoned abroad on title-pages," is imprinted like his business name on a commodity, his books. Hawthorne's ambivalence about operating in the marketplace is signaled by a fantasy of commercial circulation coupled with a desire to stop his name from circulating. As with the Journal, he "smiles" to discover that his name has so easily accrued recognition even as he remains concerned about its commercial vogue. Coming directly after his ruminations about his lack of literary fame and directly before his discovery of the scarlet letter, this passage begins the project of reimagining Hawthorne's authorship as commercially successful. However, it also registers Hawthorne's fear of becoming enslaved by the market. He mediates his literary commodification through the sign of "blackness" and the metaphor of slavery. His name, stenciled in black, signifies the realm of the market in general and the commerce of slavery in particular. The commodities upon which Hawthorne's name is imprinted—pepper, anatto, cigars—are from Salem's trade with Africa, the East Indies, South America, and the Caribbean. Moreover, by turning himself into a commodity transported by a ship—a name that is "borne" on a queer vehicle of fame—Hawthorne figures himself as human property that circulates without agency. The lack of agency in this passage—it is the Custom-House marker that imprints Hawthorne's name, not Hawthorne himself transforms Hawthorne's actual role in the Custom House as the trafficker in goods into the figurative role he appropriates—the slave. Hawthorne's description of Hester as a slave in the marketplace as well as his description of authorship as a type of imprinting—the scarlet letter brands itself like a "red-hot iron" on his breast (CE 1:32)—underscores his construction of the author as a commodified object. Hawthorne's alliance with the sailor in "The Custom-House" marks the way he attempts to transform this identity. Just as he appropriates Bridge's identity in the Journal so too does he affiliate himself with his "native place" (CE 1:8) the port of Salem, and its race of men who, generation after generation, "followed the sea" (CE 1:11) and whose "strong traits of . . . nature have intertwined themselves" with his (CE 1:10). (53) Through his confederation with the sailor as well as Salem's profitable past, Hawthorne asserts mastery over a market he claims elsewhere enslaves him. Like the sailor, Hawthorne profits from Salem's commerce. Bemoaning Salem's present "decaying trade," Hawthorne turns to the past, when Salem was a "port by itself" (CE 1:6) to transform his own idle profession of writing into a profitable business. In the midst of the marketplace—the commercial documents located in the Custom House that contain the "statistics of the former commerce of Salem" (CE 1:28) and "memorials to her princely merchants" (CE 1:29)—Hawthorne discovers the treasure that eluded him in the Old Manse: the scarlet letter. Hawthorne figures his art as a profitable by-product of commerce. Instead of disassociating himself from the traffic of the market, Hawthorne capitalizes on his commercial connections in order to succeed as an author.

As in the Journal, however, The Scarlet Letter represents the sailor's trade as illicit and connected to the illegitimate economy of slavery. In the novel's closing marketplace scene, the sailors, on whose ship Hester hopes to make her escape with Dimmesdale and Pearl, are marked not only by "blackness" but also by crime: they are "rough-looking desperadoes, with sun-blackened faces" (CE 1:232) and arrive on "one of those questionable cruisers" from the Spanish Main en route to Bristol (CE 1:215). Given the repeated description of the ship's commerce as "questionable," its connection to Bristol, one of England's leading slave ports in the eighteenth century, and the negligible difference between legal and illegal commerce through slave ports such as Salem, the ship may be not only a privateer, but a slaver. Decked out with "broad-brimmed hats of palm-leaf" and belts "clasped with a rough plate of gold" that hold knives or swords, and performing the transgressive behavior of "smoking tobacco under the beadle's very nose" (CE 1:232), the sailors symbolize the violence and profit that issue from the traffic in commodities of slavery that circulate between England, New England, and the Caribbean. The narrator's comment that "the sailor of that day would go near to be arraigned as a pirate in our own" (CE 1:233) redeploys the aphorism of the Journal that all sailors have been slavers and pirates. As the Journal makes clear, legitimate and illegitimate trade existed symbiotically: to enter international commerce meant taking part in the slave trade. Moreover, the designation of slave trading as an act of piracy in 1820 further conflates these two activities.[54]

Instead of disowning the figure of the sun-blackened sailors and their questionable traffic, Hawthorne identifies with the "license . . . allowed the seafaring class" who remain unregulated by "human law" while at sea (CE 1:233). The romancer, like the sailor, transgresses "without fear or scruple, the rules of behaviour that were binding on all others" (CE 1:232). Hawthorne figures the crime of trade as a space of freedom and profit. Moreover, he mitigates the sailor's guilt by arguing that they operate under different laws: the sailor who performs "desperate deeds" at sea can "become at once, if he chose, a man of probity and piety on land" (CE 1:232). Similarly, in mediating his authorship through the sailor and his illicit trade, Hawthorne reveals the complex market relations in which his authorship operates while simultaneously deflecting their full implications. Like the sailor whose profit necessitates and justifies his crime, Hawthorne simultaneously asserts and excuses his ownership in the prefaces to his romances. He makes clear the violent forms of dispossession that sustain the market economy and his authorship even as he ultimately projects his authorship as standing outside the market and being exonerated from it. At the end of "The Custom-House," Hawthorne returns to the literary life and, in so doing, imaginatively dissolves the commercial world: the Custom-House becomes a "dream," the "men of traffic" are converted into "shadows," and the port of Salem retreats into the mist (CE 1:44). In asserting that the commercial realm "ceases to be a reality of [his] life" (CE 1:44), Hawthorne mystifies his manipulation of the marketplace. In imagining himself as a "citizen of someplace else" (CE 1:44), "transport[ed]" by "triumphant thoughts" rather than a ship, he no longer remains a slave to the market (CE 1:45). However, his attempt to move from the site of slavery—the market—at the end of "The Custom-House" is more an imaginative projection than an actual escape. His authorship's extensive commercial connections remain to be read in his romance: not only in the opening scene of Hester standing chained before the public but also through the character who serves as the embodiment of his art, Pearl.

Hawthorne's representation of his romance through the character of Pearl underscores the commercial basis of his art and its connection to the commerce of slavery. As the "scarlet letter endowed with life" (CE 1:102), Pearl serves as a symbol of Hawthorne's romance. Like romance, she has a "strange remoteness and intangibility" (CE 1:92); and in her "dark and wild peculiarity" (CE 1:90), she embodies its license, the "freedom of a broken law" (CE 1:134). Pearl's "blackness"—she has "deeply black eyes" (CE 1:92) and a "depth of hue" (CE 1:90)—associates her not only with Hester's guilty passion but also with the crime of trade. Pearl is constantly connected to the sea: she is described as a sea-breeze, a sea-bird, a mermaid (CE 1:178), and a trafficker who sends out "more ventures on the mighty deep than any merchant in New England" (CE 1:177). Moreover, through her rich dress, her name, and her description as a "wild, tropical bird, of rich plumage" (CE 1:111), Pearl is not only figured as a commodity but also associated with the Caribbean.[55] In reading her name as a nautical reference to the schooner Pearl, a ship that attempted to free seventy-six fugitive slaves from Washington D.C. in 1848 only to be recaptured (fittingly enough) by the steamboat Salem, Pearl also signifies the slave as property. (56) Finally, Pearl's relationship with the captain of the Bristol ship—whose own garments, covered in "gold lace" and "encircled by a gold chain" (CE 1:233), symbolize the profits from his questionable traffic—further connects her to the trade of the seafaring class. In one scene, the shipmaster, unable to catch her to give her a kiss, throws his gold chain to Pearl who "immediately twined it around her neck and waist, with such happy skill, that, once seen there, it became a part of her, and it was difficult to imagine her without it" (CE 1:245). Unlike the scarlet letter, which contains "traces . . . of gold embroidery" (CE 1:31), Pearl's gold chain represents the transformation of a commodity into art as well as the fortune-seeking that lies at the heart of romance writing. Just as Pearl's "happy skill" naturalizes the mechanisms by which the gold chain captures her, Hawthorne's labors aestheticize the commodities that constitute his art. In the image of Pearl, then, Hawthorne simultaneously explicates his art's dependence on a material economy tied to slavery, and reveals the romancer's role in mystifying that relation. The beauty and profit that Hawthorne weaves into the golden image of his art, however, remain embedded in the dense market relations of a commercial economy tied to the slave trade. Pearl's necklace may be of gold instead of iron, but she remains linked to the marketplace.

Realigning Hawthorne's career through his edited works and situating him within a circum-Atlantic maritime/ mercantile culture makes intelligible how the slave trade structures Hawthorne's authorship, as well as his art. Such a repositioning of Hawthorne's authorship not only provides new routes for understanding his romance but also unveils the embeddedness of antebellum authors—even those who seem most politically disconnected from slavery—in a market economy permeated by it.[57] In figuring his art, like his authorship, in commercial terms connected to slavery, Hawthorne cogently explicates the marketplace's multiple and mediated relations. While he may ultimately attempt to mystify the commercial dependencies of his art and authorship by transforming Pearl into a gentlewoman with an inheritance, or the scribbling writer into a gentleman—they remain to be read in his romances as well as in the relationship between his commercial and canonical texts. Reconstructing the material foundations of Hawthorne's romance—its dependence on coal that issues from the Boston Custom House and a magical moonlight associated with Cuba and Africa, as well as the commercial investments of his early career in the subject of slavery—makes evident the complex market relations that produce Hawthorne's authorship. For it is through editorship that Hawthorne succeeds in manufacturing a successful authorship and in turning The Scarlet Letter into gold.

NOTES

1. Sophia Peabody Hawthorne, *The Cuba Journal, 1833-35*, ed. Claire Badaracco (1981; Ann Arbor, Michigan: University Microfilms International, 1985), 576-77 (MS221). Elizabeth Peabody to Mary Peabody, n.d. June, Sept. 14, 1834, ibid., 674. Sophia Peabody, accompanied by her sister Mary, lived on the Cuban coffee plantation, "La Recompensa," in San Marcos, Cuba from December

1833 until April 1835. The letters which she wrote home were circulated in Boston to a small audience of family and friends. The journal was later bound as a book, although it was never published. For a textual history of the "Cuba Journal" see Claire Badaracco, "The Night-blooming Cereus: A Letter from the 'Cuba Journal' 1833-35 of Sophia Peabody Hawthorne, With a Check List of Her Autograph Materials in American Institutions," *Bulletin of Research in the Humanities* 81 (1978), 56-73; Claire M. Badaracco, "Sophia Peabody Hawthorne's Cuba Journal: Volume Three, 31 October 1834-15 March 1835," *Essex Institute Historical Collections 118* (1982), 280-315; and her introduction to *The Cuba Journal, 1833-35*. Despite Elizabeth Peabody's warning, Sophia's journal contains descriptions of slavery as well as discussions of Spanish colonial policy and the threatened abolition of the slave trade. Sophia mitigates these discussions through a gradualist philosophy similar to her future husband's: "I do not allow myself to dwell upon slavery for two reasons. One is, it would certainly counter the benificient influences, which I have left home and country to court, and another is, that my faith in GOD makes me sure that he makes up to every being the measure of happiness which he loses thro' the instrumentality of others. I try to realize how much shorter time is, than eternity and then endeavor to lose myself in other subjects of thought" (*Cuba Journal*, 61). See also T. Walter Herbert, *Dearest Beloved: The Hawthornes and the Making of the Middle-Class Family* (Berkeley: Univ. of California Press, 1993), 49-51.

2. Nathaniel Hawthorne, *The Scarlet Letter*, ed. William Charvat et al., *The Centenary Edition of the Works of Nathaniel Hawthorne,* Vol. 1 (Columbus: Ohio State Univ. Press, 1962), 36. Hereafter cited parenthetically by volume and page number.

3. For a history of nineteenth-century paper making, see David C. Smith, *History of Papermaking in the United States* (New York: Lockwood Pub. Co., 1970) and Judith A. McGaw, *Most Wonderful Machine: Mechanization and Social Change in Berkshire Paper Making, 1801-1885* (Princeton: Princeton Univ. Press, 1987). In the

antebellum U.S., paper was produced by cutting rags into two to four inch pieces (the scarlet letter is described as being 3 1/4 inches), breaking them down into fiber by washing them and then reforming these fibers into sheets of paper.

4. Meredith L. McGill, "The Problem of Hawthorne's Popularity," in *Reciprocal Influences: Literary Production, Distribution, and Consumption in America*, ed. Steven Fink and Susan S. Williams (Columbus: Ohio State Univ. Press, 1999), 44, 41.

5. See, for instance, Richard H. Brodhead, *The School of Hawthorne* (New York: Oxford Univ. Press, 1986); Michael T. Gilmore, *American Romanticism and the Marketplace* (Chicago: The Univ. of Chicago Press, 1985); Jane Tompkins, *Sensational Designs: The Cultural Work of American Fiction* (New York: Oxford Univ. Press, 1985).

6. "Introduction" to Nathaniel Hawthorne, *The Letters, 1813-13*, ed. Thomas Woodson, L. Neal Smith, and Norman Holmes Pearson, *The Centenary Edition of The Works of Nathaniel Hawthorne*, Vol. 15 (Columbus: Ohio State Univ. Press, 1984), 28; hereafter cited parenthetically by volume and page number. Hawthorne was familiar with Sophia's journal: he read it during their courtship and copied several passages from it into his notebooks. His tale "Edward Randolph's Portrait" is based on a passage that he copied into his notebook from Sophia's journal about restoring a painting obscured by age. See Nathaniel Hawthorne, *Hawthorne's Lost Notebook, 1835-1841*, transcript and preface by Barbara S. Mouffe (University Park: The Pennsylvania State Univ. Press, 1978), 64. Sophia writes to Elizabeth Peabody in 1838: "He said he had imagined a story, of which the principal incident is my cleaning that picture of Fernandez. To be the means, in any way, of calling forth one of his divine creations, is no small happiness, is it?" (quoted in Julian Hawthorne, *Nathaniel Hawthorne and His Wife*, Vol. 1 [1884; reprint, Hamden: Archon 1968], 185). Robert Cantwell argues that Hawthorne transported Cuba to New England in "Edward Randolph's Portrait" by rewriting Cuba's colonial crisis as New England's. See

Robert Cantwell, *Nathaniel Hawthorne: The American Years* (New York: Rhinehart and Co., 1948), 253-58. Julie Hall also claims Sophia's journal as a source for "Drowne's Wooden Image." See Julie Elizabeth Hall, "Sophia Peabody Hawthorne: The Woman Behind the Man" (Ph.D. diss, University of North Carolina at Chapel Hill, 1993). Late in her life, Mary Peabody Mann finally wrote her own novel from her experiences in Cuba, Juanita; a Romance of Real Life in Cuba Fifty Years Ago (Boston: D. Lothrop, 1887).

7. [Horatio Bridge], *Journal of an African Cruiser*, ed. Nathaniel Hawthorne (New York: Wiley and Putnam, 1845); hereafter cited parenthetically. [Benjamin Frederick Browne], "Papers of an Old Dartmoor Prisoner," ed. Nathaniel Hawthorne, *The United States Magazine and Democratic Review* 18-19 (January 1846-September 1846), 31-39, 97-111, 200-212, 360-68, 457-65, 141-48, 209-17.
8. *CE* 1:42. There is a substantial body of critical work discussing the relationship between Hawthorne's romance, most often The Scarlet Letter, and his political stance on the issue of slavery. See Jonathan Arac, "The Politics of The Scarlet Letter," in *Ideology and Classic American Literature*, ed. Sacvan Bercovitch and Myra Jehlen (Cambridge: Cambridge Univ. Press, 1986), 247-66; Sacvan Bemovitch, *The Office of The Scarlet Letter* (Baltimore: Johns Hopkins Univ. Press, 1991); Richard Brodhead, "Hawthorne and the Fate of Politics," *Essays in Literature* 11 (1984): 95-103; Jennifer Fleischner, "Hawthorne and the Politics of Slavery," *Studies in the Novel* 23 (1991), 96-106; Allen Flint, "Hawthorne and the Slavery Crisis," *The New England Quarterly* 41 (1968), 393-408; Eric Cheyfitz, "The Irresistibleness of Great Literature: Reconstructing Hawthorne's Politics," *American Literary History* 6 (1994), 539-58.
9. Hawthorne's romances have been traditionally read as bearing no relationship to slavery. Jean Fagan Yellin argues, for instance, that Hawthorne's romances operate in terms of a "strategy of avoidance and denial" since the "link between . . . metaphorical slavery and the literal

enslavement of blacks is conspicuously absent" in his romances. See Jean Fagan Yellin, "Hawthorne and the American National Sin," in *The Green American Tradition*, ed. H. Daniel Peck (Baton Rouge: LSU Press, 1989), 88, 97. There is, however, a growing body of criticism that marks the importance of race and slavery in Hawthorne's texts. See Jay Grossman, "'A' is for Abolition?: Race, Author ship, The Scarlet Letter," *Textual Practice* 7 (1993), 13-30; Mara L. Dukats, "The Hybrid Terrain of Literary Imagination: Maryse Conde's Black Witch of Salem, Nathaniel Hawthorne's Hester Prynne, and Aime Cesaire's Heroic Poetic Voice," *College Literature* 22 (1995), 51-61; Caroline Woidat, "'Talking Back to School-teacher: Morrison's Confrontation with Hawthorne in Beloved," *Modern Fiction Studies* 39 (1993), 527-46; Jane Cocalis, "The 'Dark and Abiding Presence' in Nathaniel Hawthorne's The Scarlet Letter and Toni Morrison's Beloved," in *The Calvinist Roots of the Modem Era*, ed. Aliki Barnstone, Michael Tomasek Manson, and Carol J. Singley (Hanover: Univ. Press of New England, 1997), 250-62; Deborah L. Madsen, "'A is for Abolition': Hawthorne's Bond-servant and the Shadow of Slavery," *Journal of American Studies* 25 (1991), 255-59; Laura Hanft Korobkin, "The Scarlet Letter of the Law: Hawthorne and Criminal Justice," *Novel* 30 (1997), 193-217; Walter Benn Michaels, "Romance and Real Estate," in *The American Renaissance Reconsidered*, ed. Walter Benn Michaels and Donald E. Pease (Baltimore: Johns Hopkins Univ. Press, 1985), 156-82; Shawn Michelle Smith, *American Archives: Gender, Race, and Class in Visual Culture* (Princeton: Princeton Univ. Press, 1999); Nancy Bentley, "Slaves and Fauns: Hawthorne and the Uses of Primitivism," *ELH* 57 (1990), 901-37; and David Anthony, "Class, Culture, and the Trouble with White Skin in Hawthorne's The House of the Seven Gables," *The Yale Journal of Criticism* 12 (1999), 249-68.

10. Patrick Brancaccio, "'The Black Man's Paradise': Hawthorne's Editing of the Journal of an African Cruiser," *The New England Quarterly* 53 (1980), 41.

11. Hawthorne to Duyckinck, July 1, 1845, Nathaniel Hawthorne, *The Letters, 1843-53*, ed. Thomas Woodson,

L. Neal Smith, and Norman Holmes Pearson, *The Centenary Edition of The Works of Nathaniel Hawthorne*, Vol. 16 (Columbus: Ohio State Univ. Press, 1985), 105; hereafter cited parenthetically by volume and page number. Hawthorne writes: "My story makes no good progress . . . I am fit for nothing, at present, higher or finer than such another piece of book-manufacture as the Journal."

12. Arlin Turner, *Nathaniel Hawthorne: A Biography* (New York: Oxford Univ. Press, 1980), 155. This critical paradigm replays Sophia's construction of Hawthorne's relationship to Bridge. Sophia Hawthorne exposes the complex debt economy between the two men in her letter to Bridge congratulating him on the publication of the Joumal: "In the most unconscious & innocent way possible, you have suddenly found yourself an author of note. How impossible to find a limit to the consequences of a good action. Through your magnanimous desire to benefit my husband, you have caused your name to be entered upon 'Fame's eternal bead-roll,' as Spenser sings. Now my husband has returned your favor of the past with regard to his Tales. You first procured his appearance in a book, & now he introduces you in a fair volume to the present age." Sophia rewrites the economic transaction of Hawthorne's editorship in terms of a gift economy based on magnanimous actions and favors between friends. Authorship is described as an unconscious and innocent act, editing as a form of gentlemanly introduction, and books as "fair volumes" that earn eternal fame rather than money. Hawthorne's own postscript to this letter, which instructs Bridge to go ahead with a Plan to introduce him to influential officials who could help win him a government position, contradicts Sophia's construction of Hawthorne's editorial largess. Sophia Hawthorne to Bridge, July 4, 1845 (CE 16:108).

13. Bridge was commissioned on Commodore Perry's frigate the Saratoga, which was part of the African Squadron that joined the British, as a result of the Webster-Ashburton Treaty of 1842, in policing the coast of Africa for slavers. See Edward M. Barrows, *The Great Commodore: The Exploits of Matthew Calbraith Perry*

(Indianapolis: The Bobbs-Merrill Co., 1935), 156-77, and Alan R. Booth, "The United States African Squadron 1843-1861" in *Boston University Papers in African History*, Vol. 1, ed. Jeffrey Butler (Boston: Boston Univ. Press, 1964), 79-118. As Booth points out, the African Squadron was more interested in fostering American trade than in suppressing the slave trade (97). The Journal underscores this point when it states "It will not have escaped the reader's notice, that the foregoing journal of our cruise records not the capture of a single slave vessel" but then goes on to state that "[t]he trade of the United States has been protected" (177, 179). See also "Slaves and Slavery," *The United States Magazine and Democratic Review* 19 (Oct. 1846), 250-51 for a discussion of the slave trade.

14. Hawthorne also thought about having "Papers of an Old Dartmoor Prisoner" published in the Library of American Books. He writes to Duyckinck in January of 1846: "you can decide for yourself whether they will suit the Library . . . My own opinion is, that they have quite sufficient interest and novelty (especially the portions relating to the mode of life and economy of the prison) to entitle them to a place in the series" (CE 16:139). "Papers of an Old Dartmoor Prisoner" was not published in the Library of American Books; it first appeared in book form in the twentieth century under the title *The Yarn of a Yankee Privateer*, intro. Clifford Smyth (New York: Funk and Wagnalls, 1926). "Nathaniel Hawthorne," *US Magazine and Democratic Review* 16 (April 1845), 276-84. For a history of the Library of American Books, see Ezra Greenspan, "Evert Duyckinck and the History of Wiley and Putnam's Library of American Books, 1845-47," *American Literature* 64 (1992), 677-93.

15. Nathaniel Hawthorne, *The Snow-Image and Uncollected Tales*, ed. William Charvat et al., *The Centenary Edition of the Works of Nathaniel Hawthorne*, Vol. 2 (Columbus: Ohio State Univ. Press, 1974), 5. Patrick Brancaccio argues that Hawthorne's identification with Bridge's pro-colonization stance helped him to curry favor with the Democrats and, hence, to gain him the surveyorship at Salem (23-24). The Journal was positively reviewed and

extensively excerpted in *The African Repository and Colonial Journal* 21 (August, November, December 1845), a publication of the American Colonization Society. The preface to the Journal also sees Liberia as the book's central selling point: "If, in any portion of the book, the author may hope to engage the attention of the public, it will probably be in those pages which treat of Liberia" (v). However, it argues that the work's value depends upon the author's "freedom from partizan bias" (v), his being "neither an Abolitionist nor a Colonizationist" (vi). "Papers of a Dartmoor Prisoner" also helped Hawthorne gain the Salem surveyorship since Browne, the Salem postmaster, wrote to President Polk to recommend Hawthorne for the position (CE 16:140 n.1). After writing eighteen new tales during 1842-44, Hawthorne only produced three pieces of his own work during 1844-1845. See John J. McDonald, "The Old Manse and Its Mosses: The Inception and Development of Mosses From an Old Manse," *Texas Studies in Literature and Language* 16 (1974), 77-108.

16. Hawthorne, *The Snow-Image*, 4. Hawthorne addresses the entire preface of *The Snow-Image to Bridge*.

17. Horatio Bridge writes that be assented to the book under the condition that if Hawthorne "should take the trouble of editing and bringing out the volume . . . be should have the copyright and the sole profit of the publication." *Personal Recollections of Nathaniel Hawthorne* (New York: Harper and Brothers Publishers, 1893), 87-88. It would appear that Bridge didn't receive any payment for the book since, when Hawthorne sends him copies of the book, he reploes: "this fifty copies will be paid for out of my avails from the book; for it would be rather too severe a joke to make your work an actual expense to you." May 2, 1845 (CE 16:92). Hawthorne also writes to Duyckinck that he "should prefer a per-centage on the sales, rather than to dispose of the book outfight" since he looks "for a considerable circulation." April 7, 1845 (CE 16:87).

18. Hawthorne to Bridge, March 25, 1843 (CE 15: 683); Hawthorne to Bridge, April 1, 1844 (CE 16:26). James

Mellow writes: "Duyckinck had insisted that Hawthorne's name should appear on the title page in order to enhance the sale value." *Nathaniel Hawthorne in His Times* (Boston: Houghton Mifflin, 1980), 260.

19. April 1, 1844 (CE 16:26).

20. Hawthorne to Duyckinck, April 7,1845 (CE 16:86). See Brancaccio for a discussion of Hawthorne's extensive role in creating the book: "the thematic organization and ironic and morally ambiguous point of view clearly betrays Hawthorne's hand," Brancaccio states (33). In claiming that Hawthorne "re-wrote" Bridge's journal, Duyckinck also suggests that Hawthorne did more than simply edit Bridge's text. Evert A. Duyckinck, and George L. Duyckinck, *Cyclopaedia of American Literature*, Vol. 2 (New York: Charles Scribner and Co., 1855), 503.

21. *Journal of an African Cruiser*, vi. Hawthorne underscores Bridge's authorial luck when he writes to Bridge on April 17, 1845: "I am happy to announce that your book is accepted, and will make its appearance as one of the volumes of 'Choice Reading.' Few authors make their bows to the public under such favorable auspices; but you always were a lucky devil" (CE 16:89).

22. *Hawthorne to Duyckinck*, July 1, 1845 (CE 16:105). *Hawthorne to Hillard*, March 24, 1844 (CE 16:23).

23. *Hawthorne to Bridge*, April 1, 1844 (CE 16:27).

24. For a description of the cut-throat competition of the literary marketplace in the early 1840s, see William Charvat, *Literary Publishing in America* (Philadelphia: Univ. of Pennsylvania Press, 1959), 8, and Michael Davitt Bell, "Conditions of Literary Vocation" in *The Cambridge History of American Literature, 1820-1865*, Vol. 2, ed. Sacvan Bercovitch (New York: Cambridge Univ. Press, 1995), 16-17. Charvat argues that the retail price of American books was driven down in the 1840s due to a severe economic depression and the competition to reprint British books.

25. Nathaniel Hawthorne, *Mosses from an Old Manse*, ed. William Charvat et al., *The Centenary Edition of the*

Works of Nathaniel Hawthorne, Vol. 10 (Columbus: Ohio State Univ. Press, 1974), 34. Hereafter cited parenthetically by volume and page number.

26. *Hawthorne to Duyckinck,* March 2, 1945, April 7, 1845 (CE 16:82, 87).

27. For historical accounts of the commercial and slave trades in West Africa, see Warren S. Howard, *American Slavers and the Federal Law 1837-1862* (Berkeley: Univ. of California Press, 1963); Norman R. Bennett and George E. Brooks, ed. *New England Merchants in Africa* (Boston: Boston Univ. Press, 1965); George E. Brooks, *Yankee Traders, Old Coasters and African Middlemen: A History of American Legitimate Trade with West Africa in the Nineteenth Century* (Boston: Boston Univ. Press, 1970).

28. Luther S. Luedtke, *Nathaniel Hawthorne and the Romance of the Orient* (Bloomington: Indiana Univ. Press, 1989), 19. Luedtke shows how Hawthorne came from a long line of seafarers. Beginning in the eighteenth century with the third generation of Hawthorne's, most of the sons turned to the sea. As Vernon Loggins states, Hawthorne's great grandfather, Joseph, occasionally brought back slaves from his voyages. Vernon Loggins, *The Hawthornes* (New York: Greenwood Press, 1968), 157. Hawthorne's grandfather, Daniel, was a well-known privateer during the revolutionary war. Hawthorne's father, Captain Nathaniel Hawthorne, died in Surinam of yellow fever in 1808. The young Nathaniel read his father's log book. See Margaret Moore, *The Salem World of Nathaniel Hawthorne* (Columbia: Univ. of Missouri Press, 1998) and Loggins for the seafaring histories of both the Hawthorne and Manning families.

29. Moore, *The Salem World of Nathaniel Hawthorne*, 81, 188-89. During the War of 1812, "Papers from an Old Dartmoor Prisoner" also describes the merchants of Salem "converting their heretofore peaceful vessels into privateers" (31). "Papers from an Old Dartmoor Prisoner" was attributed to Hawthorne's "great-uncle John Lord, until Browne's claim was revealed" (CE 16:140 n.2).

30. Brooks, *Yankee Traders*, 105, 4. Brooks observes that "Salem, Massachusetts was long the chief port for African trade. As late as 1860 Salem fitted out more vessels than the next two American ports combined" (128). For a history of Salem's trade, see James Duncan Phillips, *Salem and the Indies: The Story of the Great Commercial Era of the City* (Boston: Houghton Mifflin Co., 1947). Salem had a lengthy history of participating in the slave trade. As early as 1638, slaves were imported from the West Indies on the Salem ship Desire. James Rawley argues that Boston and Salem were both active in the slave trade, especially in the mid-1780s. For a history of Massachusetts' role in the slave trade, see James A. Rawley, *The Transatlantic Slave Trade: A History* (New York: W. W. Norton, 1981), 323-53. Margaret Moore also reports that the slave trade existed in Salem from the Pequod War forward and that Hawthorne's family once held slaves. *The Salem World of Nathaniel Hawthorne*, 12-13, 136-37, 142. See Jean Fagan Yellin, "Hawthorne and the American National Sin," for an account of Hawthorne's extensive knowledge about slavery and Salem's specific role in the slave trade.

31. April 15, 1848 (CE 16:223). James R, Mellow recounts a remark made by Hawthorne to Ellery Channing in 1847 that reveals Hawthorne's intimate acquaintance with the Salem Custom House's trade with Africa: "I am determined the niggers shall have as good liquor as anyone gets from New England" (Nathaniel Hawthorne in His Times, 288). Salem traded rum, tobacco, and guns with African villages for palm-oil, ivory, gold dust—and sometimes slaves.

32. Nathaniel Hawthorne, "Chiefly About War-Matters," in *Miscellaneous Prose and Verse*, ed. Thomas Woodson, Claude M. Simpson, and L. Neal Smith, *The Centenary Edition of the Works of Nathaniel Hawthorne*, Vol. 23 (Columbus: Ohio State Univ. Press, 1994), 420.

33. From his study of the portion of Bridge's manuscript still in existence, Brancaccio argues that Hawthorne "tempered and further moralized" Bridge's version of events (34). Hawthorne's position on the issue of slavery

is most succinctly summarized by his statement in The Life of Franklin Pierce that slavery is "one of those evils which divine Providence does not leave to be remedied by human contrivances, but which, in its own good time, by some means impossible to be anticipated, but of the simplest and easiest operation, when all its uses shall have been fulfilled, it causes to vanish like a dream." (CE 23:352).

34. April 1, 1844 (CE 16:26).

35. CE 16:27.

36. Many of the reviews comment on the "freshness" of the field of Africa. The Examiner (August 9, 1845) states: "This Journal is freshly and cleverly written, and touches on a scene little hacknied by journalists or travellers" (499); *The Democratic Review* 16 (May 1845) says: "we are enabled to lay before our readers, in advance, a few pages of a book which, from the comparative novelty of the subject, its home interest, and the simple, sincere style in which it is written, cannot fail of proving widely attractive" (482); Hunt's Merchant Magazine and Commercial Review 29 (August 1853) reviews the 1853 edition of the book by saying: "This little volume contains information touching an interesting part of the world that will be new to many. The author's accounts of Liberia and descriptions of the settlements of the various nations of Europe along the western coast of Africa, and of their tribes, and their trade and intercourse with the whites, will add much to our stores of knowledge" (267). *The Critic* 2 (August 16, 1845) focuses on the book's romantic image of Africa:

> The coast of Africa has not been quite as often described as most of the shores which exercise the descriptive powers of modern tourists. The interest which it possesses has not lost its novelty, and probably an interest would be felt in any thing that was to be told about this singular continent long after its novelty had subsided. The realm to which ancient mystery looked, the home of gigantic marvels, the region around which obscurity and fable in all ages have woven an almost impenetrable veil, it seems to repel, by its noisome pestilence and fever, and by its

wild tribes of unreclaimed savages, the inquiry and investigation which its strange position among the nations of the world necessarily invites. (321)

The reviews note Africa's inaccessibility to the average tourist due to its enervating climate, and discuss Liberia as well as slavery and the slave trade.

37. May 3, 1843 (CE 15:686-87).
38. *Hawthorne to Duyckinck*, March 2, 1845 (CE 16:82).
39. Nathaniel Hawthorne, *The Blithedale Romance and Fanshawe*, ed. William Charvat, Roy Harvey Pearce, and Claude M. Simpson, *The Centenary Edition of the Works of Nathaniel Hawthorne*, Vol. 3 (Columbus: Ohio State Univ. Press, 1964), 3.
40. Nathaniel Hawthorne, *The House of the Seven Gables,* ed. William Charvat, Roy Harvey Pearce, and Claude M. Simpson, *The Centenary Edition of the Works of Nathaniel Hawthorne,* Vol. 2 (Columbus: Ohio State Univ. Press, 1965), 1, 3. *The Marble Faun: Or, the Romance of Monte Beni,* ed. William Charvat, Roy Harvey Pearce, Claude M. Simpson, and Matthew J. Bruccoli, *The Centenary Edition of the Works of Nathaniel Hawthorne,* Vol. 4 (Columbus: Ohio State Univ. Press, 1968), 4.
41. James C. Keil argues that Hawthorne's early career was based on reproduction—the recycling of other people's texts rather than invention; however he claims that Hawthorne "turns his back on this method of composition" (238) in the 1850s. See "Reading, Writing, and Recycling: Literary Archaeology and the Shape of Hawthorne's Career," *The New England Quarterly* 65 (1992), 238-64.
42. *Hawthorne to Bridge*, May 3, 1843 (CE 15:687).
43. *The Critic* 2 (August 30, 1845), 360; *The Spirit of the Times* 15 (Sept. 13, 1845), 337; *The Biblical Repository and Classical Review* 3 (October 1845), 776; *The New-York Mirror*, 2 (June 14, 1845), 159; *The Rover* 5 (June 26, 1845), 240; *The Southern and Western Magazine Review* 2 (August 1845), 130; *Duyckinck to Hawthorne*, October 2, 1845, quoted in Bridge, *Personal Recollections*, 106; Nathaniel Hawthorne. *Twice-Told Tales*, ed. William

Charvat, Roy Harvey Pearce, and Claude M. Simpson, *The Centenary Edition of the Works of Nathaniel Hawthorne*, Vol. 9 (Columbus: Ohio State Univ. Press, 1974), 3. The Journal sold well and was widely excerpted. In the same letter, Duyckinck writes: "The 'Journal of the Cruiser' has just gone to a second edition of a thousand copies, the first I believe, having been two thousand. W. & P. project cheap series of these books for the school district libraries, in the first of which the Journal will be included" (Personal Recollections, 106). Robert Cantwell states that the Journal sold five thousand copies (380). A second edition of the book was planned by Hawthorne and Bridge as early as 1846, but was never completed. The Journal was reissued in 1853 under both Bridge's and Hawthorne's names in Putnam's Popular Library: "By Horatio Bridge, U.S. Navy. Edited by Nathaniel Hawthorne," according to the title page of *Journal of an African Cruiser* (New York: George P. Putnam and Co., 1853).

44. McGill, 41.

45. CE 16:92; 94. April 17, 1845 (CE 16:89).

46. "Notices of New Books," *The Democratic Review*, 17 (October 1845), 317; "The Library of Choice Reading," *The Democratic Review* 20 (March, 1847), 238. The advertising notice in the back of the Journal about the Library of Choice Reading underscores how a book's substance is reinforced by its style: *The New York Tribune* states, "This library is put up in beautiful style, as well as offered at a very cheap rate. We are pleased to see such good paper and print, for we think the habit of reading ill-printed, dingy books deteriorates not only the eye-sight but the taste. Books, if good for anything, deserve a cleanly dress. To degrade them, even outwardly, has the same tendency as the use of tobacco, to pollute and vulgarize all the habits of life" (i). The review of the Journal in the Boston Post (June 24, 1845) also notes the form of the book: "In truth there is a simplicity and freshness about the 'Journal,' . . . which, in connection with its neat print and clear paper, must give it a very large circulation" (1). For a history of the Library of

American Books see Ezra Greenspan, "Evert Duyckinck and the History of Wiley and Putnam's Library of American Books, 1845-1847," *American Literature*, 64 (1992): 677-93. See Richard Brodhead, *The School of Hawthorne*, 48-66, for a discussion of Duyckinck's and Fields' role in the cultural production of Hawthorne's authorship. As Brodhead notes, besides publishing Hawthorne in the Library of American Books, Duyckinck wrote four reviews between 1841 and 1851 that helped to establish Hawthorne's canonical status (54).

47. The Democratic Review excerpted the Journal in May and June of 1845; it also noted the Journal in its literary bulletin in June and August of 1845. The first excerpt does not refer to Hawthorne's editorship but subsequent references do. Duyckinck's review of Hawthorne's career appeared in the April 1845 issue, where Hawthorne also published his tale "P's Correspondence." Hawthorne's name, therefore, was in front of *The Democratic Review* readership consistently throughout those months in a number of different guises: author, editor, genius.

48. After the publication of *The Scarlet Letter in 1850*, Hawthorne writes to Bridge in regard to the second edition of the Journal: "As I am busy with my own literary matters, and as you have probably a fair share of leisure, I should be glad if you would leave me very little to do . . I shall ask Duyckinck to announce your forthcoming book with the author's name." The 1853 edition of Journal was the first to bear Bridge' s name (August 7, 1850; CE 16: 355). By October 1, Hawthorne writes, "I am getting so deep into my book, that I am afraid it will be impossible for me to attend properly to my editorial duties, in respect to yours, till after the completion of the former" (CE 16:368). In reply to the request that he edit "A Slayer's Log Book; or 20 Years' Residence in Africa" by Theophilus Canneau, Hawthorne replies: "I have not been able to accept his proposition, on account of previous engagements." February 13, 1853 (CE 16:638). See *Captain Canot: or, Twenty Years of an African Slaver*, ed. Brantz Mayer (New York: D. Appleton and Co., 1854; repr. New York: Arno Press and The New York Times, 1968).

49. Evert A. Duyckinck, *Cyclopaedia of American Literature*, 504. Nina Baym, *The Shape of Hawthorne's Career* (Ithaca: Cornell Univ. Press, 1976), 8. In its first year of publication, *The Scarlet Letter* was, in Michael Winship's terms, "a moderate success." See Michael Winship's "Hawthorne and the 'Scribbling Women': Publishing The Scarlet Letter in the Nineteenth-Century United States" in this issue for a full publication history. See also Bertha Faust, *Hawthorne's Contemporaneous Reputation: A Study of Literary Opinion in America and England 1828-1864* (New York: Octagon Books, 1977).

50. During the mid-nineteenth century, Salem was losing much of its commerce to the larger ports of Boston and New York. However, this period was also the height of its trade with West Africa. Salem became the chief U.S. port for African trade in the mid-nineteenth century. As Brooks states, "One of the reasons for Salem's specialization in the African trade was the shallowness of its harbor" (Yankee Traders, 128). Joseph B. Hoyt argues that West Africa was the trade "partner of [Salem's] old age" (37). See Joseph B. Hoyt, "Salem's West Africa Trade 1835-1863 and Captain Victor Francis Debaker," *Essex Institute Historical Collections* 102 (1966), 37-73.

51. A key example of Hawthorne's conflation of "blackness" and commerce occurs in The House of the Seven Gables when he describes Hepzibah's entrance into the "sordid stain" of commercial enterprise as the selling of a gingerbread Jim Crow (GE 2:51). For a reading of property in The House of the Seven Gables in relation to the slave economy, see Benn Michaels, "Romance and Real Estate." Another episode in The House of the Seven Gables—Clifford's observation of the Italian barrel-organ grinder and his monkey from his arched window—also signifies the market economy through the racial signifier of the black monkey. The monkey holds out his "small black palm" that "plainly signifi[es] his excessive desire for whatever filthy lucre might happen to be in anybody's pocket" (CE 2:164). In using the monkey to "symboliz[e] the grossest form of the love of money" and to represent the New Englander's "own moral condition" (CE 2:164),

Hawthorne is not only drawing on racial stereotype but also his knowledge of commercial trade. Monkey skins were a central import from Salem's West African trade. The Journal recounts the "black monkey-skins" for sale by the natives (140) and Bridge also sent monkey skins from Africa to Una and Sophia. Hawthorne writes to Bridge (Feb. 21, 1846): "Your monkey skins have been converted into a splendid muff—the handsomest, the manufacturer says, that he has made this season; and Sophia wears it herself, until such time as Una shall be of an age to need it" (CE 16:142).

52. Hawthorne writes to Hillard about his *Twice-Told Tales*: "I wish the devil had the books—for I suppose he is a member of the 'Trade.'" May 14, 1844 (CE 16:35). As Michael Newbury shows in his article on slavery and celebrity in antebellum America, Hawthorne was not alone in describing the artist's growing commodification in the literary marketplace as a type of slavery. In occupying "the increasingly conspicuous cultural stage," Newbury argues, "the celebrity and the slave were united through their shared cultural configuration as consumable workers, laborers whose bodies, rather than their labor or production, were available for consumption." Newbury, *Figuring Authorship in Antebellum America* (Stanford: Stanford Univ. Press, 1997), 84. Hawthorne describes his own relationship to the marketplace in similar terms. Upon resigning from the Boston Custom House, he writes to Longfellow: "I have broken my chain and escaped from the Custom-House" (October 12, 1840; CE 15:497). Throughout his tenure in the Boston Custom House, Hawthorne's letters conflate the "blackness" of the commodity he trades in—coal—with the market economy to which he sees himself enslaved. He writes to Sophia: "your poor husband has been engaged in a very black business—as black as coal" (Feb. 11, 1840; CE 15:413). He pictures himself to Sophia as a "captive" who "feels the iron of his chain" and who desires to be freed from his "very grievous thralldom" (CE 15:445,428, 422). While coal is not a commodity specific to the slave trade, Hawthorne's characterization of commerce as a type of slavery and his racialization of its "blackness" suggests

a connection between his general construction of the commercial marketplace and his specific knowledge of the slave trade.

53. Hawthorne's alliance with the sailor, as Luther Luedtke notes, has strong biographical resonances as well. He had a passion for the sea, and declared that "if he had not been an author be should have been a sailor" (quoted in Luedtke, *Romance of the Orient*, 16). In a letter to Longfellow, June 4, 1837, he recounts his failed attempt to gain a position on the U.S. Exploring Expedition to the South Seas and Antarctica: "If such a post were attainable, I should certainly accept it; for, though fixed so long to one spot, I have always had a desire to run round the world" (CE 15:253).

54. See Alan Booth, "The United States African Squadron," 82. An 1820 amendment was added to the 1819 Slave Trade Act that made "slave trading an act of piracy, punishable by death" (82). The Journal reiterates this fact: "The laws of the United States declare the slave-trade, if exercised by any of its citizens, to be piracy, and punishable with death" (177).

55. Hawthorne's notebook entry from Sophia's "Cuba Journal," which describes a Cuban ball dress, associates pearls with the Caribbean: "A blue satin-boddice laced in front over a white satin chemisette, and a bird of Paradise, & blue silky dress; a necklace of pearl, and pearl fillet round her head, and pearl ear-rings" (63).

56. See Richard C. Rohrs, "Antislavery Politics and the Pearl Incident of 1848," *Historian* 56 (1994), 711-24. As Jean Fagan Yellin points out, Hawthorne had a connection to this event through Horace Mann, "the antislavery congressman married to Sophia's sister Mary" who defended the Pearl's owner in court ("Hawthorne and the American National Sin," 87). Harriet Beecher Stowe discusses the Pearl in both *Uncle Tom's Cabin* and *A Key to Uncle Tom's Cabin*. See Harriet Beecher Stowe, *Uncle Tom's Cabin*, ed. Ann Douglas (New York: Viking Penguin, 1987), 619 and *A Key to Uncle Tom's Cabin* (1853: repr. Salem, N. H.: Ayer Co., 1987), 306-30. William Wells Brown includes the Pearl in one of his sketches in

Original Panoramic Views of the Scenes in the Life of an American Slave (London: Charles Gilpin, 1849), 12.

57. In doing so, Hawthorne takes his place along side other antebellum authors—such as Emerson, Melville, and Thoreau—who explicitly linked the commodification of their art with the economy of slavery. Emerson, for instance, not only describes Boston as a slave port but explicitly links the book profession to the economy of slavery: "a strong desire to keep the peace and good humor with [southern slaveholders1 is felt not only by the financial authorities in State street and Wall street, but also by the cotton-spinners, the freighters, the shoe-dealers, the cabinet makers, the printers, the booksellers, and by every description of Northern salesmen." *Emerson's Antislavery Writings*, ed. Len Gougeon and Joel Myerson (New Haven: Yale Univ. Press, 1995), 42.

4

The Adulteress in the Market-place: Hawthorne and The Scarlet Letter

—Jr. Ken Egan

Readers have long lamented the absence of Arthur Dimmesdale's Election Sermon, the inspiring though pathetic discourse which serves as prelude to the tragic conclusion of The Scarlet Letter. But perhaps all along we have been overlooking the obvious: Hawthorne did in fact transcribe such a sermon, but he did so under the cover of his autobiographical sketch. "The Custom-House." Written before the final three chapters of the novel were composed (that is, before the sermon is described in the text), "The Custom-House" conforms to the "jeremiad" tradition of election-day sermons.[1] Though cast in a satiric mode, the "sketch" balances the elements of guilt and redemption, past and future, sin and salvation typical of the Puritan genre. However, this is a jeremiad with a difference, for as the autobiographical narrator reminds us repeatedly, while he "represents" his Salem progenitors he is by no means identical with them. Thus it should not be surprising to discover that Hawthorne's "Election

Sermon" is written from a distinctly different vantage point than that of the Puritan minister. Indeed, it is as artist and author that Hawthorne comes before the public to condemn the sins of his generation and project his own future fulfillment. Put differently, Hawthorne's "sermon" recounts his own election as "author," a sanctification which issues from the terrible suffering of his "decapitation." Rather than celebrating a communal victory over Satan and sinfulness, "The Custom-House" employs a form of Puritan discourse to celebrate the individual artist's prevailing over oppression.

Art and artistry are crucial to the novel as well. Joel Porte has put the case most succinctly when he writes, "The Scarlet Letter, in short, can be read as an allegory of art."[2] Porte calls our attention to Hawthorne's struggle to justify romantic art in a culture dominated by pragmatic concerns. Not surprisingly, then, we have focused on correspondences between the writer of the text and his artistic rebel, Hester Prynne. Both Hawthorne and Hester can be seen as subversive artists who must enter "the market-place" with a scarlet letter, signifier of pride and shame, achievement and alienation. However, we have not paid sufficient attention to role of adultery in this "allegory of art."[3] Though Hester's "sin" is never openly announced, the text cleverly alludes to adultery and "adulteration" throughout, creating a kind of fetishistic fascination with the "nameless" crime. Granting that the novel and its prefatory sketch are concerned with the artist's role in antebellum America, the reader can fairly ask, "in what sense is artistic reproduction an act of adultery"? But I want to push this issue even farther by insisting on the question, "in what sense is the male author an adulteress?" Put in these terms, the issue resonates with concerns about Hawthorne's attitude toward women in general and female writers specifically. I will argue that, for Hawthorne, to be a male writer in his culture was necessarily to be an "adulteress," that is, a feminized adulterer of "the truth." Furthermore, his status as "adulteress" virtually required him to enter "the marketplace" of literature, for his transgressions of gender role and vocation forced him out of the paternalistic "house of custom" into the masculinist market. That is, having violated the expectations of a cultural son, the hermaphroditic writer must compete in the acquisitive, rowdy capitalist economy of antebellum America. Thus, the figure of the adulteress serves as a nexus for complex issues of vocation and gender Hawthorne had to confront at the moment of composing his novel and sketch.

In Adultery and the Novel, Tony Tanner asserts that the adulteress represents the violation of social contract and the harmonic interrelation of clearly defined roles:

> The figure of the wife ideally contains the biological female, the obedient daughter (and perhaps sister), the faithful mate, the responsible mother, and the believing Christian, and harmonizes all the patterns that bestow upon her these differing identities. But if the marriage starts to founder, then the different identities and roles fall apart or come into conflict . . . [I]t is now perhaps clear why adultery should be the main, if the undescribed, topic for the bourgeois novel. For without anything or anyone necessarily having changed place or roles (in social terms), the action of adultery portends the possible breakdown of all the mediations on which society itself depends, and demonstrates the latent impossibility of participating in the interrelated patterns that comprise its structure.[4]

This strikes me as an extraordinarily important description of both Hester and Hawthorne's dilemmas. Hester is indeed a kind of "liminal" character, caught betwixt and between social roles as a result of her passionate transgression.[5] That liminality is emblemized by her virtual marginality, her abode located in the border region between city and forest, between the urban and the wild. Furthermore, as she attempts to fulfill her roles as mother and mate following the adulterous act and its issue, Hester struggles to meet the social demands of those roles. Her psychological traumas largely result from her confused desire to fulfill socially defined obligations while at the same time living on the margins of those obligations. Put differently, Hester attempts to be a "good" wife and mother while living out the legacy of her social disgrace.

Likewise, the Hawthorne represented in "The Custom-House" suffers from a crisis of "mediation" between himself and his society. More specifically, he struggles to keep in balance conflicting roles within antebellum culture, and his failure to achieve that balance leaves him in the interstices of his culture. Hawthorne initially hoped to sustain two contradictory roles, those of "public man" and "author." His letters to friends just prior to his dismissal as a surveyor for the Salem custom-house indicate that, in Hawthorne's eyes, his literary vocation should have provided a kind of "immunity" for him as public man, for he expected protection from partisan political decisions. As he wrote to his friend George Hillard on March 5, 1849, "it seems to me that an inoffensive man of letters - having obtained a pitiful little office on no other plea than his pitiful little literature — ought not to be left to the mercy of these thick-skulled and no-hearted ruffians."[6] And again, writing to Longfellow in anticipation of his vengeance against such "ruffians," he remarked, "This I will do [wreak vengeance], not as an act of individual vengeance, but in your behalf as well as mine, because he [an unnamed 'high official'] will have violated the sanctity of the priesthood to which we both, in our different degrees, belong. I do not claim to be a poet; and yet I cannot but feel that some of the sacredness of that character adheres to me, and ought to be respected in me, unless I step out of its immunities, or make it a plea for violating any of the rules of ordinary life."[7] Hawthorne's faith rests on at best a naive and at worst a demeaning concept of his own art, for he should be protected as long as he is not "dangerous," as long as he is "normal" in outward aspect. Hawthorne does not yet perceive that to be an author in America is, by its very nature, to "violat[e] . . . the rules of ordinary life," one of the bitter discoveries forced upon him by his ouster.

If his artistic vocation should provide Hawthorne political immunity, conversely, a secure public appointment should provide the financial cover to achieve his artistic ambitions. Some six years earlier, upon the birth of his daughter Una, Hawthorne had written to Hillard, "God keep me from ever being really a writer for bread! If I alone were concerned, I had rather starve; but in that case, poor little Una would have to take refuge in the alms-house — which, here in Concord, is a most gloomy old mansion. Her 'angel face' would hardly make a sunshine there."[8] The passage is typical of Hawthorne's financial worries both before and after his marriage. Uncannily, the letter anticipates key imagery in "The Custom-House" itself, for the narrator implies that the official building has become a kind of alms-house for the ancient crew, and a "gloomy" one at that. In a sense Hawthorne had already imaginatively rejected the Custom-House as safe haven before he took up his duties there. Nonetheless, financial security was very much on Hawthorne's mind when he accepted the post. For instance, the autobiographical subject ruefully observes of custom-house documents, "But, then, what reams of other manuscripts — filled, not with the dulness of official formalities, but with the thought of inventive brains and the rich effusion of deep hearts — had gone equally to oblivion; and that, moreover, without serving a purpose in their day, as these heaped-up papers had, and — saddest of all — without purchasing for their writers the comfortable livelihood which the clerks of the Custom-House had gained by these worthless scratchings of the pen!"[9] Thus Hawthorne initially saw the Custom-House position as enabling his "participat[ion] in the interrelated patterns of his culture," specifically, the activities of the commercial man and the artist, the financially secure and the ideologically protected.

Ironically, neither expectation was realized, and "The Custom-House" records those discoveries in the strongest possible terms. First, Hawthorne came to realize (much as he had at Brook Farm) that the weight of daily experience pressed hard upon his artistic faculties. Far from creating the economic space necessary for his composition, the job as surveyor made authorial activity impossible. As Hawthorne phrased it in an oft-quoted passage,

> My imagination was a tarnished mirror. It would not reflect, or only with miserable dimness, the figures with which I did my best to people it. The characters of the narrative would not be warmed and rendered malleable, by any heat that I could kindle at my intellectual forge. They would take neither the glow of passion nor the tenderness of sentiment, but retained all the rigidity of dead corpses, and stared me in the face with a fixed and ghastly grin of contemptuous defiance. "What have you to do with us?" that expression seemed to say. "The little power you might once have possessed over the tribe of unrealities is gone! You have bartered it for a pittance of the public gold. Go, then, and earn your wages!" (pp. 34-35)

Hawthorne suggests, then, that art and commerce are mutually exclusive, or at least exercise a deleterious effect on each other. Curiously, as I will show later, through artistic adultery Hawthorne seems to find a means out of this self-defeating opposition between Mammon and Art.

If the writer came to see that wages conflicted with his art, he discovered even more painfully that art could not protect him from politics. Hawthorne learned that in the house of "custom" his art was either worthless or a source of suspicion. It is suggestive that the sketch focuses on the fellow-workers' "accustomed corners" (p. 14), emblematic of their "sluggish and dependent mode of life" (p. 16). From the perspective of this "customary" position, Hawthorne's artistic ambitions were absolutely meaningless: "It is a good lesson - though it may often be a hard one - for a man who has dreamed of literary fame, and of making for himself a rank among the world's dignitaries by such means, to step aside out of the narrow circle in which his claims are recognized, and to find how utterly devoid of significance, beyond that circle, is all that he achieves, and all he aims at" (pp. 26-27). Hawthorne's discoveries about art's relationship with "custom" take on a more dire cast when he considers his ancestors. The critic Evan Carton has been especially sensitive to this play upon the sketch's title, observing that "throughout the essay, 'custom' is a rich and ambivalent symbol for Hawthorne: it is a duty that he collects and a less tangible but more burdensome one that he pays; it stands for the materialistic present in which, as a customs house officer, he is mired and for the most real and valuable portions of the legacy of the past to which that same customs house lends him access."[10] Carton calls our attention to "custom" as accrued tradition, the weight of the past upon the present character. In this context, Hawthorne can only sense hostility toward his role as author, for he imagines his progenitors heaping scorn upon "'a writer of story-books'" (p. 10). Indeed, Hawthorne focuses upon his ancestors' persecution of women and witches, crucial because Hawthorne saw himself as a kind of latter-day witch. In yet another letter inspired by the Custom-House controversy (his expulsion fueled some of his finest correspondence), Hawthorne playfully remarks to Horatio Bridge, "I feel an infinite contempt for them [the Salem people], and probably have expressed more of it than I intended; for my preliminary chapter has caused the greatest uproar that ever happened here since witch-times. If I escape from town without being tarred-and-feathered, I shall consider it good luck. I wish they would tar-and-feather me — it would be such an entirely novel kind of distinction for a literary man! And from such judges as my fellow-citizens, I should look upon it as a higher honor than a laurel-crown."[11] One needs no further proof of the writer's identification with Hester Prynne, for Hawthorne melodramatically reenacts the scaffold scene which begins the novel proper, casting himself as heroine scornful of the unjustified judges!

Hawthorne's unconscious identification with the Salem witches suggests a more profound sense of transgression than we have uncovered so far. Under the hegemony of the Jacksonian "cult of manhood," the male writer was already a suspect figure, a kind of hermaphrodite.[12] After all, his letter to Bridge hints at similarities between "the literary man" and the victims of "witch-times." Furthermore, in the letter to Hillard quoted above, Hawthorne explicitly chastises "thick-skulled and no-hearted ruffians," a conventional description of aggressive masculinity in the antebellum United States. The acquisitive male, on the make in the capitalist economy, was assumed to lack the intelligence and the affections of womanhood.

As an author of "minor literature," Hawthorne saw himself in conflict with the dominant image of male available within his culture. In his important study of women and masculine aesthetics during the nineteenth century, Leland S. Person, Jr. has addressed precisely this crisis of gender definition, observing that "given the identification of masculinity with vigorous, self-reliant activity both inside and outside the home, it must have been difficult indeed for male writers to reconcile their profession with their masculinity."[13] Like Hester, the male writer must dwell among multiple, conflicting personae while somehow making a living and maintaining an imaginative integrity. A father, a husband, a son, a worker, Hawthorne must yet acknowledge his "feminine" qualities, those qualities associated with his "authorship."[14] In light of the writer's much discussed diatribe against "the d—— d mob of scribbling women" and his unkind cut of Margaret Fuller after her death, perhaps this claim for sympathy with women seems overstated. But as one critic has recently asserted, for Hawthorne, "in their marginal relation to American political and economic life, their uneasy submission to or rebellion against the ideology of domesticity, and their use of fiction and poetry as indictment, revenge, and compensation, these women [Fanny Fern, Margaret Fuller, and Julia Ward Howe] are the perfect images of the artist in America, including [himself]."[15] A remarkable verbal echo reaching over five years from the composition of the novel to his comments on Ruth Hall provides dramatic evidence that in fact Hawthorne felt sympathy for the devil, that is, for enraged femininity. In a letter to Horace Conolly, dated June 17, 1850, Hawthorne sarcastically thanks his reader for helping evict him from office: "If I had stayed four years longer in the Custom House, I should have rusted utterly away, and never have been heard of more, but being kicked out (through your good offices) just at the nick of time, I came forth as fresh as if I had been just made, and went to work as if the devil were in me, if it were only to put my enemies to the blush."[16] Compare this language with the description of Fanny Fern included in a letter to William D. Ticknor dated February 2, 1855: "The woman writes as if the devil was in her; and that is the only condition under which a woman ever writes anything worth reading."[17] Given his earlier reference to his own "deviltry," Hawthorne might have written that it is only under possession by such agency that he himself "writes anything worth reading."

What, then, does it mean to say that the devil inspires a literary text? In part, of course, the male writer refers to a wrath generated by social injustice. But surely Hawthorne also has in mind what might generally be termed "desire" and more specifically termed "sexuality."[18] Here is another, more specific sense in which Hawthorne identifies with the adulteress. In addition to transgressing social contract and defined roles, adultery openly announces sexual desire. For unlike sex in the nineteenth-century marriage, which at best would serve the purpose of procreation and at worst serve to allay male passion, adultery nakedly asserts pleasure in sex. In that remarkable forest scene in The Scarlet Letter, the long repressed/suppressed sexuality of Hester is suddenly exposed when she releases her hair. The reader immediately recognizes that the complex art of her sewing, her re-presentation of her sin and art in Pearl, and her subversive political visions largely originate in that passionate core. So, too, did Hawthorne describe the libidinal origins of his art in his love letters to Sophia. In a remarkably frank passage (remarkable in part because Sophia chose not to excise it), the male writer indulges in a complex sexual metaphor to describe his creative activity: "Dearest, would it be unreasonable for me to ask you to manage my share of the correspondence, as well as your own? — to throw yourself into my heart, and make it gush out with more warmth and freedom than my own pen can avail to do?"[19] Not only is this letter notable for the implied connection between sexual love and verbal expression, but it suggests as well a cross-gender fantasy in which Sophia plays the part of the penetrative male and Nathaniel plays the part of the receptive female.[20] In fact, throughout the love letters of the late 30s and early 40s, Hawthorne characterizes Sophia as an "inspiring" agent who helps him produce his correspondence. No doubt we are witnessing the recurring mythology of the female muse, but Hawthorne's imagination seems to go beyond this facile cliche to project the possibilities of giving birth to utterance. Here, also, we see a remarkable and revealing correspondence between the adulteress and the male writer, for as her "devilry" issues forth in a "scarlet letter endowed with life" (p. 102), so does the author bring forth his novel, an animated version of the scarlet letter discovered in the Custom-House. As Zelda Bronstein has cleverly remarked of the novel, "like Pearl, 'The Scarlet Letter' issues from an illicit union of an artist and a public man."[21] In that formulation we find a convergence of the senses of "adulteress" we have explored to this point: the failed mediations of defined vocational and gender roles result in a "corrupt" offspring, the novel itself.

If comparisons between authoring and birthing seem far-fetched, we should recall, first, that "to author" originally meant "to make to grow, originate, promote, increase."[22] While the root suggests insemination, it is useful to notice the connection between writing and procreation. Hawthorne himself called attention to this analogy, most notably in "The Artist of the Beautiful," surely his most important meditation on his role as artist prior to the major novels. In that story the narrator contrasts the "offspring" of the idealistic artist Owen Warland (who is, true to his name, his "own war land"), and that of the carnal couple, Robert and Annie Danforth. In what seems like an authorial regression to his pre-married life, Hawthorne stages a dramatic conflict between these "children," for Owen's "spiritualized" butterfly, the product of an almost autistic artistic sensibility, is crushed by the "natural" child of the married couple: "With a wavering movement, and emitting a tremulous radiance, the butterfly struggled, as it were, towards the infant, and was about to alight upon his finger. But, while it still hovered in the air, the little Child of Strength . . . made a snatch at the marvellous insect, and compressed it in his hand . . . The blacksmith, by main force, unclosed the infant's hand, and found within the palm a small heap of glittering fragments, whence the Mystery of Beauty had fled for ever."[23] It is apparent, then, that in this 1844 story Hawthorne could not imagine a meeting point between the natural and the ideal, the biological and the cultural forms of creation. By contrast, the adulteress represents a fusion of these creative processes. In an obvious sense she incorporates the dichotomies of "The Artist of the Beautiful," for in her giving birth to Pearl she emulates (if illicitly) the creativity of Robert and Annie, while in projecting her social reforms for women she models the idealistic thoughtwork of Owen. However, at a kind of juncture or meeting point between the biological and the cultural, Hester produces her astonishing art: "She had in her nature a rich, voluptuous, Oriental characteristic, — a taste for the gorgeously beautiful, which, save in the exquisite productions of her needle, found nothing else, in all the possibilities of her life, to exercise itself upon" (p. 83). The passage carefully balances "voluptuous" against "exquisite," the passional against the refined, suggesting a more complex understanding of authorial creativity than Hawthorne demonstrated in "The Artist of the Beautiful."[24] Not only did Hawthorne reveal a similar "voluptuousness" in his love letters, but upon the birth of Una he expressed a similar sense of "falling" into the biological, material world, a fortunate fall into the realm of care, human relations, and pain:

> I find it is a very sober and serious kind of happiness that springs from the birth of a child. It ought not to come too early in a man's life — not till he has fully enjoyed his youth — for methinks the spirit never can be thoroughly gay and careless again, after this great event. We gain infinitely by the exchange; but we do give up something, nevertheless. As for myself, who have been a trifler preposterously long, I find it necessary at last to come out of my cloud-region, and allow myself to be woven into the sombre texture of humanity. There is no escaping it any longer. I have business

> on earth now, and must look about me for the means of doing it.[25]

It is as if Hawthorne were announcing his transformation from an Owen Warland into a Hester Prynne, a conversion from the inhabitant of a "cloud-region" to a participant in "the sombre texture of humanity." For writer and protagonist both, the child is mother to the authentic artist.

To this point I have emphasized what might be termed the "empowering" or "liberating" qualities of Hawthorne's identification with the adulteress. At the very least, Hawthorne sets aside a trivializing self-image as artist in favor of a "devilish" author who "gushes forth" his words. As part of that transformation, Hawthorne identifies with females in general and female writers in particular in their struggle with marginality and silence. At the same time, Hawthorne seems to affirm the carnal origins of his own creativity, ironically dismissing the "shrunken" male artist such as Owen (and one might speculate, Dimmesdale as well). Yet, as Frederick Crews has forcefully observed, "even for the most bounteously passionate of Hawthorne's characters . . . art and guilt are intertwined."[26] The novel registers this sense of guilt, for despite Hester's obvious appeal — her heroism, her endurance, her daring — she remains a censured figure, not only by surrounding characters, but by the narrator himself. No doubt this censure issues from Hawthorne's complex filiopiety, for not only does he relish the differences between himself as writer of story-books and his ancestors, but he also acknowledges the correspondences.

More importantly for purposes of this analysis, Hawthorne's often critical characterization of Hester leads us to consider additional meanings of "adulterate." What about the process of "adulteration" might cause Hawthorne to feel guilt or shame? Or, pursuing another possibility, might Hawthorne need to adulterate in order to succeed as an artist, especially in his treatment of the adulterous heroine? In its widest application, "to adulterate" means "to render spurious or counterfeit; to falsify, corrupt, debase, especially by the admixture of baser ingredients."[27] Hawthorne lived in a kind of global terror of "adulteration," a dread that he practiced such "counterfeiting" every time he took up the pen. Terence Martin makes a crucial observation when he writes, "'The bane of your life has been self-distrust,' wrote Horatio Bridge to Hawthorne in 1836; and, although he meant that Hawthorne distrusted the quality of his work, he might correctly have added that the primary difficulty derived from a fundamental doubt about the efficacy of fiction. Having decided to be a writer, Hawthorne found it extremely difficult to sustain a belief in the value of his fiction."[28] In part, as Martin has helped us see, Hawthorne battled a common-sense philosophy of art which elevated the "fanciful" and chastised "the imaginative." Though Hester seems to provide a new conception of the romantic artist, at the same time Hawthorne continues to wrestle with these latent demons of artistic guilt. It is at least suggestive that as Hester confronts the community upon the scaffold, the narrator directs the reader's vision to "the unadulterated sunshine" (p. 65), an apt figure for divine judgment, "the light of common day," and perhaps even a Platonic realm beyond this fallen world. Hester's adultery transgresses all three worlds, for she has sinned against her religion, evicted herself from the "common" world, and "fallen" into "the sombre texture of humanity" out of the "cloud-regions" (to quote once again Hawthorne's letter to Hillard). Hawthorne as author also "adulterates" the truths of these three realms, as well as the interior regions of his psyche. His famous "definition" of romance (surely it is more an atmospheric evocation of that genre) suggests a desperate need to "balance" the competing demands of world (the furniture in the room), the heart (the firelight), spirit (the moonlight), and imagination itself (the mirror). He seeks a formula for mixing these ingredients into an attractive, "probable" concoction. But notice that by the very act of "mixing" Hawthorne has succumbed to "adultery," for he must by necessity "falsify" and "corrupt." Hawthorne even confesses to his "crime" as romancer when he suggests that he might have written far better had he "attempted a different order of composition," say a more straightforward narrative of the "veteran shipmaster," "since scarcely a day passed that he did not stir me to laughter and admiration by his marvellous gifts as a storyteller" (p. 37). More generally, Hawthorne remarks, "the wiser effort would have been, to diffuse thought and imagination, through the opaque substance of to-day, and thus to make it a bright transparency" (p. 37). Granted, there would still be an element of adulteration in this latter scheme, but one might say that the artistic "corruption" would be less. That is, in the "wiser effort" the author would reduce the elements under consideration, simplify the task, mix fewer ingredients, and remain truer to the "unadulterated sunshine" of our common world. Certainly the author would be less dangerous, less subversive, less peculiar. This famous caveat by the romancer has struck readers as amusing and perhaps a bit trivial. However, I take the autobiographical subject at his word here, accepting as authentic his sense of failure, his sense of sin, his sense of adulteration.

I suggest, then, that the novel censures Hester in part because her "sin" of "adultery" implicitly recalls for the writer his own sins of authorial "adulteration." But in another sense, a far more cynical and yet self-protecting sense, the author uses adulteration to his advantage, and his female protagonist practices this same cunning art. In addition to the general definition discussed earlier, "adulterate" has traditionally referred to a process of preparing a product for sale by "mixing in baser elements."[29] Unquestionably Hawthorne sensed that he could achieve an authorial "ten strike" by "mixing in the baser elements" of sex, adultery, and ministerial misdeeds. In his study of popular culture during the antebellum era, David S. Reynolds points to common motifs in sensational literature available to the author of The Scarlet Letter. Reynolds observes, for instance, the popularity of "the justified pariah" and "the reverend rake."[30] Despite his ennobling claims for his "spiritualized" art, Hawthorne surely knew what he was about when he "mixed in" these lurid character types. But he adulterates in the other direction as well, for having introduced these sensational themes, Hawthorne refuses to exploit their libidinous potential fully. Indeed, carefully balancing desire and repression, curiosity and primness, Hawthorne "adulterates" the story of Hester by questioning her morality and her repentance. Once again, I am convinced Hawthorne as professional writer knew he was playing with fire and chose to temporize. Writing to his publisher James T. Fields prior to the novel's publication, Hawthorne remarked, "'The Scarlet Letter' is rather a delicate subject to write upon, but in the way in which I have treated it, it appears to me there can be no objections on that score."[31] The same "Fanny Fern" (Sarah Parton) praised by Hawthorne for her deviltry provides testimony to just how dangerous adultery could be for antebellum women and writers. We need only consider the debacle of Parton's second marriage, a marital disaster in which the future writer was accused of adultery by her husband, resulting in a divorce. The event was so devastating that Parton refused to discuss it openly in later years. Even more significantly from our present perspective, Parton deleted the entire episode from the otherwise faithfully autobiographical Ruth Hall. Adultery not only threatened Parton as a wife and mother but as a writer.[32] Though Hawthorne could not have known of this incident in the life of a contemporaneous writer, it suggests that his caution in representing adultery was well-founded.

We know (and Hawthorne anticipated) that The Scarlet Letter was a modest commercial success, and thus the writer's acts of adultery paid off. If we feel inclined to accuse Hawthorne of hypocrisy or acting in bad faith toward his protagonist, we need only recall what Nina Baym has written about Hester's art: "in a society that does not recognize and provide forms for imaginative expression, the artist of the private must always make her statement covertly by distorting the available public forms of expression. The executed product therefore involves a compromise, sometimes a very radical one, between the conception and its final shape. In the interplay between Pearl and the letter, Hawthorne and Hester both wrestle with the problem of bringing together the artist's 'idea,' which is nonsocial and even nonverbal, and the eventual product."[33] To survive in the marketplace, the author/adulteress must compromise, must balance internal vision against external form, subversive drives against communally sanctioned genres. Ironically it is as an adulteress that Hawthorne found the resolution of that conflict between "public man" and "artist," between the financially solvent and imaginatively inspired personae. Once he had entered the marketplace as a scandal, he could exploit the "shame" for financial benefit, an attitude made transparent by his composing "The Custom-House." Indeed, Hawthorne frequently mentioned that it was the satiric sketch which drew the most attention to his text.[34]

But the question remains: by what logic must the adulteress (either Hester or Hawthorne) enter the marketplace at all? Put simply, by transgressing paternalistic norms, the adulteress perforce must pay his/her own way in the world. Once the individual citizen becomes an "author," a creative, self-authenticating individual, he/she must by necessity step outside the protection of "authority." As Hester Prynne exchanged the protective custody of "Chillingworth" for the site of the male gaze, so too must the androgynous author.[35] Hawthorne makes this point eminently clear in "The Custom-House." He places stress upon his felt dependence while employed as surveyor, as in this comment: "while [a Custom-House officer] leans on the mighty arm of the Republic, his own proper strength departs from him. He loses, in an extent proportioned to the weakness or force of his original nature, the capability of self-support" (p. 38). Hawthorne elaborates upon this theme of financial and emotional dependence by calling attention to the "patriarchal" qualities of his fellow-workers, reminding the reader several times that these ancient personages are the models of dependence and "custom" (that is, conformity to the norms of the Custom-House). Furthermore, the sketch highlights the "unadulterated" quality of its key inhabitants, including the permanent Inspector and the "man of business." In one of the more memorable moments in the text, the narrator cannot repeat often enough the shallow, superficial, spirit-less qualities of the Inspector, who is the "unmixed" image of man as animal: "The careless security of his life in the Custom-House, on a regular income, and with but slight and infrequent apprehensions of removal, had no doubt contributed to make time pass lightly over him. The original and more potent causes, however, lay in the rare perfection of his animal nature, the moderate proportion of intellect, and the very trifling admixture of moral and spiritual ingredients; these latter qualities, indeed, being in barely enough measure to keep the old gentleman from walking on all-fours" (p. 17). If anything, the "man of business" is even more perfectly suited to the scene than "the father of the Custom-House," for "would he forthwith, by the merest touch of his finger, make the incomprehensible as clear as daylight" (p. 24). Set against these "person[s] thoroughly adapted to the situation which [they] held," Hawthorne could only appear an oddity, a disturbing mixture of artist and surveyor, one who ultimately must fall back on his idolatrous art for sustenance because he cannot "adapt" himself to the mind-numbing, spiritless routines of the Custom-House.

Thus Hawthorne the artist was indeed a kind of adulteress, for he transgressed vocational and gender boundaries, acknowledged sexuality as a prime mover in art and culture, confessed to "adulterating" the truth in all its possible manifestations, and made due with an independent source of income closely linked to his "adulterous" behavior. "The Custom-House" remains the eloquent testimony of the outsider who cannot quite accept that status, the liminal writer who chastises his commercial culture while at the same time longing for its emoluments. If the analogy between Hawthorne and Hester still seems far-fetched, I would refer the reader to yet another treatment of the male artist and the "sinful" female, The Blithedale Romance. Hawthorne's fourth novel provides a parodic revision of many elements of his earlier prose, especially in his characterization of gender roles and the function of the narrative consciousness.[36] It is as if Hawthorne asked himself, "what sort of story would an 'inoffensive man of letters' produce, especially upon confronting a powerful, intelligent, expressive female character such as Zenobia?" The result is the comic, often squeamish, ultimately evasive narrative of Miles Coverdale. By contrast, the narrative consciousness of "The Custom-House" and The Scarlet Letter, endowed with "deviltry" and made arrogant by justified wrath, produced a classic study of the artist's complex fate in American culture.

NOTES

1. For the definitive scholarly treatment of this sermonic tradition, see Sacvan Bercovitch, *The American Jeremiad* (Madison: Univ. of Wisconsin Press, 1978). Interestingly, in *The Puritan Origins of the American Self* (New Haven: Yale Univ. Press, 1975), Bercovitch has interpreted Hester's story as an eschatological "sermon" (pp. 176-78). As Bercovitch remarks, we might add "America" to the list of referents for the scarlet A, symbolic of Hester's role as prophet in the future glory of the United States.

2. *The Romance in America: Studies in Cooper, Poe, Hawthorne, Melville, and James* (Middletown, CT: Wesleyan Univ. Press, 1969), p. 99. See also Nina Baym, *The Shape of Hawthorne's Career* (Ithaca: Cornell Univ. Press, 1976), esp. pp. 142-51; Michael Davitt Bell, "Arts of Deception: Hawthorne, 'Romance,' and The Scarlet Letter," in *New Essays on The Scarlet Letter*, ed. Michael J. Colacurcio (New York: Cambridge Univ. Press, 1985), pp. 29-56; Rita K. Gollin, "'Again a Literary Man': Vocation and The Scarlet Letter," in *Critical Essays on The Scarlet Letter*, ed. David B. Kesterson (Boston: G. K. Hall, 1988), pp. 171-83; and most recently, Jon B. Reed, "'A Letter, — the Letter A': A Portrait of the Artist as Hester Prynne," *ESQ* 36 (1990): 79-107.

3. In "His Folly, Her Weakness: Demystified Adultery in The Scarlet Letter," in *New Essays on The Scarlet Letter*, pp. 137-59, Carol Bensick locates Hawthorne's novel in the tradition of "the novel of adultery," asserting that while The Scarlet Letter employs key motifs of that tradition, it violates generic expectations by creating "the happiest possible ending," that is, by allowing the adulteress to live. In *Secrets and Sympathy: Forms of Disclosure in Hawthorne's Novels* (Athens: Univ. of Georgia Press, 1988), Gordon Hutner comments on Hawthorne's "attraction" to the theme of adultery: "In the novel, Hawthorne makes metaphoric the literal charges against him by enlarging the allegation of political misconduct, which so mortified him, into an indictment significant enough to include the social extent of private transgressions . . . Perhaps as a guilty consequence of blinking at Custom House graft, Hawthorne believed his transgression betrayed an image of himself, thus violating Sophia's redemptive love in being untrue to the spirit of bourgeois respectability that he believed had graced his marriage" (pp. 27-28). I do not so much take issue with these readings as build upon them.

4. *Adultery in the Novel: Contract and Transgression* (Baltimore: Johns Hopkins Univ. Press, 1979), p. 17.

5. For an excellent discussion of Hester's liminality and her empowerment through that marginal status, see Reed,

"'A Letter, — the Letter A': A Portrait of the Artist as Hester Prynne," especially pp. 90-93.

6. *The Letters, 1843-1853*, ed. Thomas Woodson, L. Neal Smith, and Norman Holmes Pearson (Columbus: Ohio State Univ. Press, 1985), p. 264.
7. *The Letters, 1843-1853*, p. 270.
8. *The Letters: 1843-1853*, p. 23.
9. *The Scarlet Letter* (Columbus: Ohio State Univ. Press, 1962), p. 28. Further quotations from this text will cited parenthetically.
10. *The Rhetoric of American Romance: Dialect and Identity in Emerson, Dickinson, Poe, and Hawthorne* (Baltimore: Johns Hopkins Univ. Press, 1985), p. 156.
11. *The Letters, 1843-1853*, pp. 329-30.
12. For the most complete discussion of masculinity and creativity in the antebellum United States, see David Leverenz, *Manhood and the American Renaissance* (Ithaca: Cornell Univ. Press, 1989), esp. Chapter One, "'I' and 'You' in the American Renaissance," pp. 9-41.
13. *Aesthetic Headaches: Women and a Masculine Poetics in Poe, Melville, and Hawthorne* (Athens: Univ. of Georgia Press, 1988), p. 8.
14. In an intriguing (though speculative) analysis of Hawthorne's relationship with his daughter Una, T. Walter Herbert, Jr. has aptly described Hawthorne's place in the interstices of his culture, observing that "Hawthorne's unstable fusion of feminism and misogyny is one feature of the interference pattern set up by ceaselessly colliding self-appraisals, the convulsive uncertainties regarding his sexual identity that permanently characterized his emotional life" ("Hawthorne, Una, and The Scarlet Letter: Interactive Selfhoods and the Cultural Construction of Gender," *PMLA* 103 [1988]: 285). Milton R. Stern has stated Hawthorne's dilemma in even stronger terms: "Disconnected from the work of the world, like Owen Warland, Hawthorne's Artist of the Beautiful, the male

writer was too easily disowned as 'unmanly' — a person of vaguely epicene uselessness or detriment to the mainstream of Americans fulfilling God's plan among the important actualities of life" (*Contexts for Hawthorne* [Urbana: Univ. of Illinois Press, 1991], p. 40). For a thorough discussion of Hawthorne's ambivalent attitude toward women and his own femininity, see Jennifer Fleischner, "Female Eroticism, Confession, and Interpretation in Nathaniel Hawthorne," *Nineteenth-Century Fiction* 44 (1988): 514-33.

15. James D. Wallace, "Hawthorne and the Scribbling Women Reconsidered," *American Literature* 62 (1990): 221-22.

16. *The Letters, 1843-1853*, p. 345.

17. *The Letters, 1853-1856*, ed. Thomas Woodson, James A. Rubino, L. Neal Smith, and Norman Holmes Pearson (Columbus: Ohio State Univ. Press, 1987), p. 308.

18. In *The Romance in America*, Porte has argued, "in a remarkable insight underlying much of his work and clearly anticipating Freud's notions, not only of the sources of art in general, but more particularly of those dreams and fantasies which are the type of romance, Hawthorne suggests that there is a connection between 'sin' (by which he means sexual knowledge and passion) and artistic understanding and power" (pp. 102-03). Joanne Felt Diehl has recently developed this interpretation by focusing on the "family romance" inscribed in the novel. See "Re-Reading The Letter: Hawthorne, the Fetish, and the (Family) Romance" in *New Literary History* (1988): 655-73.

19. *The Letters, 1813-1843*, ed. Thomas Woodson, L. Neal Smith, and Norman Holmes Pearson (Columbus: Ohio State Univ. Press, 1984), p. 388.

20. In "Hawthorne's Love Letters: Writing and Relationship," *American Literature* 59 (1987), Person comments on this letter:

"[Hawthorne] seems to offer Sophia a kind of 'male drag.' He resigns control over his own interior space and invites her to take his place, speaking and writing in her own voice after reading his thoughts. The imagery he employs, furthermore, is striking for its suggestion of gender reversal. Instead of penetrating Sophia, Hawthorne himself is penetrated and virtually — verbally — impregnated. With Sophia empowered in his 'inmost regions,' he will in effect give birth to a new, more self-expressive kind of writing, gushing out in 'warmth and freedom' as he has not been able to do before." (pp. 223-24)

Later in the same article Person speculates that Hawthorne identifies with Dimmesdale, who is "inspired" by Hester. I would suggest that we pursue the logic of this cross-gender fantasy to its conclusion, considering the possibility that Hawthorne identifies with his powerful heroine and associates Sophia (in part) with Dimmesdale.

21. "The Parabolic Ploys of The Scarlet Letter," *American Quarterly* 39 (1987): 206. My analysis of Hawthorne's cross-gender fantasy of birthing is indebted to Bronstein's insight that, for Hawthorne, "procreation figures literary production" (p. 205).

22. *The Compact Edition of the Oxford English Dictionary* (New York: Oxford Univ. Press, 1971), p. 143.

23. "The Artist of the Beautiful," in *Tales and Sketches* (New York: Library of America, 1982), p. 930.

24. In *The Shape of Hawthorne's Career*, Baym comments, "At the core of 'The Artist of the Beautiful' is Hawthorne's recognition of how inadequate a figure Owen is for the vocation he has chosen, how timid and shrunken his conception of art. The narrative belies the narrator's claim for Owen's artistic stature and calls for another kind of artistry than his" (p. 111). Thought of in these terms, Owen represents the "minor" artist Hawthorne characterizes in his letters to Hillard and Longfellow, the artist who is deposed and goes on to write his "h-ll-fired story." Significantly, Baym later observes that *The Scarlet Letter* echoes but "goes beyond" "The Artist of the Beautiful" in its characterization of the artist (p. 148), an argument I develop in this section of the article.

25. Letter to G. S. Hillard dated March 24, 1844, in *The Letters, 1843-1853*, pp. 22-23.

26. *The Sins of the Fathers: Hawthorne's Psychological Themes* (New York: Oxford Univ. Press, 1966), p. 158.

27. *The Compact Oxford English Dictionary*, p. 33.

28. *Nathaniel Hawthorne*, rev. ed. (Boston: Twayne, 1983), p. 8.

29. *The Compact Oxford English Dictionary* cites nineteenth-century uses of "adulterate" in this sense, including a passage from 1822 which refers to the adulteration of bread with alum and chalk (p. 33).

30. *Beneath the American Renaissance: The Subversive Imagination in the Age of Emerson and Melville* (New York: Alfred A. Knopf, 1988), p. 260.

31. *The Letters, 1843-1853*, p. 305.

32. For a thorough discussion of this crisis in Parton's life, see Mary Kelley, *Private Woman, Public Stage: Literary Domesticity in Nineteenth-Century America* (New York: Oxford Univ. Press, 1984), pp. 264-68.

33. *The Shape of Hawthorne's Career*, pp. 132-33.

34. It is on these grounds that I take issue with Michael T. Gilmore's important analysis of *The Scarlet Letter* in *American Romanticism and the Marketplace* (Chicago: Univ. of Chicago Press, 1985). Gilmore distinguishes between the artistic endeavors of Hester and Dimmesdale in these terms: "The difference in status and behavior of Hawthorne's principal characters dramatizes the conflict in his mind between two radically opposed conceptions of the artist's role and relation to the public. On one side is the version of the artist represented by Hester, a scorned outcast who makes no compromises with her audience and is indifferent to its approval . . . Dimmesdale, who embodies the other side of Hawthorne's thinking, is a type of the artist for whom fame and popularity are everything" (p. 76). Gilmore rightly emphasizes recurring puns on "market-place" within the novel and Hester's reticence in her transactions with the surrounding

community. However, he overemphasizes the symbolic import of her scenes in the literal marketplace, arguing that her silence about her lover is writ large throughout the text in her artistic or authorial silence. But as I have just suggested, Hester's relationship with her culture is far more complex than Gilmore allows, for she does extract a modest living for herself and her child through her art. She does so by "accommodating" her passionate designs to the prescribed patterns of her community's needs.

35. For an illuminating analysis of the antebellum literary marketplace and Hawthorne's vexed relationship with it, see Stern, *Contexts for Hawthorne*, "A Marketplace Context," pp. 36-105.

36. See my "Hawthorne's Anti-Romance: Blithedale and Sentimental Culture," *Journal of American Culture* 11:4 (Winter, 1988): 45-52 for an analysis of Hawthorne's parodic tactics, especially in his characterization of Coverdale and the "minor poet's" relationship with Zenobia.

5

Domesticating Hawthorne: Home is for the Birds

—John Dolis

At the head ("Custom-House") of a tale (The Scarlet Letter), where its author ("Hawthorne"), as we discover at "The End"—in the rear, if you will—has been missing from the outset, decapitated up front, in a pre-face whose face is missing (even more so) once this headless talking body turns around, on this pretext alone, this rear-end disclosure, it should come as no surprise to learn that the House of Custom is always and everywhere a chopping block. This hors-d'oeuvre prefigures the dirty work (oeuvre) in advance, announces—in good taste, nonetheless—the body of the work to follow, whose main course would be most unsavory were it to arrive with its head still on. At the head of this scenario (The Letter), the head(less: body [of Hawthorne])—lacking nothing of foresight—previews a veritable panorama of butchery: "One fine morning, I ascended the flight of granite steps, with the President's commission in my pocket, and was introduced to the corps of gentlemen who were to aid me in my weighty responsibility, as chief executive officer of the Custom-House."[1] For "corps of gentlemen" we'd best be advised to read, instead, "corpses of gentlemen."

For what, after all, is this "patriarchal body of veterans" (1:12) upon which Hawthorne's authority is brought to bear if not a brain-dead body as a (w)hole, a body whose head has never been present in the first place: "They seemed to have flung away all the golden grain of practical wisdom, which they had enjoyed so many opportunities of harvesting, and most carefully to have stored their memories with the husks. They spoke with far more interest and unction of their morning's breakfast, or yesterday's, today's or tomorrow's dinner, than of the shipwreck of forty or fifty years ago, and all the world's wonders which they had witnessed with their youthful eyes" (1:16).

From the outset, the head of this (uncivil) "body" has lost its sense, feeds on the husk rather than the grain. Its heart (Kern) keeps pace with nothing, survives upon a kernel of nonsense, the idle chitchat that inhabits the heart of this house, the inarticulate murmur of custom. Its body hasn't a grain of sense, this body of old crows whose custom it is to align itself along a wall—like a row of birds along a fence—and chirp: "it was pleasant to hear them chatting in the back entry, a row of them all tipped against the wall, as usual" (1:15). Hawthorne will have a crow to pluck regarding this chatter: "it would have been nothing short of duty, in a politician, to bring every one of those white heads under the axe of the guillotine" (1:14). Yet Hawthorne will keep a cool head. The discourse will prevail, will talk things out. If there's an axe to grind, the pen itself will be the (s)word that lops things off, that cuts to the bone. Upon this site, these heads will talk, wag their tongues, recite the scene in which all discourse will be missing (from) itself.

Here talk turns the table, to table talk. Around its customary decor, within the bounds of propriety, the discourse will come to roost. Its representative, the rooster, ironically appears in the (dis)guise of a hen. "The father of the Custom-House," its "patriarch"—"a certain permanent

Inspector"—betrays a matriarchal disposition at heart: "he seemed—not young, indeed—but a kind of new contrivance of Mother Nature in the shape of a man" (1:16, 17). And like the rest of this impotent (patriarchal) body, his head is missing—his discourse nonetheless puffed up: "His voice and laugh, which perpetually reechoed through the Custom-House, had nothing of the tremulous quaver and cackle of an old man's utterance; they came strutting out of his lungs, like the crow of a cock" (1:17), a cock that crows most vocally of feathered friends. Indeed, where and whenever talk turns (around) the tables, a bird's not far away. Here, the custom of the house dictates that table talk itself (re)turns always and everywhere to dinner:

> One point, in which he had vastly the advantage over his four-footed brethren, was his ability to recollect the good dinners which it had been no small portion of the happiness of his life to eat. His gourmandism was a highly agreeable trait; and to hear him talk of roast-meat was as appetizing as a pickle or an oyster. As he possessed no higher attribute, and neither sacrificed nor vitiated any spiritual endowment by devoting all his energies and ingenuities to subserve the delight and profit of his maw, it always pleased and satisfied me to hear him expatiate on fish, poultry, and butcher's meat, and the most eligible methods of preparing them for the table. His reminiscences of good cheer, however ancient the date of the actual banquet, seemed to bring the savor of pig or turkey under one's very nostrils. There were flavors on his palate, that had lingered there not less than sixty or seventy years, and were still apparently as fresh as that of the mutton-chop which he had just devoured for his breakfast. I have heard him smack his lips over dinners, every guest at which, except himself, had long been food for worms. (1:18-19)

It's not by chance the house of custom serves only what culture cooks up: that is, (good) taste itself. The recollection of its sense re-members only the sensation. Hence, disappointment resembles an after-taste in one's mouth:

> a particular chicken, or a remarkably praiseworthy turkey, which had perhaps adorned his board in the days of the eider Adams, would be remembered; while all the subsequent experience of our race, and all the events that brightened or darkened his individual career, had gone over him with as little permanent effect as the passing breeze. The chief tragic event of the old man's life, so far as I could judge, was his mishap with a certain goose, which had lived and died some twenty or forty years ago; a goose of most promising figure, but which, at table, proved so inveterately tough that the carving knife would make no impression on its carcass; and it could only be divided with an axe and handsaw. (1:19)

The axe and handsaw return again and again in this tale without a head. Those who fall under its spell, within the path of the blade, will be cut to the quick, just as those bodies at the opposite end of a bayonet "at Chippewa or Fort Erie" (1:22) succumbed to the blade of "the Collector, our gallant old General" (1:20)—indeed, "had fallen, like blades of grass at the sweep of a scythe" (1:22). Among the instruments of bureaucracy, its "inkstands, paper-folders, and mahogany rulers," the old General might seem as much out of place "as an old sword—now rusty, but which had flashed once on the battle's front, and showed still a bright gleam along its blade" (1:23). What's missing from the scene of such bureaucracy, from the site of its political domestication—its inkstands, paper-folders, and rulers—is, of course, the very instrument by means of which bureaucracy as such recites itself, carves out the space of its perpetuation. Regarding the path of the sword, its curvature, the space of its cut (coup), the pen takes (up) its place. Here nothing will escape the chopping block, the niche of a pen, its (pen)manship—"the bright gleam along its blade." Those heads it cuts become the meat of its discourse:

> after living for three years within the subtile influence of an intellect like Emerson's; after those wild, free days on the Assabeth, indulging fantastic speculations beside our fire of fallen boughs, with Ellery Channing; after talking with Thoreau about pine-trees and Indian relics, in his hermitage at Walden; . . . after becoming imbued with poetic sentiment at Longfellow's hearth-stone;—it was time, at length, that I should exercise other faculties of my nature, and nourish myself with food for which I had hitherto had little appetite. Even the old Inspector was desirable, as a change of diet, to a man who had known Alcott. (1:25)

If these impotent, emasculated, castrated—that is, beheaded—birds within this hen house of custom speak only of what they eat, Hawthorne eats the very thing of which his discourse speaks (cannibalism is not far off). His pen cuts up (coup) these birds, dismantles the chicken coop to which they have become accustomed: the hens will be served up as tasty morsels, these headless birds his nourishment. In the meantime, talking heads will croak. In between time, Hawthorne eats their words. Between time, within the timeless (non)duration of custom, confined to the paucity of its diet—its fowl taste—Hawthorne eats crow. Beyond the frame of this hen house, "The Custom-House," the narrative, moreover, will not forget its talk of birds, the bird talk of its recit. Birds configure several scenes within The Letter—not to mention the central scene of Hawthorne's letters (the primal scene [hors] of the oeuvre), where a bird (re)turns with a vengeance as but the supplement of talking heads (but I'm ahead of myself).

At one point, separated from Hester, Pearl, perceiving "a flock of beach-birds," gathers pebbles in the apron of her dress and, "creeping from rock to rock after these small sea-fowl, displayed remarkable dexterity in pelting them. One little gray bird, with a white breast, Pearl was almost sure, had been hit by a pebble, and fluttered away with a broken wing" (1:177-78). In (the) light of its desire, its metonymic displacement, this moment simultaneously figures Pearl's hostility toward Hester as well as its effect upon herself, for "the elf-child sighed, and gave up her sport; because it grieved her to have done harm to a little being that was as wild as the sea-breeze, or as wild as Pearl herself" (1:178). This identification is reinforced, as James Mellard observes, when Pearl returns to her mother, "flitting along as lightly as one of the little sea-birds" (1:178)wan identification whose desire, in turn, reveals its symptom as a chain of metaphoric substitutions.[2] Up ahead, the forest scene of The Letter will further reconfigure this scenario. Here, the "great black forest" puts on "the kindest of its moods" to welcome Pearl: "It offered her the patridge-berries, the growth of the preceding autumn . . . These Pearl gathered, and was pleased with their wild flavor. The small denizens of the wilderness hardly took pains to move out of her path. A partridge, indeed, with a brood of ten behind her, ran forward threateningly, but soon repented of her fierceness, and clucked to her young ones not to be afraid. A pigeon, alone on a low branch, allowed Pearl to come beneath, and uttered a sound as much of greeting as alarm" (1:204).

It would be hasty, however, to think such birds are yarded by the confines of The Letter. The gourmandizing bird talk of "The Custom-House," for instance, parrots the insignificant chatter of another scene whose bird-brained scenario chirps endlessly of birds (and of a certain bird chirping), a scene whose figures rec(o)uperate those brainless birds at the head of Hawthorne's tale who figure the headless body of custom—a senseless corpse, a body that doesn't figure—cannot make sense of signs. In "Circe's Palace," such chatter becomes the very stuff(ing) of myth: a tale, moreover, in which a king-transformed-to-bird peeps unheeded warnings at sailors who—rather than bite—would eat the hand that feeds them: "This troublesome and impertinent little fowl ... would make a delicate tit-bit to begin dinner with! Just one plump morsel, melting away between the teeth" (VII:272). Here talk turns everywhere to table: Ulysses's crew of "terrible gormandizers" (VII:266) speaks only of dinner—and "any hour of the day was dinner-time with them" (VII:279). Here, too, significance is found only in the promise of food: hence, the general failure of the crew to read signs—above all, those of danger.

Ironically, the purple bird itself appears as the first sign of danger: the sailors, as usual, see only food. Ulysses, on the other hand, unable to interpret its chirping, nevertheless reads into its appearance the possibility of being other than it seems. When the gluttonous crew, perceiving only growls of the stomach, insists it search the island, despite its previous encounter with the Sirens, "those bird-like damsels" (VII:276), Ulysses gives in: mother hen must feed her brood. Little wonder that Circe so easily turns them into swine, transforms them into the very dinner they desire, despite Ulysses's caution: "if we go to yonder palace, there can be no question that we shall make our appearance at the dinner-table; but whether seated as guests, or served up as food, is a point to be seriously considered" (VII:270).

Unlike "The Custom-House," however, narration here (a)voids the (primal) scene, the site of sightlessness, the failure of insight, blindness to signs and their significance, what's missing (a/head). No heads need fall where cool heads prevail. In keeping with this logic, Circe must be defeated, as Laura Laffrado suggests, "but she need not—either in traditional myth or in Hawthorne's version of it—be decapitated.[3] Thus, seizing Circe by her ringlets, Ulysses "made a gesture as if he meant to strike off her head at one blow" (VII:291) unless she restore his crew to human form. Yet even the body might be a form of deception: "When men once turn to brutes, the trifle of man's wit, that remains in them, adds tenfold to their brutality" (VII:293). In the wrong place, wit breeds absolute brutality. To wit, wisdom requires the subject's displacement from the heart of nature to the nature of (its) heart, the heart of (its) reason, reason's heart—the security (that lies) ahead of its voyage: hearth and home. Missing (what's) a/head (the voyage), nature is left behind. With this reversal, hospitality (re)claims its customary ("unnatural") place within the "enchanting" confines of the house and its domestic "charms": "they all made themselves comfortable in Circe's enchanted palace, until quite rested and refreshed from the toils and hardships of their voyage" (VII:295).

Birds similarly (re)appear elsewhere and otherwise to populate Hawthorne's oeuvre, his House of Fiction. I needn't recall you to another house, beside whose seven gables, in its backyard, its rear (if you've been following me), appears a certain "hen-coop, of very reverend antiquity" (II:88), with its inhabitants, whose descendants "had existed . . . ever since the House of the Seven Gables was founded, and were somehow mixed up with its destiny" (II:89). Mixed up with its destiny indeed: this scene—primal, if you must (a tergo, no less)—this backyard scene is but the scenic behind of the barnyard itself, the derriere of Hawthorne's oeuvre, and in whose name an-Other bird takes (its) place, displaces the discourse of "Hawthome"—in the end. But here, too, I'm ahead of things. For the moment, I recall you to the discourse at hand (what's in the bush comes later). Regarding this "feathered society," their "generally quiet, yet often brisk, and constantly diversified talk, one to another, or sometimes in soliloquy . . . had such a domestic tone, that it was almost a wonder why you could not establish a regular interchange of ideas about household matters, human and gallinaceous" (II:150-51). These hens are now the end of a line whose talking heads had long since fallen in order to still the likes of the mouths of those very heads talking around the table. This ironic inversion will stimulate but further talk, will itself become the topic of conversation. The body of these birds will offer yet another occasion for discourse. Dinner, here, stops short of the cannibalism taking place just beyond this barnyard scene (the backyard of the House itself), just beyond the confines of Hepzibah's shop, where other heads have fallen for less—to wit, the gingerbread "Jim Crow," whose fate it was to fall into the hands of little Ned Higgins: "No sooner had he reached the sidewalk (little cannibal that he was!) than Jim Crow's head was in his mouth" (II:50). All talk stops here.

At the end of this scenario (The House), what once brought up the rear-the behind—of The House (the hens and their head, Chanticleer) is sent ahead of Clifford, Hepzibah, Phoebe, and Holgrave, into the future, to another house, the country-seat of the late Judge Pyncheon: "Chanticleer and his family had already been transported thither; where the two hens had forthwith begun an indefatigable process of egg-laying, with an evident design, as a matter of duty and conscience, to continue their illustrious breed under better auspices than for a century past" (II:314). Repression stages this recuperation, its own return: these previously barren hens take up the line precisely where the sterile Pyncheon women drew its end. In turn, Phoebe will follow their lead: more eggs will be hatched. Hawthorne's Gentle Reader discovers its ecstasy, its jouissance, in this (Oedipal?) intersection of story line and destiny, its (own) end. Finally full, replete, stuffed, it identifies as a (w)hole with this biological arrangement, this coup/coop, the domestic scene (at the heart) of The House (The House): Propter solum ovanum muller est id quod est: solely because of the ovary, a woman is what she is.[4]

This country theme anticipates an urban variation in both Blithedale and The Faun. Across from his hotel room in town, Coverdale espies, on the peak of a dormer-window, a dove: "looking very dreary and forlorn; insomuch that I wondered why she chose to sit there, in the chilly rain, while her kindred were doubtless nestling in a warm and comfortable dove-cote. All at once, this dove spread her wings, and launching herself in the air, came flying so straight across the intervening space, that I fully expected her to alight directly on my window-sill. In the latter part of her course, however, she swerved aside, flew upward, and vanished, as did likewise the slight, fantastic pathos with which I had invested her" (III:152). Coverdale's "pathetic" investment, here, silhouettes another bird nestling in the "comfortable dove-cote" of Blithedale—Priscilla, whom Coverdale, we can imagine, envisions alighting at the window that opens onto his own domestic dream. This vision will likewise vanish. And if this correspondence is too easy, too facile, as Kenneth Dauber suggests, since "there is practically no dove imagery elsewhere in Blithedale," the dove maintains a constant vigil in Hawthorne's oeuvre, just as, after Priscilla had disappeared from the boudoir, "the dove still kept her desolate perch, on the peak of the attic-window" (III:159).[5] It's neither the first nor last time this love bird comes calling in the House of "Hawthorne": its coo (coup/coop) reverberates throughout the oeuvre (but I'm ahead of things once more).

The Faun (re)marks the scene of homecoming, the site of the dove's return, recites this bird until it knows it by heart, knows that the dove, at heart, reverberates the heart of a virgin—Hilda, "the Dove, as her well-wishers half-laughingly delighted to call her" (IV:59). Domiciled in her tower, Hilda keeps a vestal vigil—no home fire as such, no heart(h)—trimming the lamp before the Virgin's shrine, ceaselessly paying homage "to the idea of Divine Womanhood" (IV:54) while "keeping a maiden heart within her bosom" (IV:328). Here chastity transfigures the domestic scene, transforms motherhood into the "purity" of an idea(l), just as Hilda's occupation as copyist, handmaiden of "Art" (to wit: "The Handmaid of Raphael, whom she loved with a virgin's love" [IV:61]), translates art into the sterile space of imitation. Genealogy here disdains (its own) experience, owes nothing to itself, hands over its technique(s) of reproduction to another.

Hilda's avocation similarly reflects this test-tube technology, its occupation as proxy, standing in for another, ensuring hereditary succession, the success of a (family) "line." Here she fails to draw the line. For "handmaid" read, instead, "housemaid": connected with Hilda's tower and its lofty shrine, "a lamp has been burning before the Virgin's image, at noon, at midnight, and at all hours of the twenty-four, and must be kept burning forever, as long as the tower shall stand; or else the tower itself, the palace, and whatever estate belongs to it, shall pass from its hereditary possessor, in accordance with an ancient vow, and become the property of the Church" (IV:52). In (the) place of keeping the home-fire burning, Hilda tends (to) a lamp, the heart(h) of a bird house, the space of a dovecote: "Here she dwelt, in her tower, possessing a friend or two in Rome, but no home-companion except the flock of doves, whose cote was in a ruinous chamber contiguous to her own. They soon became as familiar with the fair-haired Saxon girl as if she were a born sister of their brood; and her customary white robe bore such an analogy to their snowy plumage, that the confraternity of artists called Hilda The Dove, and recognized her aerial apartment as The Dove-cote" (IV:56). Similarly, Miriam remarks of Hilda, "how like a dove she is herself, the fair, pure creature! The other doves know her for a sister, I am sure" (IV: 52-53). Even her "art" betrays a bird-like quality, her copies revealing a "flitting fragrance, as it were, of the originals" (IV: 58, italics mine).

It's not for nothing the Gentle Reader takes her to heart: she's one of them, one of the flock, part of that con-maternity of gentle readers: the readerly counterpart of Hawthorne's "scribbling women." They can produce but chicken scratch. Just so, it's best they stick to "reproduction." So too, the world is better off with Hilda's copies: "Would it have been worth Hilda's while to relinquish this office, for the sake of giving the world a picture or two which it would call original; pretty fancies of snow and moonlight; the counterpart in picture, of so many feminine achievements in literature!" (IV:61). Notice, in passing, the exclamation point: this is not a question. So much for (popular) taste: hardly a cuisine. Similarly, the anonymous portrait of Hilda reflects the vaudevillian variation of this popular "snow and moonlight" sentiment, its contamination, the defloration of this hen house, the rooster as part of the scene. Despite the disruption of this idyllic cliche, itself a cliche, the "modem artist" nevertheless "strenuously upheld the originality of his own picture, as well as the stainless purity of its subject, and chose to call it, (and was laughed at for his pains,) `Innocence, dying of a Blood-stain'" (IV:330). We'd do well to call it, instead, "The Gentle Reader Deflowered." The rooster's been at work, has ruffled some feathers and would be finished with the cackling. Unlike the archangel Michael, whose feathers remain untouched in his fight with Lucifer (IV: 184), The Gentle Reader's not a saint. Its reputation's on the chopping block.

The text inters this issue, lays the issue of getting laid (to rest): the hens croak. In its final chapter, The Faun recites the (primal) scene of "Art" at the site of a coincidence: the Pantheon—where Western art transfigures pagan religion, its figures domesticated now as household deities. It's not by chance the text recuperates the "Gentle

Reader" in sight of this domicile—the house of (dead) Artists, the tomb of art. On first glance, this house possesses all the earmarks of home, including "a very plump and comfortable tabby-cat . . . [that] had established herself on the altar" (IV:458). Kenyon, however, recalls its unhomely (uncanny?) resemblance to other figures that populate the oeuvre, figures without heads. The Pantheon, too, is missing its head, has a hole in its roof: "I think ... it is to the aperture in the Dome—that great Eye, gazing heavenward—that the Pantheon owes the peculiarity of its effect. It is so heathenish, as it were;—so unlike all the snugness of our modern civilization" (IV:457). The end of The Faun returns the Gentle Reader to (the) dispossession (of) itself: no homecoming here—and this in face of nothing but talk about home: "I have neither pole-star above, nor light of cottage-windows here below, to bring me home. Were you my guide," beseeches Kenyon, "with that white wisdom which clothes you as with a celestial garment, all would go well. Oh, Hilda, guide me home" (IV:460-61). Hilda concurs: "We are both lonely; both far from home" (IV:461). The same desire thus structures both the forward glimpse of domestic serenity and a backward glance toward the "mother" land, to recollect, to return, home—to inhabit, once again, the homeland:

> So, Kenyon won the gentle Hilda's shy affection [not to mention the Gentle Reader's], and her consent to be his bride. Another hand must henceforth trim the lamp before the Virgin's shrine; . . . they resolved to go back to their own land; because the years, after all, have a kind of emptiness, when we spend too many of them on a foreign shore. We defer the reality of life . . . until a future moment, when we shall again breathe our native air; but, by-and-by, there are no future moments; or, if we do return, we find that the native air has lost its invigorating quality . . . Thus,

> between two countries, we have none at all . . . It is wise, therefore, to come back betimes—or never. (IV:461)

Upon the site of the Pantheon, in this uncanny home, in sight of the gods, Hilda (ex)changes "place," transforms from maid to deity—a household god: "for Hilda was coming down from her own tower, to be herself enshrined and worshipped as a household Saint, in the light of her husband's fireside" (IV:461). The hen comes home to roost, becomes herself (the rooster of the coop). In this coup, we know who wields the blade and who wears the pants. The Gentle Reader, likewise, wants nothing more than to be in on this game, the promise of domestic bliss—to be part of Hawthorne's House (of Fiction), let into its most intimate space, its sacred mystery, the Author's intention. The Author, however, refuses to parrot this (domestic) scene, to traffic in this coo(p), bearing the balm of sympathy like Hilda's doves, "uttering soft, tender, and complaining sounds, deep in their bosoms" (IV:331). Instead, the Author claims ignorance of his (own) text: "Hawthorne" claims ignorance of itself. In the "Postscript," questioning his characters "with a curiosity similar to that which he has just deprecated on the part of his readers," Hawthorne tells us that, once upon a time, he took occasion "to cross-examine his friends, Hilda and the sculptor, and to pry into several dark recesses of the story" (IV:464). Inquiring of Hilda, for example, about the contents of Miriam's mysterious package, Hawthorne remarks of her answer, "it is clear as a London fog" (IV:465). Regarding the disappearance of Miriam and Hilda, and Kenyon's reply ("with a glance of friendly commiseration at my obtuseness"), Hawthorne ironically concedes, "How excessively stupid in me not to have seen it sooner" (IV:465). When he asks of Hilda's whereabouts during her disappearance, "Hilda threw her eyes on all sides, and seeing that there was not even a bird of the air to fly away with the secret," responds so inconclusively that

Hawthorne once again remarks, ironically, "The atmosphere is getting delightfully lucid" (IV:466). If ignorance, here, removes the Author from the work, it similarly removes the Gentle Reader from the oeuvre, evicts the hens from the House itself. Within the Post Crypt, the Author "lies"—forever interred. Intentionality is set against itself, beside itself, beyond itself: the Author is dead—and with him, the Gentle Reader as well. The Reader has traveled this infinite "distance," the space of the oeuvre, only to be refused admittance. In sight of its mysteries, of sharing the Author's insight into the text, Hawthorne's refusal to let the Gentle Reader in on these secrets incites hysteria. Denied this entr(e)e ("if only you had told me; I too can keep a secret"), domestic civility defenestrates the scene. The hens go wild.

(Hen) COOP

In itSelf, the Gentle Reader does nothing if not consume. Consumption fuels its own desire, becomes, indeed, the reader's own "issue." In taking the "Author" to heart, the Gentle Reader recuperates the heart(h) of its domestic topography: colonialization, incorporation as a whole. At home, amid the alchemy of the coop, the heart(h) of the love-nest, the "two" become "one" (Plato's not far behind [hen]: Fuller's up ahead). Domestic economy demands as much. And yet, in "Hawthorne," domesticity intrudes upon the oeuvre, usurps its space, creates an occupied territory—at times, a battle zone. I recall you to Dorcas, in "Roger Malvin's Burial," whose song of "domestic love and household happiness" amid "her preparations for their evening repast" is interrupted "by the report of a gun"—her husband killing their son (X:357-58). There's something dangerous, immanently threatening, about "home" in "Hawthorne," something uncanny. Over and against the sentimental tranquillity of nineteenth-century domestic ideology, "Hawthorne" stages a different scene, one implicated in passion, disturbed by violence. Witness, for instance, the band of dead Puritans, in "Alice Doane's

Appeal," who "groaned horribly and gnashed their teeth," beholding their "homes of bliss" with "glances of hatred and smiles of bitter scorn" (XI:276).

More often than not, the domestic "cannibalizes" the oeuvre, disrupts "Hawthorne" from without. Just so, the discourse of cannibalism anxiously mirrors domesticity's desire to feed on itself, its will to self-sufficiency, to secure a space of its "own," its "proper" space, entirely within, secured, its property cut off from outside, from without, from what is other than its own. Distancing itself from the "other" (the foreign, the exotic, the alien, the uncivilized, the unfamiliar), domestic economy repeats the very thing it would exclude, the duplicity of its incestuous desire—reflects it in the discourse of an-"other" taboo. Cannibalism lies outside the domestic scene, and yet inhabits its discourse from the inside out as well, the heart(h) of its desire—that is, the desire to have no outside. (Is "Melville" behind [the staging of] this scene?) Domestic economy capitalizes on itself.

(Bird) HOUSE (cont.)

So too, the Gentle Reader seeks intercourse with the "Author," wants to be invited in, wishes for "familiar terms," desires to know the narrative itself, the narrative's desire, the "inside" story, the story from within, its (hidden) meaning, its secret. These house-bound hens would gobble up "their" Author, devour him (something he disagreed with ate him). Incorporation hence characterizes the Gentle Reader's delusion, the delusion of the Gentle Reader it-Self being ONE with the Author as a whole. Nothing foreign must remain, nothing outside—nothing "other" whatsoever. The scope of such desire does not exclude its own ironic inversion: "Now, there aren't any more cannibals in our region. Yesterday we ate the last one."[6] "Hawthorne" will have nothing to do with this yoke (zeugma). The Faun thus turns the tables on this crack-brained idea(l), serves up the Gentle Reader as entree—its (point of) departure the main course. I've done this elsewhere.[7] By placing the Author in the postscript of his text, "Hawthorne" returns as but the ghost of himself: entombed in its Post Crypt, the Author is always already dead. Outside the script, beyond the text, "Hawthorne" knows nothing of its secret(s). Narration falls apart, loses its thread—its ideal commun(icat)ion scrambled. The post does not arrive, has gone astray. Romance re(as)sembles nothing (if not a dead letter office), entombs the oeuvre itself. Meaning lies buried in the post. Indeed, the office of The Letter has always already positioned it thus: delayed, belated, postponed. The Faun buries the plot, denies narration its end, recites its very time (recit) as yet an "other" plot, an empty plot, a vacant space, the grave. The story knows nothing, not even itself; the author knows nothing, not even his story. The tale ("The End") now leaves the Gentle Reader hanging by its tail, likewise bereft of its head, squawking, beside itself, dispatched. His readership disowned, the "Author" finds jouissance in impropriety. Precisely here, where nothing is proper, the Gentle Reader gets it (in the end), becomes itself antique, remaindered, the "antique fashion of Prefaces" that "Hawthorne" has always already fashioned as out-of-fashion from the outset, old-fashioned from the start: "If I find him [the Gentle Reader] at all, it will probably be under some mossy grave-stone" (IV: 1-2).

Hospitality aside, the "Author" no longer indulges the (over) "Indulgent Reader," no longer dispenses free meals. Like Hilda's "eleemosynary doves" (IV:52), these birds depend upon the Author's charity, require mothering, just as Hilda finds solace in the Virgin—"a child, lifting its tear-stained face to seek comfort from a Mother" (IV:332). Such gratuity emasculates the Author, transforms paternity to baby-sitting the text. Notice, furthermore, the "capital" (Mother) in the above quote on which depends this vertical configuration (the child left hanging) and that, ironically, sustains this "column" from above (its head, if you will). A similar structure mirrors the "columns" supporting the

Custom House, those mother hens nurturing (the) custom, inhabiting "The Custom-House." The House of Custom replicates the custom of "the house," the cult of domesticity, the cult(ure) of (Mother) hens and Gentle Readers, the cult of The Virgin, the sterile culture of the Motherland. The rooster's flown the coop: those foolish enough to stick around must lose their heads. Such is the defining gesture of (a) culture transported to the kitchen, transfigured as cuisine, transformed by popular "taste": the dominion of women, as Catherine Beecher would have it, whose influence "the heart is proud to acknowledge."[8]

Lest we linger in the rear, I return you to the head of "The Custom-House" (now dispossessed) and to the Head of the house (whose head is missing). Here custom itself is for the birds. It's not for nothing that Hawthorne recalls this birdhouse (and the "point" of its pillars) at its peak: mother hen transformed to eagle, transfigured as symbol of the nation. This icon guards the entrance to both House and text. I give you the quote whole. Chew it slowly:

> Its front is ornamented with a portico of half a dozen wooden pillars, supporting a balcony, beneath which a flight of wide granite steps descends towards the street. Over the entrance hovers an enormous specimen of the American eagle, with outspread wings, a shield before her breast, and, if I recollect aright, a bunch of intermingled thunderbolts and barbed arrows in each claw. With the customary infirmity of temper that characterizes this unhappy fowl, she appears, by the fierceness of her beak and eye and the general truculency of her attitude, to threaten mischief to the inoffensive community; and especially to warn all citizens, careful of their safety, against intruding on the premises which she overshadows with her wings. Nevertheless, vixenly as she looks, many people are seeking, at this very moment, to shelter

> themselves under the wing of the federal eagle; imagining, I presume, that her bosom has all the softness and snugness of an eider-down pillow. But she has no great tenderness, even in her best of moods, and, sooner or later,—oftener soon than late,—is apt to fling off her nestlings with a scratch of her claw, a dab of her beak, or a rankling wound from her barbed arrows. (I:5).

"If I recollect aright": he doesn't: on purpose. This feigned amnesia performs the work of condensation and displacement. In (the) place of an olive branch, thunderbolts echo the malignity of "Mother," her incipient violence-treacherous, traitorous, ready at the moment to "fling off her nestlings."[9] Dispossessed, evicted, the citizen is de trop, the homeland defunct. Such is the House of State, the state of the nation, divided against itself: (the temple of) Olympian Zeus reduced to national bird. This overgrown hen portrays the nation as a (w)hole: emasculated, lifeless, without direction or purpose: the nation runs in circles—a rooster with its head cut off, Uncle Sam in drag. To vary the theme, Uncle Sam and National Bird play house: Mother's at home; so is Uncle. Their very treachery points to what has always already been missing: where's the father? The "where" of this Hamletesque scenario, however, resembles child's play in light of a more serious question that raises the "issue" of National Identity: who is the Father? There's only the Uncle (Sam). To further mix the metaphors (symptoms), this "play house" parrots a burlesque variation of "Leda," gender reversal and all. Here Uncle Sam beds down with Mother. Make no mistake: the country's going to the birds. No wonder the Citizen feels betrayed, a cuckold in his own house—a house, moreover, wherein presides the icon of (the power of) Rome (Romance), and in whose maternal bosom reside its patriarchal castrati, mere ghosts of men transformed to (Mother) hens. The chicken coop is dark; the lights are out. How ironically Melville positions that dimension of blackness he attributes to Hawthorne's oeuvre which, as he remarked in his review of Mosses, the "eagle-eyed reader" perceives.[10] Ahead of this tale, in a preface ahead of another tail (the tales [Mosses] that follow), Hawthorne already faces the double-edged coup of this bind, the cut that goes both ways. Already he holds "The End" in sight. The menacing presence of the chopping block steals the scene (of writing) from the outset. Nonetheless, despite (in spite of) the Gentle Reader's demand, here Hawthorne refuses to lose his head. He'll not go off half-cocked. In "The Old Manse," he cautions the reader: "So far as I am a man of really individual attributes, I veil my face; nor am I, nor have ever been, one of those supremely hospitable people, who serve up their own hearts delicately fried, with brain-sauce, as a tidbit for their beloved public" (X:33).

We've fallen behind again. I'd best make headway the reality, returning to the head of this scenario, the (headless) figure (no longer head of house) at the head of the Custom-House. Once in the house of custom, on the hither side of the cutting edge, as it were, the scene appears upside down, turned on its head (or so it seems). Here Hawthorne forewarns his Gentle Reader in advance: "Some authors . . indulge themselves in such confidential depths of revelation as could fittingly be addressed, only and exclusively, to the one heart and mind of perfect sympathy; as if the printed book, thrown at large on the wide world, were certain to find out the divided segment of the writer's own nature, and complete his circle of existence by bringing him into communion with it. It is scarcely decorous, however, to speak all, even when we speak impersonally" (I:3-4). That is to say: even when we speak without a head. At any rate, the unity of this ideal communion between "Author" and "Gentle Reader" betrays the shape of its delusion, its desire to be an undivided whole, to be One with itself: to be no one in particular. Short of this, the Gentle Reader must settle for talking meat, must take its cannibalism to heart, the desire to incorporate the

Author's body—the body of the Author's text—as its own: it's good to eat meat that talked with us.

"The Custom-House" regurgitates this scene: "It is a little remarkable, that . . . an autobiographical impulse should twice in my life have taken possession of me, in addressing the public. The first time was three or four years since, when I favored the reader . . . with a description of my way of life in the deep quietude of an Old Manse. And now . . . I again seize the public by the button" (I:3). For "button," read, instead, an object close to the "heart" of the Gentle Reader's "lips" by means of which (manipulation) the Gentle Reader, now given (over) to ecstasy, is nothing but a whore. Upon this site, Hawthorne recites the scene of the whole within the space of a hole—that very place in which the head is missing. Once caught in this bind (the Gentle Reader's "lips"), the logic of the double-edge, the cut that goes both ways, Hawthorne would appear to be its victim. The missing head's his own—or so it seems. In its ironic inversion, however, the cut will go both ways. Hawthorne loses interest, the penalty for early withdrawal. Without a head, the Gentle Reader, left to its own devices, spread-eagled and panting, now occupies the site of a gaping hole.

Despite its desire to be one, to be whole, to be stuffed, the Gentle Reader will never be full. Full-figured? Verily! To be correct, this gentle one's a being of size, indeed—its stomach bigger than its eyes. Its appetite exceeds all bounds, knows nothing of desire itself. The Gentle Reader occupies, in fact, the place we would expect to see appear this matriarchal body of patriarchs who have come to inhabit the hen house of custom. Upon this site, the sight of its domicile, these birds will nest; in sight of the erotic, these birds recite the scene of taste. Yet in the nest of custom, bliss—if such there can be—is not paroxystic. Here everything vegetates. Desire itself is absent from the head of this lethargic scenario. Hawthorne observes as much:

"Literature, its exertions and objects, were now of little moment in my regard . . . A gift, a faculty, if it had not departed, was suspended and inanimate within me . . . [T]his was a life which could not, with impunity, be lived too long; else, it might make me permanently other than I had been, without transforming me into any shape which it would be worth my while to take" (I:25-26). At present, the course of Hawthorne's shape will run to fat, obesity. At every turn, the table's but an elbow away, its talk within earshot. In custom's house, digestion is (mis)taken, misconstrued, for life itself. Yet, lust and gastronomy (Brillat-Savarin, where are you?) know nothing of each other, as Roland Barthes suggests: "between the two pleasures, a crucial difference: orgasm, i.e., the very rhythm of excitation and its release. Pleasures of the table include neither ravishments nor transports nor ecstasies—nor aggressions; . . . no mounting of pleasure, no culmination, no crisis; nothing but a duration; as if the only critical element of gastronomic joy were its expectation; once satisfaction begins, the body enters into the insignificance of repletion (even if this assumes the demeanor of gluttonous compunction)."[11] The headless environment of the custom house leaves room for only the stomach, knows only repletion, the fullness beyond desire: these birds sense nothing but torpor, timelessness, constipation. No wonder the Letter turns up as simply one of the innumerable pieces of dead weight which clutter the House itself: mere ghosts of men who through the repetition and redundancy of bureaucratic scribbling have come to occupy this dead letter office. It is, indeed, their office to repress—by means of idle chitchat and procrastination—the very thing bureaucracy perpetually defers: the dead line. Here it is (mis)construed, of course, that life goes on forever. How else are we to understand the overpowering lethargy that befalls Hawthorne in "the" place of dead being (l'etre mort / lettre morte), these dead letters (being[s]-of-no-consequence) who because they always talk can therefore never write (a thing): a veritable dead end which by its impotence leaves everything unfinished?[12] Thus, time stops cold. Regarding the fullness, the oneness, the uniformity, of this body of custom, moreover, Hawthorne is but a remainder, a supplement, a leftover. His goose is cooked.

(Love) NEST

The step ("trans-") is short from (custom) house to home. The space is one and the same: from kitchen to hearth: the space of the Freudian fort-da (0,1). In "Hawthorne," the step (pas) beyond (au-delhi) stumbles, is "other"-wise, mistaken, a mistep; it returns, always and everywhere, home. Movement, here, repeats the progress of the "proper," the properly familial, the homely (Heimlichkeit), trans-forms eventuality to advent of one's "own," issues of propriety.[13] Home knows simply the (shortest way to a man's) heart(h). Forget the head. The Custom House both stages and (re)enacts this scene: domestication in "Hawthorne," the oeuvre as a (w)hole, a headless corpse. Its domesticated fowl know nothing of the wild, care only for security, the lethargy of the nest, the indolence of incubation, and return us to that Other bird I mentioned in back of this scene, behind the scenic backyard of the barnyard, the homely bird of Hawthorne's letters that hovers over The Letter, that hovers over the scene of domesticity itself—yet hovers behind it as well, that constitutes its very end, the derriere of Hawthorne's house of fiction, regarding whose "feathered society," like the Pyncheon fowl, has always already been given to coo(p)s, to chatter, to bird talk: whose "generally quiet, yet often brisk, and constantly diversified talk . . . had such a domestic tone" (II: 151-52).

What does "The Custom-House" conceal, behind the space of a bird house, if not the (primal) scene of domesticity as such? Is not the bird house, in effect, a love nest? Is not the bird in the bush the very one that sends two love birds on their way—the chick behind Geschick? Here discourse is always already reduced to silence, the dumbness of a chirp, the murmur of a coo. Let's nestle into a familiar instance: "Boston, October 23d. 1839—1/2 past 7.—P. M. Dear little Dove, Here sits your husband, comfortably established for the evening in his own domicile, with a cheerful coal-fire making the room a little too warm. I think I like to be a very little too warm. And now if my Dove were here, she and that naughty Sophie Hawthorne, how happy we all three-two—one—(how many are there of us?)—how happy we might be!" (XV:357).

To wit: to woo: those familiar with Hawthorne's letters know all too well the frequency with which this appellation appears. "Dove" stages the scene of culture, custom, propriety: Sophia as health provider, hospital room; the oeuvre as patient—anaesthetized, sanitized. "Dove" stages the scene of domesticity: Sophia as hen, housekeeper, homemaker; the oeuvre as hen-house. I recall you to Sophia's editorial broomplay.

(Nest) EGG

Lest feathers get ruffled, I caution you in advance: when the table is turned, the genders reversed, those readers with axes to grind will snatch their jouissance from pleasures that exceed the table's borders, that border on excess, pleasures that border the border, rites of passage. The border patrol secures its own, its own propriety, its precinct: the liminal, the sanctity of the hymen. Disowning ownership, gender nonetheless still claims propriety. Fuller harps on this. Reworking Plato, working him over, Fuller will sanitize his thought, transport the sage to Sparta—whose women "were as much Spartans as the men." In that community, he'd not have thought the souls of "vain and foppish men will be degraded after death, to the forms of women, and if they do not there make great efforts to retrieve themselves, will become birds." Transmigration disfigures itself: "By the way it is very expressive of the hard intellectuality of the merely mannish mind, to speak thus of birds, chosen always by the feminine poet as the symbols of his fairest thoughts."[14] (By the way) sex is power—always and everywhere.

(Broom) CLOSET

The oeuvre's overworked, worked over by domestic manipulation both within and without. In sight of this handiwork, a privileged bird abridges "Hawthorne" from oeuvre to homework, reduces writing to housework, reworks the house of fiction as a (w)hole, transposes public to private, masculine to feminine, head to heart. "Hawthorne," here, is but another name for dirty-work, the oeuvre (re)moved indoors, tamed, cleaned up: Hawthorne deferred to woman's work, referred to feminine domains, domiciled, grounded: "Hawthorne" in transit, prior to public scrutiny, itself a rite of passage, translated at the threshold, (re)produced, a captive of the hymen. This spectre (re)claims the oeuvre from the inside out: a Dove transfigures technique, eliminates the "dirt," disinfects (the) language, transforms a "public" transaction to matters of propriety, reduces the oeuvre from marketplace to housebound work. Restoring "Hawthorne" to the proper, love cleans house, returns the "Author" to its proper self, redeems the "Author" from the wild: domestic ideology now hands the "Author" over to the nest, settles "Hawthorne" down, discards the inappropriate, secures the oeuvre from within—against the threat of all contamination without, what doesn't belong. The Author's under house arrest.

(Bird) CAGE

Custom, likewise, knows its own domestic technique: subscribes to those advantages ascribed to good housekeeping. After all, what generates the Custom House if not the politics of cleaning? This gesture, ironically, now opens up desire, frees Hawthorne for jouissance, frees "Hawthorne" for its self (Hawthorne), enables "Hawthorne" to reflect (about) itself, the generation of The Scarlet Letter, its gestation, incubation: how the plot is hatched. The "Author" inscribes itself, makes its self at home in the work. With publication, moreover, the "Author" exposes itself, emerges to the public, to popularity: "Hawthorne" becomes a household word. Prescribing a domestic ideology, the need to clean (Uncle Sam's) house, he is accused of impropriety. "The Custom-House" breaches decorum. How could it not? Like the custom house itself, publication is, by definition, open to the public—the oeuvre an open house. Housework thus reworks these scenes from top to bottom, a politics of the person(al)and of empowerment—"at home." Once set in place, domestic ideology-"an ideology of love proffered throughout the 1850s as a solution to inequalities of power"—controls the oeuvre in its entirety.[15] The "house" holds sway (oiko-nomia: at once both "home" and "cage" [especially for domestic birds]). This house-hold captures "Hawthorne" entirely. Indeed, it governs the site on which arises the institution of the (Gentle) "Reader."

If "Hawthorne" (con)figures the "Author" within the confines of the "Reader," that Reader is yarded as well, produced by reading's own techniques, techniques whose very lessons engender the installation of an ideological apparatus: domestic ideals: the home(stead), love's domicile. Staging this scene involves duplicitous scenarios. It's custom's way to capture the subject thus.

SCENE 1 (child's play): let's set the stage. McGuffey's Reader, Lesson #23 (woodcut): in the foreground, a young boy kneels next to an open bird cage, hands open, arms outstretched, gazing toward the middle ground; in the middle ground, above and beyond the boy, a bird in flight approaches the left-hand border of the frame; in the background, a house recedes toward the horizon, diminished in size by the distance that places it in opposition to the open, unoccupied bird cage of the foreground.

SCENARIO: "it would be cruel to keep the bird."[16]

SCENE 2 (adult's only): let's set the stage. Graham's Magazine, "The Willing Captive" (engraving): in the foreground, lower right, an open bird cage sits, unoccupied; in the middle ground, a young boy, seated, gazes at a bird perched on his hand, eye-level: the bird returns the gaze, wings poised for flight; in the background, there is nothing—no horizon, no "distance" beyond the central scene which monopolizes the space of the image, captures it.

SCENARIO: (there's only the caption) "The Willing Captive."[17]

(School) HOUSE

Lesson #23: "I hope that no boy who reads this book, will ever rob a bird's nest. It is very cruel and wicked and none but naughty boys will do so.[18]

(Play) HOUSE

Return of the Repressed: The Old Manse: 10 October 1842, three months after Hawthorne's marriage: "Just now, I heard a sharp tapping at the window of my study; and looking up from my book (a volume of Rabelais) behold the head of a little bird, who seemed to demand admittance! . . . This incident had a curious effect on me; it impressed me as if the bird had been a spiritual visitant—so strange was it that this little wild thing should seem to ask our hospitality" (VIII:363). Rabelais indeed!

(Post) CRYPT

Forget the New Historicist ca(w)-ca(w). Desire is on the outside looking in (the Wolf Man's here). It looks toward hearth and home, the (primal) scene where nothing takes place, takes up its place, and does so from the outset, the scene that engenders a scenario. Domesticity and emptiness are not "extremes," as Douglas Anderson suggests, "between which human existence is poised."[19] Rather, they configure the same event. Nothing (always already) happens at home.

It happens by surprise (die Unheimlichkeit): nothing happens by surprise. In "Hawthorne," home configures the space that anxiously awaits some "thing" (res), something that "matters," that waits for something to take place, to begin, the space that knows not (what it awaits), the space that waits for discourse, the space that engenders narration itself: the site of lethargy, ennui, incubation. Home itself is nothing, nothing in itself. It simply waits (for something): it waits (for life to begin): the nothing that waits for something. In this, it waits for nothing. Let's hurry to catch up.

In "Hawthorne," nothing happens at home. It happens by surprise. In the meantime (for all time), everyone walks on eggs. Sublime, inhuman, monstrous, original, unspeakable, literal: at heart, the home—its heart(h), the heart of domesticity—embraces (nothing [but ghosts, skeletons]) death. Literally, nothing (fort) is there (da). Death occupies home, preoccupies the oeuvre, inhabits (the heart of) Hawthorne's house ("Hawthorne"), just as the figure (the dead [Judge]) of nothing occupies the heart of the House, its last judgment.[20] Doubly so for The Faun: death inhabits the very heart of the "Eternal City." Its ruins contain, within themselves, the ruins of (human) ruins (skeletons): death itself is haunted, the specter beside itself, ghost of a ghost.[21]

It's (not) for nothing that the Custom-House is haunted by ghosts—and by the specter of the "Author," the shadow of Hawthorne, whose very presence is (itself) uncanny, absent, always already dead, beheaded, missing (from) itSelf. Thus, in The Faun, the "Author" returns (to itself) too late, belated, missing (from) the story, missing (its own) meaning, missing (out on) itself from the outset. Here nothing belongs to the Author—not (the fiction of) itself, not even the fiction (itself): nothing is rendered to Hawthorne. The "Author" surrenders itself. Authority pays with its head. "Hawthorne" knows only this: the "Author" knows nothing.

Dying to know, however, the Gentle Reader demands "further elucidations respecting the mysteries of the story," regarding which the "Author," likewise "troubled with a curiosity similar to that which he has just deprecated on the part of his readers," now looks to the imaginary (characters) for answers; he cross-examines Hilda (who circumspectfully consents, "seeing that there was not even a bird of the air to fly away with the secret") and Kenyon "to pry into several dark recesses of the story," promising his characters "it shall be kept a profound secret" while instantaneously entrusting their revelations to writing, the public, the "Reader" (IV:463, 464, 466, 464, 466). If the "Author" cannot keep a secret, perhaps there's nothing to keep. Nothing is hidden. To this effect, Hawthorne defenestrates the frame of the recit, abandons the body of this tale, hangs itself at "the end," outside—a ghost—as an appendage, its tail, its "postscript": a crypt to which the "Author" now re-signs itself (a dead letter, a blockhead, a dummy). Secrecy but marks the place of containment to which the Gentle Reader is dispatched. The Faun entrusts this secret to its (post) crypt, and hence enshrines (inters) itself in the Pantheon at its end (in The End): the temple of "Artists," tomb of "Authors." Such is the scenario to which (the identity of) the Gentle Reader has been appended from the head of this tale. Such is its destiny, its fate, its end. For with the disappearance (death) of the Author, the (Gentle) Reader now loses its head.

Out of its mind from the beginning, the disembodied head of this tale (Hawthorne's preface) consigns the Gentle Reader, this Ideal "other" ("this Representative Essence of all delightful and desirable qualities which a reader can possess" [IV:1]), to the grave, its proper home, "to the Paradise of Gentle Readers" (IV:2). In returning, it does so as a ghost ("under some mossy gravestone"), a dead letter ("inscribed with a half-obliterated name"), and from some point in time so prior that the author, the name "Hawthorne," can be only the belated image of itSelf—"I cannot precisely remember the epoch" (IV:2, 1). The epoch is, of course, the very scene of its own decapitation: The (Custom) House of The Letter. Rehearsing those halcyon days, The Faun now lays (to rest) the Gentle Reader. Amnesia this is not. Hawthorne will not remember the "Hen" (Plato's "One"). The honeymoon is over. Thus with authority, the "Author" (un)dresses these chickens with a coup (de grace) regarding which the flirtation, the courtship, the seduction is cut off regarding which the Gentle Reader itself is disregarded, taken from behind, upended, stuffed from the rear. Hawthorne inters, forthwith, all presumptuous familiarity, dispatches this "familiar," disposes of this ghostly double once and for all with but a single gesture of formality. Here, night falls like a curtain: "I stand upon ceremony, now, and, after stating a few particulars about the work which is here offered to the Public, must make my most reverential bow, and retire behind the curtain" (IV:2). Amid their cackling, the hens will never hear this swan song.[22]

The oeuvre represents the act of representation (narration) in its abysmal de-sign: to (k)not the tail of its tale, the head must have been missing, severed, from the beginning—rendering up its secret of the executioner's block, a crypted remainder.[23] "Hawthorne" (re)iterates that tale to which is appended the remnant of itself: the "Author" is (nothing but this) tail. Hawthorne is, at best, to call upon Lacan, an hommelette—at worst, a limp souffle(e).[24] Beneath its plot, Romance conceals a "dead" line ("Ha[w]thorne"): the "Family Romance," The Fall of the House of "Hawthorne"—a haunted house. Romance is ruined; it lies (in ruins)-"The End" its ruination. There's nothing (more) to know. Commemorating the (Gentle) Reader's demand to know (the truth), (the truth of)

Romance gives (up) itself; it gives to be rendered.[25] The "Author" endures this separation—surrenders to nothing:

> P.S(sssssssst).
>
> Salem, 20 January 1850: "My dear Fields, I am truly glad that you like the introduction . . . If `The Scarlet Letter' is to be the title, would it not be well to print it on the title-page in red ink? I am not quite sure about the good taste of so doing; but it would certainly be piquant and appropriate—and, I think, attractive to the great gull whom we are endeavoring to circumvent" (XVI:308).

NOTES

1. *The Centenary Edition of the Works of Nathaniel Hawthorne*, ed. William Charvat, et. al, 23 vols. (Columbus: Ohio State University Press, 1962-1997), I:12. Subsequent references to Hawthorne are hereafter cited parenthetically in the text by volume and page number.
2. James M. Mellard, *Using Lacan, Reading Fiction* (Urbana: University of Illinois Press, 1991), 75.
3. Laura Laffrado, *Hawthorne's Literature for Children* (Athens: University of Georgia Press, 1992), 120.
4. See Thomas Laqueur, "Orgasm, Generation, and the Politics of Reproductive Biology," *Representations* 14 (1980): 27, and Cathy N. Davidson, "Photographs of the Dead: Sherman, Daguerre, Hawthorne," *South Atlantic Quarterly* 89 (1990): 696.
5. Kenneth Dauber, *Rediscovering Hawthorne* (Princeton: Princeton University Press, 1977), 183.
6. Slavoj Zizek, *For They Know Not What They Do: Enjoyment as a Political Factor* (London: Verso, 1991), 233.
7. John Dolis, *The Style of Hawthorne's Gaze: Regarding Subjectivity* (Tuscaloosa: University of Alabama Press, 1993). 196-211.

8. Catherine E. Beecher, *Suggestions Respecting Improvements in Education* (Hartford, 1829), 53.

9. Cf. Lauren Berlant, *The Anatomy of National Fantasy: Hawthorne, Utopia, and Everyday Life* (Chicago: University of Chicago Press, 1991), 169-70.

10. Herman Melville, *The Piazza Tales and Other Prose Pieces, 1839-1860* (Evanston: Northwestern University Press, 1987), 250.

11. Roland Barthes, *The Rustle of Language, trans. Richard Howard* (New York: Hill and Wang, 1986), 267.

12. Dolls, *The Style of Hawthorne's Gaze*, 194.

13. Cf. Jacques Derrida, *The Post Card: From Socrates to Freud and Beyond*, trans. Alan Bass (Chicago: University of Chicago Press, 1987), 397.

14. Margaret Fuller, "Woman in the Nineteenth Century" and Other Writings (New York: Oxford University Press, 1994), 32.

15. Lesley Ginsberg, "'The Willing Captive': Narrative Seduction and the Ideology of Love in Hawthorne's A Wonder Book for Girls and Boys," *American Literature* 65 (June 1993): 271.

16. William H. McGuffey, *McGuffey's Newly Revised First Eclectic Reader* (Cincinnati: Winthrop B. Smith, 1848), 42-43.

17. "The Willing Captive" (engraving), "by Deshay's, W.E. Tucker, S.C.", *Graham's Magazine* 41 (July 1852): 41.

18. McGuffey, *McGuffey's Reader*, 42-43.

19. Douglas Anderson, *A House Undivided: Domesticity and Community in American Literature* (Cambridge: Cambridge University Press, 1990), 200.

20. John Dolls, "Hawthorne's Circe: Turning Water to (S)wine," *Nathaniel Hawthorne Review* 24.1 (1998): 42-44.

21. See Edgar A. Dryden, *The Form of American Romance* (Ithaca: Cornell University Press, 1988), 41.

22. Dolis, *The Style of Hawthorne's Gaze*, 205-11.

23. Cf. Jacques Derrida, *The Truth in Painting*, trans. Geoff Bennington and Ian McLeod (Chicago: University of Chicago Press, 1987), 381-82.

24. Jacques Lacan, *The Four Fundamental Concepts of Psycho-Analysis*, trans. Alan Sheridan (New York: W. W. Norton, 1978), 197.

25. Cf. Derrida, *The Truth in Painting*, 382.

6

The Marble Mother: Hawthorne's Iconographies of the Feminine

—Todd Onderdonk

To participate in the critical discourse on Hawthorne is to step into a fast-rushing stream, crowded with fishermen of varying orientations, all in hot pursuit of a specimen that, no matter how many times it is caught, always ends up back in the water. Thus the sport of Hawthorne criticism has its pleasures and short-lived rewards, but perhaps the most characteristic aspect of the catch has not been its flesh, but its slipperiness, the accompanying sense that the canonical "big one" always gets away. Textually well-supported arguments, often diametrically opposed—we might want to call them studied and elaborate fish stories—are advanced with great regularity, but only seem to incite further discourse. The famously ambiguous Hawthorne has maintained his claim on critical attention by just this capacity of his work to sustain widely disparate readings. As preamble to my own—perhaps similarly foredoomed—reading, I would like to suggest that the undecidability we are faced with in Hawthorne's work was deliberately cultivated by the author himself, and that equivocal qualities of Hawthorne's writing are better understood as the manipulations of a highly subtle and self-conscious artist who knows only too well what he is trying to say, yet feels he must not say it.

But why would Hawthorne dissimulate his views in his romances? We should consider the nature of the romance itself, the genre that the author claimed for his work, in explicit opposition to the novel. As Hawthorne's prefaces assert, indirection is the soul of the romance, both representationally and in its "moral." It is impossible not to note this prefatory Hawthorne's rather extreme aversion to being pinned down by his "Gentle Reader." The keynotes everywhere are unease, circumspection and an insistent, even combative, modesty. This passive-aggressive mode is reflected even in his syntax. Observe Hawthorne as he simultaneously avers and defers in the preface to The Marble Faun: "Therefore, I have little heart or confidence (especially writing as I do in a foreign land, and after a long, long absence from my own) to presume upon the existence of that friend of friends, that unseen brother of the soul, whose apprehensive sympathy has so often encouraged me to be egotistical in my prefaces, careless though unkindly eyes should skim over what was never meant for them."[1] A major author more sensitive to the influence of these "unkindly eyes" may never have written, and it is in this habitually defensive mode, I contend, that Hawthorne gravitated toward the romance over the more nakedly moralizing and topical domestic and sensationalist novels then ruling the marketplace. These novels Hawthorne tended to lump together as "trash," and associated—rightly or wrongly—with the famous "damned mob" of female authors whose sales dwarfed even The Scarlet Letter, his most commercially successful work.[2] This is not to say, of course, that Hawthorne rejected self-expression in his fiction. Nina Baym has suggested that Hawthorne's career-long tendency to "put himself forward as an author who declined engagement with issues of public moment," was a strategy that differentiated this writer of romances from the participants of a public sphere he saw as dominated by women.[3] Not many issues were more clearly of "public moment" in Hawthorne's time than the proper role and place of woman herself, and the problem unquestionably glared at Hawthorne as a writer of imaginative fictions.

Michael T. Gilmore has recently suggested that Hawthorne wrote against "the tyranny of knowing," championing "distanced and guarded forms of disclosure" in a time when "a continuum of [antebellum] social, political, and cultural practices" insisted on legibility and transparency.[4] The novel, for Hawthorne, exemplified this "tyranny" in literature, and in a powerfully gendered way. The prefaces depict the novel as participating in a kind of gross literary materiality, whether in too-solid or literal representations of everyday realities, or in unyielding and artless moralizing. In response to these solidifies, Hawthorne yearns to spiritualize, to rise above his "material" in representing not the rudely real, but the higher or deeper truths that phenomenal realities only exemplify. Thus the trope of ethereality that runs through the prefaces, and his almost squeamish delicacy toward meaning. This approach is apparent in "The Custom House," where Hawthorne laments "the materiality of daily life pressing so intrusively upon [him]."[5] In that deadening commercial setting, Hawthorne would, by writing, "spiritualize the burden that began to weigh so heavily"; he would "seek, resolutely, the true and indestructible value that lay hidden in the petty and wearisome incidents, and ordinary characters, with which [he] was now conversant" (SL, 29). This passage not only suggests Hawthorne's own literary aims, but also implicitly critiques fictions that would depict such "intrusively" familiar realities and "home"-truths. Strikingly, Hawthorne chooses the homely sitting room, that most literally familiar of domestic spaces, to illustrate the task of the romancer. He describes the transformative, liberating effect of moonlight on "the little domestic scenery" of the room, with its center-table shared by "a workbasket, a volume or two, and an extinguished lamp"(SL, 28). The departed female denizen of this genteel setting, her sex distinguished by the iconographic implements she has left behind, needle and book, child's shoe and wicker carriage, leaves the detached romance-writer not to capture her reality, but to dematerialize it, to render it a thing "of the intellect": "At such an hour, and with this scene before him, if a man, sitting all alone, cannot dream strange things, and make them look like truth, he need never try to write romances" (SL, 28). Seemingly defining his art against woman herself, Hawthorne gives us this defamiliarized image of the parlor, with its sofa, idle pastimes and accoutrements of motherhood suggesting femininity as a state of irreducible situatedness. To be a woman is a state of embodiment and near immobilization; in several senses here, women are sitters, encumbered with bodies and the consequences of their bodies—in short, deeply seated in the material world. Thus as well, then, the realistic novel, mired in a distasteful intimacy with the concrete and the passing, is a low art in its "feminine" (or feminizing) relation to the worldly and timebound. Meanwhile, sitting in that same chamber, the male romancer utilizes the effects of moonlight to step outside and above this ineluctable embodiment into an objective realm of timeless, bodiless truth. In Donna Haraway's words, he pulls the "god-trick" of infinite vision, transcending his own situatedness—he makes us forget that he, too, "sits."[6]

Such codings illustrate Hawthorne's tendency to construct his own art against the all-too legible realism of the novel, and perhaps against the all-too bodily real of femininity itself. Direct meaning, and especially heavy-handed moralizing, was an even greater novelistic transgression. In the preface to The House of Seven Gables, Hawthorne expresses an aversion to this practice not only on aesthetic grounds, where it results in "ungainly and unnatural" representations, but as a distinctly phallic excess. While refusing "relentlessly to impale the story with its moral as with an iron rod," he mockingly defers to the need for an explicit moral by providing one—in the preface. But if Hawthorne regarded novel writing as a feminine vocation, his apparent refusal to moralize would not differentiate him from phallic males, but from the phallic female.[7] Baym points out that Hawthorne admires or decries this figure depending on who he is addressing, but the romancer was clearly disturbed by the loss of delicacy and propriety that occurred when a female writer came "before the public stark naked, as it were" in her writing.[8] I would argue that Hawthorne, in defending the "immunities" of the romance in contradistinction to the female-identified moralizing of the novel, advocates not against the moral or didactic function itself, but against this phallic nakedness, which we might interpret as a kind of artistic immodesty. Meaning, like the Marvelous, should be judiciously bestowed. Like a flavor, it should be "slight, delicate, and evanescent," and, also "difficult of attainment"—or in other words, "dressed" in art. If in this aesthetic context Hawthorne was to assert directness as a properly masculine mode of writing, it would not be a reclamation, but an imitation of the supposedly dominant female mode, a circumstance to be avoided at all costs. As Baym puts it, "He was making a name for himself with fictions that seemed to be characterized by ethereality and a rejection of the actual world, at the very moment when women writers were laying literary claim to the real world he was rejecting."[9] The key word here is "seemed," as Hawthorne's choice of the romance's ethereality over novelistic "actualities ... so terribly insisted upon," was not so much a rejection of authorially directed meaning itself, as an intensely gendered aesthetic question about the form in which that meaning should—or, more accurately, should not—be presented.[10]

The choices he made have paid off in a wealth of critical prestige and attention. Hawthorne's equivocations manifest to the critical eye a fascinating textual richness and multiplicity that seems lush with options. The verdancy of this interpretive landscape has invited—indeed generated—almost 150 years of conflicting exegesis, a perpetual motion that, if tendentious sell concealment was his aim, has amply served the author's design. The key ideological moments of Hawthorne's texts are sedulously blurred, as if they were designed to both invite and thwart attempts at interpretive closure. This indirection makes any positive position one might attempt to ascribe to the author—such as the anti-feminist one I will suggest here—subject to a store of textual equivocalities laid in to be readily available for his "defense"; in this way Hawthorne ensures that the positions he may in fact espouse cannot be "held against him" with any certainty. And of course, as game poststructuralists, we love multiple meanings, and have learned our own subtle ways to "mean" without closing down meaning. Yet considering this systematic modus operandi in the context of the author's oeuvre as a whole, with its obsessively reworked thematic formulations, and equivocations at every crisis, it might be desirable to spy out the more partisan Hawthorne by resisting his strategies of textual "deniability," and the distorting effects of irony and bi-vocality so pervasive in his texts. Indeed, Hawthorne's "ambivalence" has long been an answer all too ready at hand.

Re-revising Hawthorne's Women

Reading for a purposeful obscurantism is most necessary if we seek to better understand Hawthorne's representations of women. Throughout his career, the author consistently argued—and just as consistently blurred his argument—that only the narrowest role was acceptable for women, that of submissive wife and mother, a role demanding the highest level of sexual purity. The importance of women in Hawthorne's life and career, and his awareness of their substantial capabilities, have been well documented, yet this awareness should not be equated with a feminist position. Interpreters have assigned to Hawthorne a confusion of positions on women, especially as the scope of criticism has broadened to consider the author's politics, psychology, homoerotic impulses, attitudes toward history, toward race, toward writing, revolution, mother, daughter, wife; with each new area of inquiry, new significations fill in the blanks the author so kindly left open. My contention here, however, is that, with some notable exceptions, Hawthorne's anti-feminist gender politics have too often been either misidentified or deprioritized in the critical literature, however much the issue bristles with the energy of deep emotional investment in his works.

Hawthorne's attitude toward women is most suggestively articulated in his textual treatment of the issue of sexual purity. T. Walter Herbert has shown that the author's marital life was organized according to fairly orthodox nineteenth-century tropes of femininity and domesticity in all their inequalities and fraught sexual dynamics—but most especially in the Victorian insistence on feminine purity.[11] Early in his career, Hawthorne depicts this imperative scathingly as a destructive male pathology, but at the same time, he never disavows the demand for feminine purity itself. In The Marble Faun, the issue is highlighted thematically, and, although a number of critics have, of course, arrived at the opposite conclusion, this essay argues that Hawthorne's last romance should be read as manifesting more clearly the partisan, not the ambivalent, "moral" about feminine purity that his artistry had seemingly better concealed previously. Perhaps we might see The Marble Faun as a case where the aging Hawthorne's desire to mean finally outweighs his desire to veil. Other reasons for this greater transparency, whether his heightened anxiety about mortality and his literary legacy, a decline in Hawthorne's skills, his feelings of dislocation as ambassador and European traveler, the illness of his daughter Una with "Roman fever," or all of these and more, are as open to debate as the meanings of the romance itself. Yet in examining this final pass at themes that are obviously Hawthornian obsessions, we are given insight into anxieties that the author saw fit to willfully entomb in his earlier fiction. To unearth these anxieties we must travel to that "deep grave in which old Rome lies buried," where Hawthorne's own obsession with feminine purity, like the darkly figured model who emerges from the catacombs, might finally be seen to walk abroad.[12] But I begin by tracing some of the author's surprisingly consistent earlier treatments of the theme of feminine purity, which evidence both his fixation and his evasiveness.

Iconographic Sisters

The critical recognition of static types of female characters in Hawthorne's work has a long tradition, though the significations that critics accord to these types are—by, as I suggest, authorial design—still much in play. The repeated pairings of women representing values of purity or chastity with others who are tainted by sensuality and tendencies toward philosophical speculation is a constant in his oeuvre, though the texts themselves can seem to sanction readings according authorial sympathy to either term of the equation. I read Hawthorne's persistent recycling of these character types not as an exploratory variability of sympathies and positions, nor a progressive conceptual development, but as an increasingly obsessive desire to concretize the values these women represent to the author, and justify those values with greater persuasiveness. In this sense his character types are truly iconographic, if we take that word to signify enduring symbolic meanings attached to some sort of a sign. "Divided," as Baym puts it, "along the axis of guilt and purity, or knowledge and innocence," Hawthorne's women seem again and again to rehearse familiar stances in new contexts, angelically innocent victims of destructive male projections of purity or sin, or essentially tainted embodiments of "carnal pride" and dissenting social tendencies.[13]

Sometimes, paradoxically, they are both at once. In the opening to "Young Goodman Brown," the title character suspects that his new wife senses his evil intentions in journeying into the forest: "Methought, as she spoke, there was trouble in her face, as if a dream had warned her what work is to be done to-night." But he quickly comforts himself by asserting her incapacity for even conceiving of the possibility: "But, no, no! 'twould kill her to think it. Well; she's a blessed angel on earth; and after this one night, I'll cling to her skirts and follow her to Heaven."[14] Hawthorne's narrator mocks this "excellent resolve," marking Brown's image of Faith's purity as selfishly enabling and willfully self-deluding. And when, upon his return, Brown judges her tainted on the dubious evidence of his phantasmagoric experience, we see that the story is clearly an indictment of his projecting self-deceit. But do Brown's anxieties belong to Hawthorne's character only? Faith's womanly subjectivity, her sensuously whispered invitation to bed, and later almost-public kiss of her husband upon his return make her, even without the possibility of her participation in the Satanic ritual, among the earliest avatars of female characters whom Hawthorne himself shadows with mysterious sexual guilt. Consider the darkly Edenic depiction of husband and wife in the forest, "hesitating on the verge of wickedness." Hawthorne gives us this infernal baptismal font:

> A basin was hollowed, naturally, in the rock. Did it contain water, reddened by the lurid light? Or was it blood? Or, perchance, a liquid flame? Herein did the shape of evil dip his hand and prepare to lay the mark of baptism upon their foreheads, that they might be partakers of the mystery of sin, more

> conscious of the secret guilt of others, both in deed and thought, than they could now be of their own. (146)

The passage suggests graphically that the "fall" of these newlyweds is their initiation into the communal, adult world of sexual knowledge, identified negatively with the female reproductive system. Like the "sulphurous pit" of King Lear in his madness, the mysteries of this "naturally hollowed" uterine "basin," with its aspect of blood evoking menstruation, defloration and childbirth, are represented with a masculine sexual horror that suggests that attitudes about the sinfulness of sexuality have poisoned even licit intercourse.[15] But Hawthorne obscures these (perhaps extremely personal) sentiments in multiple ways: by the intervening, first, of the ironic screen of the narrator, then by the unreliable consciousness of Brown; next, by the open questions in the description, and finally, by the narrator's repeated suggestion that we cannot know whether the experience was vision, dream, or reality. The possibility that the story might be allegorical—Brown's "faith" on trial in the forest—further obscures the actual source of the horror expressed by the passage. But let us resist these detours the author has prepared for us, and suspect that the feelings are in some part, and more than just imaginatively, the author's own. Had Shakespeare in his career so persistently circled around the misogynistic ideas he puts in the mouth of the mad Lear, had he depicted and censured the same values in like characters time and again, we would naturally read such sentiments in his work more warily. To read "Young Goodman Brown" suspiciously, then, is to unite our sense of the weird intensity and vividness of this scene in the forest with our awareness of the rhythmic frequency with which bloody and grotesque images of sexualized women appear in Hawthorne's work—clues that the issue is, at the very least, deeply and disturbingly personal to the author. Reading for obscurantism yields the suggestion that the powerful critique of patriarchy in "Young Goodman Brown" serves to veil the author's own anxieties about sexual purity, and that his discomfort about these feelings may indeed be the story's genesis.[16] Safely externalized into the pathological Brown, anxieties are also visible in the tale's opening lines, in the carefully mixed depiction of Faith on the "threshold," telling her husband, "A lone woman is troubled with such dreams and such thoughts, that she's afeard of herself, sometimes" (133). With these frightening, adult thoughts and her girlish pink ribbons, Faith liminally combines aspects of both guilt and innocence, "dark" and "fair" ladies, that in later works are split into paired and opposed "sisters" such as Zenobia and Priscilla in "The Blithedale Romance," and The Marble Faun's Miriam and Hilda. Brown's suspicions are shown to be not utterly baseless, as a feminist Hawthorne might have written it, but a distorted magnification of Faith's slightly suggestive sexual deportment. What we see as tragic in the context of "Young Goodman Brown" is not of course Faith's slight taintedness, but her husband's victimizing projeotions. Yet her womanly sexuality, and the disturbance it occasions in her husband, place her in a plentiful company among Hawthorne's women, many of whose fictional fates are even more dismal than Faith's own.

For the author's female characters are often subject to speculation and innuendo about their sexual purity, and are seldom exonerated. In "Alice Doane's Appeal," in which the title character's brother is tortured by the idea of the virtuous Alice's sexual guilt, the taint can only finally be removed by the extreme solution of a supernatural intervention, an affirmation from the ghost of her dead suitor of her purity—from which "ghost and devil fled as from the sinless presence of an angel."'[17] More often the result of impurity, imputed or otherwise, is either a lifelong penitence, as with Hester Prynne and Miriam, or death, as with Georgiana Aylmer in "The Birthmark," Beatrice in "Rappaccini's Daughter," and the voluptuous Zenobia of The Blithedale Romance. Though Hawthorne sometimes offers compensatory penances through "good works" to the female characters he allows to live, their roles as vital, central, and, as I will argue, procreative beings are terminated, and the narratives offer little prospect for redemption.

The disturbing violence and intransigent "justice" that Hawthorne brings to bear on his "tainted" characters is frequently overlooked, while critics laud his sensitive and unquestionably insightful portrayals of feminine victimhood, his complicated understanding of their persecutions, and his harsh portrayals of the patriarchal perpetrators of these wrongs. Roy Male most succinctly expresses these critical sentiments: "Before The Scarlet Letter no American writer understood the values of time, tragedy, or womanhood well enough to create a woman in fiction."[18] Harold Bloom sees Hester as a "national heroine," calling Hawthorne's characterization of her "the most representative fictive portrait of an American woman."[19] And, of course, Nina Baym calls the author a male feminist, rightly calling the question of women, "the determining factor in Hawthorne's work."[20] Baym argues against reductive treatments of the dark/fair axis among Hawthorne's women, but herself merely reverses their positions, making the dark lady the representative of desirable traits and leaving the fair lady, "the stereotypical Victorian priss," to bear the Hawthorne's "feminist" Critique.[21] To discuss the issue in these terms acknowledges the radical interchangeability of these highly symbolic figures in their main attributes, despite the obvious differences in their contexts and details. Describing Hawthorne's women as "signifiers dressed up in the garments of the real," Baym would align the author's sympathies with the "signifiers" he invariably silences or destroys.[22]

In Pictures of Romance, Wendy Steiner bases her interpretation of The Marble Faun on this same notion of Hawthorne's "feminist" sympathies.[23] Steiner directs the author's disapprobation at the character of Hilda, an interpretation attractive to the twentieth-century reader, who sees modern femininity better mirrored in the articulate and bodily Miriam than in her prudish, virginal friend. This reading is made available textually by the sophistication and pervading irony of the narration, which authorizes the liberal reader to regard the speaker as a reasonable fellow who would naturally be on the "right" side of these vexing issues. He could not possibly prefer this vapid, intolerant "Victorian priss," could he? Thus we take the ironic bait proffered by the author as a decoy to his deeper, more conservative sentiments, which are expressed covertly. Scott Derrick counsels us to distinguish between sentiments Hawthorne expresses in mid-composition, and those he ends with, which carry considerably more weight.[24] During the course of a tale, Hawthorne cultivates a fund of trust in the narrator's fair-mindedness and seemingly feminist sympathies; at the end, he draws upon this "fund" to obtain our endorsement of the "necessary" denouement. Hawthorne's stunningly sympathetic depiction of Hester Prynne's rebelliousness is the best example of this; ultimately, it is elaborated only to establish more incontestably the author's right to contain and censure her at the novel's close. As Sacvan Bercovitch has emphasized, Hawthorne's return of his heroine to New England and her re-assumption of the letter there attempt to depict as just and "voluntary" Hester's renunciation of her radical views and her acceptance of her grim marginalization.[25]

With the texts larded with obfuscating evidence, our best recourse might be to read Hawthorne with prejudice, and especially with an eye for the patriarchal desires that, as Laurie A. Sterling has recently shown with regard to The Marble Faun, seem always to strive against

Hawthorne's own unbelief in the certitudes and inequities of patriarchal authority.[26] For to evaluate this author on the terms he attempts to dictate is to overlook end results in favor of their fictional means, to choose the story's telling over its telos. To understand Hawthorne as any kind of feminist is to listen to what he says, rather than observe what he does. The author clearly has an advanced sensitivity to the wrongs imposed on women, but it is precisely this well-developed sympathy that makes his "ambiguous" conclusions and closures so disturbing. Far from depicting critically and deploringly the tragedy of these women's fates, this "male feminist" in each case orchestrates as necessary their often-violent textual containments.

These operations, visible in varying intensities throughout Hawthorne's works, are central as well to The Marble Faun, with its juxtaposition of the submissive, virginal Hilda and the outspoken and sexualized Miriam. Is it fair or even possible to read The Marble Faun as a key to unlock this vexing question in Hawthorne's catalogue as whole, spanning, as his career did, decades, continents and myriad rhetorical situations? Certainly not; nor would I propose to decide here forever what Hawthorne "really" meant or what his works "mean" today. But in this politically tractionless, even regressive "post-feminist" moment, much as it seems to some that literary criticism has already "been there" and "done that" with regard to uncovering patriarchal impulses, it may be time to reclaim suspicion as a crucial tool in Hawthorne criticism.

Falls, Icons, Essences

We can best glimpse Hawthorne's gendered manipulations in three aspects of his final romance—its treatment of the motif of the felix culpa or "happy fall," its many depictions of parental models, and its thematizing of issues of purity and adulteration, especially purity in generation, expressed through the romance's meditations on art and creative essence. All three features are dichotomized by gender in The Marble Faun; what is depicted as desirable for men is vastly different from what is desirable for women. The theme of "the happy fall" most sharply dramatizes this dichotomy; the idea that sin can be beneficial for the development of the soul is intricately developed throughout the romance, but is acceptable only for males. This duality is reproduced in the critical discourse surrounding the tale, which has made the theme of felix culpa a long-standing center of controversy. Donatello has been the primary subject of this debate, notwithstanding the text's explicit representation that his guilt is shared equally with Miriam. Canonical readers F.O. Matthiessen and Hyatt Waggoner influentially concretized the terms of the discussion by not even considering Miriam's parallel fall, centering the critical attention exclusively on Donatello.[27] Waggoner malleably accepts Hawthorne's lead in asserting that "Miriam is an unregenerate character however much the modern reader may sympathize with her."[28] But why is Miriam "unregenerate"? Why cannot she, like her male partner in crime, realize potentialities through her experience with sin and guilt? For reasons we will consider presently, Hawthorne designs the couple's trajectories as diametrically opposed. Donatello's arc, despite his imprisonment, is unequivocally upward, toward spiritualization and redemption, while Miriam's carries her downward toward lifelong abasement, penitence and feminine inutility.

We see Donatello initially as more closely akin to the animal world than the human. He follows Miriam with an aspect "as gentle and docile as a pet spaniel" (39), is full of "animal spirits" (67), and never reveals the tips of his ears to vindicate his humanity when it is jocularly called into question. His likeness to the Faun of Praxiteles associates him with a prelapsarian state of being that excludes the "principle of virtue" (16). The artist Miriam, dogged by a mysterious guilt that, like her model, clings to her like a shadow, rhapsodizes on the life of such an innocent being, "enjoying the warm, sensuous, earthy side of nature . . . living . . . as mankind did in its innocent childhood, before sin, sorrow, or mortality itself had ever been thought of" (18). But Donatello's love of Miriam draws him into the sin of murder, and from that nadir he proceeds upward into the human state. Before the death of the model, Miriam and Donatello, with a party of rambling artists, visit the precipice known as the Traitor's Leap. Miriam meditatively excuses the crime in advance, saying that such as were thrown from that cliff in ancient times were "men who cumbered the world" (128). "Was it well done?" asks Donatello. "It was well done" she answers. The party leaves them there, and a dark figure, ostensibly the model, emerges from the gloom; after a silent struggle, he is thrown from the cliff. During the crime Donatello and Miriam have shared a look that unites them in guilt. They now engage in "a clinging embrace that [brings] their two hearts together, till the horror and agony of each was combined into one emotion, and that a kind of rapture" (130). Their guilty embrace—note the familiar resonance of illicit sexuality—suggests an equal culpability, but the crime transforms only the male partner, "kindl[ing] him into a man . . . develop[ing] within him an intelligence which was no native characteristic" (129). Miriam afterward stands merely "a guilty, bloodstained, lonely woman" (130). Her appeal later toward the window of the saintly Hilda is unanswered; the window shuts, and Miriam feels this to signify "the cry of her condemned spirit . . . shut out from Heaven" (133). Indeed, our last view of her in the Pantheon suggests her perpetual but unavailing penitence—the author literally brings her to her knees. She opens her hands to bless the lovers, Kenyon and Hilda, but "as if [she] stood on the other side of a fathomless abyss . . . warn[ing] them from its verge" (330).

In both her artistic and penitential aspects, Miriam is an incarnation of Hester Prynne. Like the golden needlework on Hester's scarlet letter, Miriam's artistry can only dramatize or embellish her guilt; all other themes are closed to her, as we see in her studio, where her idealized representations of conventional domestic themes are all marred with the figure of the distant and isolated onlooker, unable to participate in the distaff joy. And like Hester, she is ultimately set aside, left in a state both marginalized and irredeemable. Zenobia in The Blithedale Romance avoids this fate only through suicide, and even in death assumes a frozen pose of penitence. Whatever limited purposes Hester or Miriam might serve in their repentance should not obscure for us the fact of their practical abandonment and doom of sterility, unfit in Hawthorne's eyes for any life but that of self-abasement. This is articulated in the sanctimonious admonishment of Kenyon: "Not for earthly bliss, therefore, but . . . a severe and painful life you take each other's hands" (234).[29] Though Donatello receives this admonishment with Miriam, we will see how differently his fate is figured. Hawthorne's own censoriousness is most powerfully suggested by the acquiescence he extracts from his "dark ladies" in their fates. Hester Prynne, Zenobia and Miriam all fade (or leap) into the gloom with a complete acceptance of its necessity. Zenobia's petrified penitence in death mirrors Hester's return to New England again to take up her punishment, which mirrors Miriam's final kneeling submission in the Pantheon. The latter lacks even the pride to resent Kenyon and Hilda's self-righteous repugnance to her apparently plague-like guilt, their "suffer[ing] her to glide out of the portal, without a greeting" (330). I take Miriam's blessing, as with Hester's "voluntary" return and Zenobia's suicide, as a particularly bald gesture of self-justification in which the author, not eased by punishing his sensual "dark ladies," must displace the moral burden of their judgments onto them as well.[30]

Donatello, however, retires to his estate of Monte Beni, and, when Kenyon next sees him, has continued his ascension from animality. "In the black depths," the narrator tells us, "the Faun had found a soul, and was struggling with it towards the light of heaven" (196). Kenyon himself notes the change: "A wonderful process is going forward in Donatello's mind . . . Out of his bitter agony, a soul and intellect, I could almost say, have been inspired into him" (206). His submission to civil punishment for his crime results in his imprisonment, yet his spiritualization gives this a redemptive glow: "His aspect unconsciously assumed a dignity which, elevating his former beauty, accorded with the change that had long been taking place in his interior self. He was a man, revolving grave and deep thoughts in his breast" (234). In this regard he is like Arthur Dimmesdale, who, in his confession on the scaffold finds a transcendent power and vision, transforming him unrecognizably from the blighted apostate of the previous chapters. Dimmesdale's suddenly heavenward arc allows him to triumph over the satanic Chillingsworth, who he addresses in an access of Christ-like authority: "May God forgive thee . . . Thou too hast deeply sinned!" (SL, 173). His death is figured, in his own words, as a "triumphant ignominy" arranged by a merciful and redeeming God. Kenyon effuses about Donatello's moral growth as a similarly high victory: "He perpetrated a great crime; and his remorse, gnawing into his soul, has awakened it; developing a thousand high capabilities, moral and intellectual, which we never should have dreamed of asking for, within the scanty compass of the Donatello whom we knew . . . Sin has educated Donatello, and elevated him" (329).

Kenyon is here relaying—or plagiarizing—Miriam's idea of the fortunate fall to his newly affianced Hilda: "Did Adam fall, that we might ultimately rise to a far loftier paradise than his?" She reacts with shock: "'Oh hush!' cried Hilda, shrinking from him with an expression of horror which wounded the poor, speculative sculptor to the soul" (329). He backs down apace: "'Forgive me Hilda!' exclaimed the sculptor, startled by her agitation. 'I never did believe it!'" Critics have struggled with this sudden disavowal of a theme so painstakingly cultivated in the book. Hilda's horror however, and the resultant suppression that Kenyon affects, must be seen in terms of the dichotomized attitude toward feminine purity which pervades The Marble Faun. Kenyon cannot so quickly discount his own firsthand observation of Donatello's happy development. Rather he must compartmentalize his understanding of sin, separating its influences by gender to preserve from taint his apparently too-vulnerable "angel." Sin is danger or destruction for a woman; for a man—for Kenyon himself, for Donatello, for Dimmesdale, it can engender new virtues.

This point is asserted negatively in Hilda's own slight "fall," lingered over in The Marble Faun's last eight chapters, and given the utmost symbolical weight by Hilda's apparent abandonment of her tower and the subsequent dying of its Virgin's flame, so intimately and metaphorically associated with her in the romance.[31] Despite his conception of Hilda as invulnerable to sin, Kenyon's anxiety over her "falling" is presented as no less powerful. Indeed these anxieties, which seem to partake more of sexual fantasy than genuine apprehension, expose at once the cost and the erotic underpinnings of the ideology of purity. As T. Walter Herbert observes, "the language asserting sexual propriety itself [is] titillating," and the arousal it occasions, in both partners, is integral to the worship of purity since "a woman can hardly appear transcendently pure to a man not sexually aroused by her.[32] This eroticism is visible throughout The Marble Faun, as in the fetishized white marble hand of Hilda that Kenyon has secretly sculpted and covertly worships. Through Kenyon, Hawthorne indulges in the fantasy of Hilda's abduction in order to imaginatively and titillatingly—yet quite safely—"taint" her, so that we might marvel all the more at her emergence intact and unstained. After her disappearance, Kenyon visualizes Hilda walking "saintlike," "with white innocent feet" through the "grime and corruption" of the city, imagining pornographically "what hideous outrage might have thrust her into that abyss" (297). He "comforts" himself by imagining her inviolability—"Ah, yes, she was so pure!"—but then reverts to his graphic fantasy: "many an innocent virgin has lifted her white arms, beseeching [providence] in her extremity, and all in vain." This imagery, with its gratuitous emphasis on Hilda's sexually prized feminine whiteness, accentuates the bodily focus of these "anxieties," which seem to stem less from a desire to protect her vaunted purity, than to sully it. The narration invites us to enjoy images of Hilda's violation, but screens this erotic and misogynistic impulse behind a more paternal one. When it becomes clear finally that her abductor was doubly unsexual, a priest both elderly and celibate, we see the duplicity of this authorial gesture, in which Hilda is pruriently imagined as violated, but then presented as "proof' against what turns out to be only the weakest kind of threat, the "kindly custody of pious maidens, and . . . a dear old priest" (333). Her specious fall is dwelt upon with extreme sexual tension, and then completely withdrawn, but Donatello's fall remains, despite Kenyon's retraction, in the faun's undeniable ascent from animality.

The suggestion that true purity cannot fall, so weakly depicted in Hilda's abduction, is an attempt to obviate the argument for a feminine felix culpa. Hilda's closest real approach to sin is only by proxy, through her friend, Miriam. That Miriam's apparent sin, murder, is figured more like sexual intercourse, hints at what is, in Hawthorne's eyes, her true fault—her adult sexuality, and this is continually contrasted in the romance with Hilda's antiseptic coolness. The juxtaposition of Miriam's quasi-sexual guilt and Hilda's purity is itself depicted almost lasciviously, as a penetration in which the virginal Hilda is forced to "[hold] the knowledge of Miriam's crime within her tender and delicate soul" (238). She "stumble[s] ever and again over this deadly idea of mortal guilt," but indeed does not fall. For Victorian men, the attractive idea of benefiting from one's "lowest" impulses posed less of a threat to the individual or the social order, countered as it was with the civilizing influences of the home; the male sphere, with its corruption and competition, was always such a battleground of the moral and immoral in the standard tropes of Victorian mores. But in women, such a possibility threatens the very heart of the ideology of purity by valorizing its central taboo, feminine impurity. Thus, beside the hollow gesture of Hilda's eclipse, we see the exaggerated and persistent representations of her spotlessness. Kenyon says, "There are women of that ethereal type . . . and Hilda is one of them. She would die of her first wrongdoing—supposing for a moment that she could be capable of doing wrong" (98). As with Faith, in "Young Goodman Brown," the least imputation of sin is damning for a woman, but feasible, even sacrificial for a man: "Of sorrow," Kenyon continues, "slender as she seems, Hilda might bear a great burden; of sin, not a feather's weight. Methinks now, were it my doom, I could bear either, or both at once." When the sexualized Miriam speaks of the fortunate fall, Kenyon cannot but react with horror to hear a woman flirting with a doctrine that would not only unleash the choked temptations and chaotic influences in them both, but also remove a structural linchpin of the contemporary social order. If, as Baym suggests, "'woman' in Hawthorne's fiction, stands for a set of qualities which the male denies within himself and rejects in others," then Miriam's fate in the romance, as opposed to Hilda's, may well represent the author's own struggle to suppress a knowledge incompatible with the ideal of feminine purity through which he strives to understand the world, and on which he has structured his marital life. Thus Adam may happily fall and rise again to redemption, but Eve in falling must be destroyed lest she introduce the chaotic into a highly ordered system of repression-of men and women, as we have seen in Kenyon's self-censorship and erotic substitutions. There is of course nothing new historically in this old displacement, except as we ascribe it to Hawthorne, who is so often exempted by his ironical stance from simplistic moralities.

Mamas and Papas

With Eve so thoroughly censored and silenced, Hawthorne has little option but to replace her with a more fitting figure. Following the biblical model, then, this descendant of the Puritans does the typological thing—he replaces her with that purest of women, the virgin mother, Mary. Statues of Mary in Catholic churches sometimes depict her as the "new Eve," standing with serpent and apple trodden underfoot. Catholic doctrine holds that Mary undoes the sin of her foremother, Eve, just as Christ's sacrifice redeems the fall of Adam.[33] Consider Pope Plus IX's 1854 decree of the Immaculate Conception, four years before Hawthorne began The Marble Faun: "the most Blessed Virgin Mary was, from the first moment of her conception, by a singular grace and privilege . . . preserved immune from all stain of original sin."[34] This Roman revision of doctrine is an apt analogue for the hardened position Hawthorne himself was to take in representing feminine purity in his final work. Hilda is linked in an endless multiplication of tropes and associations with Mary, whose simultaneously virginal and maternal qualities, as opposed to, for example, Mary's role as apostle or advocate, are heavily emphasized. Hawthorne's narrator contains this provisional veneration within characteristically ironic boundaries, as a specimen of the picturesque. Mary is seen always as a pictorial supplement to Hilda—associated with "quaint" superstitious practices, or presented as a touristically picturesque feature of Italy—but her main textual function is to embody the thematically central combination of purity and maternity. In emphasizing the picturesque, Hawthorne "ambiguously" obscures her ideological role in the romance, which is as a model mother. Hilda's devotion is explicitly directed to this version of Mary:

> When she trimmed the lamp before the Virgin's shrine, Hilda gazed at the sacred image, and . . . beheld . . . a woman's tenderness responding to her gaze. If she knelt, if she prayed, if her oppressed heart besought the sympathy of divine womanhood afar in bliss, but not remote . . . was Hilda to be blamed? It was not a Catholic kneeling at an idolatrous shrine, but a child lifting its tear-stained face to seek comfort from a mother. (240)

Hilda does not pray to the Mary of Catholic dogma, but to an idealized model of the perfect woman, which means, for Hawthorne, the perfect mother. Thus paintings of the Virgin are a repeated motif in The Marble Faun, which seeks to invest as a "sacred image" this very specific and restricting iconography of womanhood. Hawthorne represents a very different iconography for men. Hilda's home in Rome is in a high tower, where she serves, as we have seen, as keeper of the flame in a shrine of the Virgin. Thus are united significations of the figurative loftiness of feminine purity, the domestic orientation of our fair Vestal virgin, and the paradox of virgin motherhood. Hawthorne positions Hilda physically "at a height above the ordinary level of men's views and aspirations" (45). Thus "ordinary men" lead their lives beneath the ideal, in the low and impure squalor that the author never tires of animadverting upon in the Roman streets. Suggestively, the only structure that Hilda's eye finds in "this airy region" above the city is "the column of Antoninus," that "thrusts itself upward . . . the sole human form that seems to have kept [her] company" (46). This juxtaposition of phallic impurity with virginal "ethereality" epitomizes the model of parenthood that Hawthorne wishes to project in The Marble Faun, dichotomizing yet uniting the earthly, earthy male and the heavenly female. The column arises from "the very heart of Rome," which Hawthorne associates motifically with decadence, impurity, and death, primarily in emphasizing Rome's history as site and tomb for patriarchal dynasties of Holy Fathers and imperial tyrants. These impure paternal figures, so frequently invoked and excoriated in The Marble Faun, are, at key moments, disassociated with their bygone sins in favor of an emphasis on their patriarchal strength and beneficence, as when the party of artists visits the statue of Marcus Aurelius. The narrator describes "the old heathen" as inspiring a will to submission, "a command that was in itself a benediction" (125). As Hilda's connection with Mary is maternal, so Kenyon frames this icon in conservative and paternal terms: "The sculptor of this statue knew what a king should be . . . and knew, likewise, the heart of mankind, and how it craves a true ruler, under whatever title, as a child its father."

Frederick Crews notes the prominence of this "pathetic homage to the idea of the benevolent parent" in The Marble Faun, but does not note the marked potential parenthood of the two couples of our central foursome.[35] It is this potentiality that gives the theme of mothers and fathers its structural power, especially in light of the exclusion from parenthood of half the foursome (Donatello and Miriam), and the idealized parental prospects of the other half (Kenyon and Hilda). For the central function of these repeated sculptural and pictorial parents is to model or reify the author's own dichotomized conception of parenthood. As a statue, the figure of Marcus Aurelius literally embodies "in stone" its ideological import of benevolent patriarchal authority. So, too, do the images of the Virgin Mary seek to freeze and codify a parental model. When the troubled Hilda begins to haunt shrines of Mary she is unable to find "just the virgin mother she needed . . . [with] a face of celestial beauty . . . human as well as heavenly" (251). Perhaps this is because she is herself the perfect embodiment of that ideal. Hawthorne was well aware of the concretizing power of art, and for this reason the narrator regrets the permanence of impurely conceived sculpture and art, as when Raphael is rebuked for depicting the features of his mistress as the Virgin Mary in the Fornarina. Hilda, on the other hand, is open to no such criticisms; she is a pure vehicle for the symbolic values Hawthorne wishes her to signify.

Another paternal correlate to Mary in the romance's symbolic diptych is, like Marcus Aurelius, also sculptural, the "bronze pontiff" of Perugia. Set in the thronging marketplace, this figure with its hand raised in benediction might be expected to represent the corruption of that "irresponsible dynasty of Holy Fathers, who seem to have aimed at making life as agreeable an affair as it can well be." (78) Yet, as with the statue of Marcus Aurelius, it now sheds those associations in exchange for strongly marked paternal values. The statue's "patriarchal majesty" (228) is such that it overcomes all impurity as well as the sordid facts of history: "no matter that it was modeled for a Catholic chief priest, the desolate heart, whatever be its religion, recognizes in that image the likeness of a father" (230). Miriam looks up to the statue's "benignant face, as if she had come thither for his pardon and paternal affection" (231). Hawthorne does not try to elide the Pope's impurity; Donatello's self-exculpatory reference to the "brazen image" erected by the Israelites in the wilderness explicitly evokes its association with what Hawthorne conceives of as illicit paganism. Instead the author's desire to codify a powerfully paternal and impure figure—such as Herbert suggests Hawthorne imagined himself to be—outweighs such considerations as it could never do for the maternal.[36] This "brazen image" is the paternal counterpart to the "sacred image" of the Virgin; together they model the dichotomized ideal of marriage that Hawthorne wished to reify. To say that this model is sell serving would be no overstatement. Herbert describes the advantage Hawthorne took in his own marriage by acknowledging Sophia's moral superiority in matters of "angelic truth," but ruling in all practical things "til she become . . ., earthly-wiselier" an event not to be anticipated considering her circumscribed role.[37]

Reproducing the Father

In seeking to codify this parental dichotomy, Hawthorne was quite in step with Victorian middle-class norms of domesticity, though his justifications are personal to a solipsistic degree—as commentators who have pointed out Kenyon and Hilda's resemblance to the author and his "dove," Sophia, have already suggested.[38] But The Marble Faun can also give us a glimpse of the anxieties behind such repressive moral structures. Hawthorne raises another issue in the romance that sheds a revealing light on the obsession with purity, and that is the question of generation, for which the tale's meditations on artistic essence metaphorically veil the more delicate topic of procreative essence. The issue is broached in multiple representations of purity and adulteration; mediation is always linked with death, or associated with the decline or decay of an originally precious essence. Kenyon's visit to Donatello's estate at Monte Beni provides several examples of this attitude toward adulteration. There the sculptor drinks "Sunshine," a wine of unique "peculiarities and subtile exquisiteness" (164). Kenyon suggests that reproduction of the wine would be like minting money, but it is so susceptible to decay that it loses its golden essence before the bottle is finished; indeed Kenyon fancies that the wine "became almost imperceptibly clouded as he approached the bottom of the flask" (164-65). Its purity is gendered female, and is suggestive of an innate positivity intended for male appreciation: the wine "has kept itself . . . as a maid reserves her sweetness till her lover comes for it."

On the walls of the hall of Monte Beni are ancient frescos that had "been rubbed and scrubbed . . . defaced .

. . and retouched . . . till the joyousness had quite vanished out of them all" (166). This decay is the shadow of death: "joy darkening into grief, and festal splendor into funereal darkness." Most disturbing to the narrator is the "grim identity between gay things and sorrowful things. Just give them a little time and they turn out to be just alike!" Things becoming all alike turns into a reproductive issue. A repeated figure in the fresco bears a resemblance to Donatello, whose ancestral line is itself a series of reproductions, descending from a mythical progenitor of mixed blood—a union of sylvan faun and mortal maid. From that primal origin, "the Faun's wild blood had necessarily been attempered with constant intermixtures from the more ordinary streams of human life. It lost many of its original qualities, and served . . . only to bestow an unconquerable vigor" (171). Yet avatars or copies of the original Faun were periodically generated, that "reproduced the character that had been assigned to it from immemorial times" (172). Donatello is one of these, a throwback to the original purity of his animal ancestor, an instance of arrested decline within the downward trajectory of reproductive adulteration.

Hawthorne's concern with perishable purities is most revealingly elaborated in the text's treatment of artistic or creative essences, though these are full of resonances of the procreative. Hilda inspects a portfolio of old drawings whose owner thinks they bear "evidence on their faces of the touch of master hands" (104). The narrator tells us that these ragged and yellowed scraps record the ephemeral moment of artistic inspiration: "the artist seemed to have bestirred himself at the pinch of the moment, snatching up whatever material was nearest . . . Thus, by the spell of a creased, soiled, and discolored scrap of paper, you were enabled to steal close to an old master, and watch him in the very effervescence of his genius" (105). This masculine "effervescence," connoting fluids, passion, volatility, and emission, might be thought a strangely sexual choice of words, but we are just beginning. The master's "effluence of divinity," his "pure light of inspiration" is, like the wine, a unique but perishable essence: "the subsequent toil of the artist serves to bring [it] out in stronger luster, indeed, but likewise adulterates it with what belongs to an inferior mood" (105). As fatherhood is to the moment of conception, so is the artist's craft to the moment of his inspiration. Hilda has a unique insight into the phenomena, and articulates the sensation for Kenyon, who laments the gap between inspiration and realization in his own sculpture of Cleopatra: "The idea leaves you an imperfect image of itself, which you at first mistake for the ethereal reality, but soon find that the latter has escaped out of your closest embrace" (273).[39] Fortunately for the artist, however, this male essence can be discerned and restored by a certain purity in the spectator.

Enter Hilda the Copyist. She states her creed: "there is a class of spectators whose sympathy will help them to see the perfect through a mist of imperfection" (273). In Rome, Hilda has abandoned her own artistic self-expression for just such an office of worshipful copyist of the works of the old masters. She is a patriarchal fantasy of adoring submission: "She had the gift of discerning and worshiping excellence in a most unusual measure . . . No other person, it is probable, recognized so adequately, and enjoyed with such deep delight, the pictorial wonders that were here displayed" (48). It is telling that "adequate" recognition is paired with "deep delight" as the most appropriate sensations for an ideal woman—the circumscription of feminine faculties Hawthorne fantasizes about here would codify a thoroughgoing mediocrity that would pose no threat to male producers of art. But the more central issue is the purity and divinity of the conception itself, the "essence," to which Hilda has a unique access. "Reverencing these wonderful men," Hilda's feminine sympathy goes "straight to the central point, in which the master had conceived his work" (48-9). The erotics of this submissivity are physical as well as aesthetic, resting in "her physical organization, which was at once healthful and exquisitely delicate," and a "command of hand, a nicety and force of touch . . . an endowment separate from pictorial genius" (48). We have seen this sexualized hand before, in the jeweled coffer of Kenyon's studio: "touching those lovely fingers . . ., you could hardly believe that a virgin warmth would not steal from them into your heart" (93).

This might all be thought enough for the romance-writing husband/artist, but Hilda's gift of reproduction goes beyond the merely superficial imitation of other copyists, who inevitably leave out "that inestimable something, that constitutes the life and soul through which the picture gets its immortality" (51). The perfect copyist provides the male essence, whether understood as reproductive or aesthetic, with immortality. As for a female essence, Hawthorne effusively lauds Hilda's sacrifice of her own creativity, which would have inevitably "fall[en] short . . . of the best that has been done" (51). Women are not to attempt excellence for their own good, so as not to inevitably fail; rather, they are to be "handmaidens" to godlike men, for whom they virginally birth "wondrous picture[s] into daylight" (51). Such a paragon of reproductive perfection must herself be without taint, transparent, in order not to shadow or subvert the precious male essence to which she is dedicated. Hilda is just such a vessel, who "look[s] . . . through the crystal clear medium of her own integrity" (276). Her contribution is to make no contribution, but to allow the male essence complete sway: "the copy would come from her hands with what the beholder felt must be the light the old master had left upon the original in bestowing his final and most ethereal touch" (50). This is the faculty Kenyon most prizes in his beloved, as when Hilda fails to meet him at the galleries of the Vatican, and he misses the "perfectly transparent medium" that only she could provide (281). Thus in response to a fantasy of overly bodily or materialistic femininity as old as the apple-coveting Eve herself, Hawthorne creates an ideal woman whose most prized attribute is a kind of non-existence.

That all of this symbolical maneuvering has reference to the future parental state of our ideal couple, artist/husband Kenyon, and reproductionist/wife Hilda, is made clear by the romance's end, which confirms the domestic telos aimed at since the first appearance of the New England Vesta. With slightly broadened sympathies, Hilda finally abdicates her virgin's office of lamp-trimmer "to be herself enshrined and worshipped as a household saint, in the light of her husband's fireside" (330). Without irony, Kenyon mirrors the fatuity of Goodman Brown's words to Faith on the threshold, perhaps signifying the author's own "fall" from his earlier skills of ideological concealment: "Were you my guide, my counselor, my inmost friend, with that white wisdom which clothes you like a celestial garment, all would go well" (329). Were the narrator to sneer at this "excellent resolve" we might still have cause to be discussing Hawthorne's ambiguity.

What this ending suggests is that the link between artistic and parental creativity in The Marble Faun was Hawthorne's anxiety about the danger feminine impurity presented to successful perpetuation of a unique male essence. Such a continuity would include nothing of the woman that could "shadow" what is individual in the man. She must make herself entirely "transparent" in favor of the paternal contribution, to ensure a line of stable and enduring reproductions of the father. In Rome, the aging Hawthorne saw the inevitability of decay and decline everywhere he looked; his response was to turn away from those "actualities . . . so terribly insisted upon," and create in the "fairy precincts" of romance, a model of stability and virtual immortality that might endlessly and purely reproduce, in all its quintessential positivity, the unique individuality and power of the father (vi). In figures like Miriam, Zenobia, and Hester Prynne, properties of individuality and sexuality that Hawthorne found seductively admirable in women, or just plain seductive, are anxiously represented as anarchic threats to stable patriarchy. These women insisted on existence—physical, mental, spiritual—and could not allow the crucial "essence" of masculinity to pass without their influence. Thus they had each to be contained or destroyed—removed from the cycle of reproduction, with their less threatening sisters placed at the center of the domestic order. This demanded of the fair ones an obeisance they had learned to be only too happy to provide. A suspicious reading of Hawthorne's fiction thus asks if this body of work includes in its aims the reactionary desire to restrict women to an ideal and invisible non-being, their bodies controlled as vessels for their one necessary function—motherhood. If this is true, the insightful sympathy Hawthorne extended in his depictions of women was all the more disingenuous for its full apprehension of what it would suppress.

NOTES

1. Nathaniel Hawthorne, *The Marble Faun or The Romance of Monte Beni* (New York: Signet, 1961), vi.

2. For an illuminating discussion of these genres and of the famous quote, see Nina Baym, "Again and Again, The Scribbling Women" in *Hawthorne's Women: Engendering and Expanding the Hawthorne Tradition*, eds. John L. Idol and Melinda M. Ponder (Amherst: Univ. of Massachusetts Press, 1999). Baym's acute readings, focusing on the exact same textual features of Hawthorne's work examined in this essay, frequently argue points directly opposed to my own—illustrating these texts' trenchant bi-vocality.

30. Baym, "Again and Again," 32.

4. Michael T. Gilmore, "Hidden in Plain Sight: The Scarlet Letter and American Legibility," *Studies in American Fiction* 29 (2001), 21.

5. Nathaniel Hawthorne, *The Scarlet Letter*, ed. Seymour Gross et al. (New York: W.W. Norton, 1988), 29; hereafter cited parenthetically as SL.

6. Donna Haraway. *Simians, Cyborgs, and Women: The Reinvention of Nature* (New York: Routledge, 1991), 189.

7. Nathaniel Hawthorne, *The House of Seven Gables* (np: Aerie, nd), xix.

8. Quoted in Baym, "Again and Again," 24.

9. Baym, "Again and Again," 32.

10. Hawthorne, *The Marble Faun*, vi.

11. See T. Walter Herbert's *Dearest Beloved: The Hawthornes and the Making of the Middle-Class Family* (Berkeley: Univ. of California Press, 1993), and "The Erotics of Purity," in *Representations* 36 (1991), 114-32. Also see Evan Carton, *The Marble Faun: Hawthorne's Transformations* (New York: Twayne, 1992), 6-7.

12. Hawthorne, *The Marble Faun*, 21.

13. Nina Baym, "Thwarted Nature: Nathaniel Hawthorne as Feminist," in Fritz Fleischmann, ed., *American Novelists Revisited: Essays in Feminist Criticism* (Boston: G. K. Hall, 1982), 59. The phrase "carnal pride" is from "Mrs. Hutchinson" in Nathaniel Hawthorne, *Selected Tales and Sketches* (New York: Penguin, 1987), 19.

14. Nathaniel Hawthorne, "Young Goodman Brown," in *Selected Tales and Sketches* (New York: Penguin, 1987), 131. Hereafter cited parenthetically.

15. "Down from the waist they are centaurs, / Though women all above. / But to the girdle do the gods inherit, / Beneath is all the fiend's. / There's hell, there's darkness, / There is the sulphurous pit; burning, scalding, stench, consumption. Fie, fie, fie! Pah, pah!" William Shakespeare, King Lear, in *William Shakespeare: The Complete Works*, ed. Alfred Harbage (New York: Penguin Books, 1977), 1095.

16. Evan Carton evaluates Hawthorne's ambiguity as a kind of farming-out of conflicting elements of the author's

own personality into his polarized characters. If this is the case with "Young Goodman Brown," then Hawthorne the young critic of patriarchy is here still viably in dialog with Hawthorne the emerging patriarch. We will see which element gets the upper hand in this internal dialogic. See "'A Daughter of the Puritans' and Her Old Master: Hawthorne, Una, and the Sexuality of Romance," in *Daughters and Fathers*, ed. Lynda E. Boose and Betty S. Flowers (Baltimore: Johns Hopkins Univ. Press, 1989).

17. Nathaniel Hawthorne, "Alice Doane's Appeal," *Selected Tales and Sketches*, 120.

18. Roy R. Male, *Hawthorne's Tragic Vision* (Austin: Univ. of Texas Press, 1957), 5.

19. Harold Bloom, introduction to *The Scarlet Letter*, by Nathaniel Hawthorne (New York: Vintage Books/The Library of America Edition, 1990), xi-xiii. Bloom excuses Hawthorne's ultimate containment of Hester by distinguishing between the novel's set-up and its resolution, saying, "the conclusion is not the book" (xiv), a reading that allows Hawthorne to have it both ways—as feminist and patriarchal oppressor.

20. Baym, "Thwarted Nature," 62.

21. Baym, "Thwarted Nature," 70.

22. Baym, "Thwarted Nature," 61.

23. Wendy Steiner, *Pictures of Romance: Form Against Context in Painting and Literature* (Chicago: Univ. of Chicago Press, 1988).

24. Scott S. Derrick, *Monumental Anxieties: Homoerotic Desire and Feminine influence in Nineteenth-Century U.S. Literature* (New Brunswick: Rutgers Univ. Press, 1997).

25. Sacvan Bercovitch, *The Office of the Scarlet Letter* (Baltimore: Johns Hopkins Univ. Press, 1991). Compare this to Lauren Berlant's reading of the novel, which, from the same words on the page, arrives at diametrically opposed conclusions about Hester's return. See Lauren Berlant, *The Anatomy of National Fantasy: Hawthorne,*

Utopia, and Everyday Life (Chicago: Univ. of Chicago Press, 1991).

26. See Laurie A. Sterling, "A Frail Structure of Our Own Rearing: The Value(s) of Home in The Marble Faun," *ATQ* 14 (2000), 93-111.

27. See F.O. Matthiessen, *American Renaissance* (Oxford: Oxford Univ. Press, 1941), and Hyatt H. Waggoner, *Hawthorne: A Critical Study* (Cambridge MA: Belknap Press, 1955). Much more recently, Emily Schiller has argued that Hawthorne's ironic narrator promotes a faux sympathy for Hilda in The Marble Faun that the author himself did not feel. The modern critical valorization of irony, or what David Leverenz calls "the modernist tradition of alienated mindplay" contributes to this tendency to credit Hawthorne with the will and ability to articulate ideas in a text absolutely contrary to its systematic thematics. See Emily Schiller, "The Choice of Innocence," *Studies in the Novel* 26 (1994) 372-92.

28. Waggoner, 198.

29. The narrator's ironic treatment of Kenyon throughout the romance is another shield protecting Hawthorne from the responsibility for these preachments, which articulate ideas the text labors intricately to express.

30. Hawthorne's narratorial ambiguity toward Coverdale authorizes Joel Pfister to read The Blithedale Romance as a feminist work revealing the social constructedness of nineteenth-century notions of femininity and beauty. For Pfister, Zenobia's self-disfiguring suicide represents her liberation from such entrapping cultural restrictions—an anachronistic reading that, powerful in itself, seems less compelling when we look at Hawthorne's praxis as a whole, which consistently encourages such interpretations as a "cover" for darker judgments. See Joel Pfister, *The Production of Personal Life: Class, Gender, and the Psychological in Hawthorne's Fiction* (Stanford: Stanford Univ. Press, 1991), 80-103.

31. "The idea of this girl had been like a taper of virgin wax, burning with a pure and steady flame, and chasing

the evil spirits out of the magic circle of its beams" (294).

32. Herbert, "The Erotics of Purity," 119.

33. *Catechism of The Catholic Church* (St. Paul: The Wanderer Press, n.d.), 128.

34. *Catechism*, 124.

35. See Frederick Crews, *The Sins of the Fathers: Hawthorne's Psychological Themes* (Berkeley: Univ. of California Press, 1989), 229-33. I draw, mostly for examples, on Crews' discussion of parenthood in "Subterranean Reminiscences."

36. Herbert, *Dearest Beloved*, 225, 264.

37. Herbert, *Dearest Beloved*, 118, emphasis in original.

38. Terence Martin, *Nathaniel Hawthorne*, rev. ed. (Boston: Twayne, 1983), 178.

43. Another appearance of the "dark" lady—voluptuous, passionate, tender, wicked . . . and full of poisonous and rapturous enchantment" (97).

7

Hawthorne's "Waking Reality"

—Benjamin Friedlander

"The Wives of the Dead" first appeared in the Token for 1832, alongside "My Kinsman, Major Molineaux," "Roger Malvin's Burial," and "The Gentle Boy." The tale remained an orphan for some twenty years — until the appearance of The Snow-Image, the last of Hawthorne's four collections — and even now stands in the shadow of those early companions.[1] An intricate knitting of interior and exterior worlds, of sleeping and waking realities, "The Wives of the Dead" nonetheless merits closer attention. Condensed, suggestive, and poetic, this brief but perplexing resurrection tale shows Hawthorne's prose at a peak of concentration.

The story concerns a difficult night passed by two widows, sisters-in-law who may or may not dream the nighttime arrival of tidings, to the effect that each sister's husband, recently reported dead, is in fact alive. The husbands — brothers, hence the legal relation of the two women, a relation spelled out in legal language when Hawthorne describes their living arrangements — are the unnamed dead of the title. The wives — "recent brides" still "young and comely" — are Mary and Margaret (61).

Their names are appropriate, for Mary's husband was lost at sea (mare), while Margaret's, a landsman laboring on the frontier (marge), was killed "by the chances of Canadian warfare" (61). We're informed early on that the sisters have "joined their hearts" for consolation, yet the story proper, the heart of the story (beginning at the "verge of evening"), gives the sisters over to our separate consideration, proposing for each a joy that asserts the possibility of a difference, a verging of fate that threatens their union (61). In two dreamily described episodes, first one, and then the other, is awakened from sleep or from disturbed contemplation by a knocking, in each case signifying the unexpected arrival of a messenger. Each in turn then goes, without waking the other, to a window overlooking the street, to be apprised that her husband is in fact alive.

Despite the symmetry of these occasions, the episodes unfold in distinctly different terms, and though each widow receives the same news, revealingly different responses are recorded. Mary, partly awake when her messenger arrives, is slow to answer the summons, and though afterward a flood of conviction swells "into her heart, in strength enough to overwhelm," her initial response is "a doubt of waking reality" (66). Margaret, by contrast, is feverish but conscious. She hears the knock and receives the visitor in a state of fretful apprehension; she screams at the messenger, and then, upon receiving the news that her husband is alive, feels a flash of joy. Soon after, however, "a thought of pain" breaks in on her, that Mary's husband is still dead (64). She feels, writes Hawthorne, "as if her own better fortune, had rendered her involuntarily unfaithful" (64). This guilt, Margaret's feeling of unfaithfulness, pierces the story's dreamy surface, allowing a revelation of hidden desires — perhaps even a revelation of adultery.

Our understanding of what transpires in this tale of broken sleep depends ultimately upon our interpretation of the final lines, the most inexplicable in all of Hawthorne's work, a body of writing well noted for its purposeful ambiguity.[2] The ending is startling, not simply for suggesting that one or another messenger has been dreamt, but because the very distinction between dream and reality is now befuddled. So all of a piece is the tale's dreamy quality, that having entertained a doubt as to one moment's facticity, the reader loses faith in the facticity of the whole. Indeed, if the narrator doesn't tell, how know the border between the sisters' waking and sleeping lives? How know if the sisters cross that border once, or repeatedly?[3] This much is clear: repeating, with certain significant differences, a sequence of steps and thoughts that each sister undertakes on her own, the narrative draws to a close by bringing the sisters face to face, a strange encounter whose precise meaning remains hauntingly in doubt. Whether this encounter is provoked or forestalled by the sudden waking which ends the story — whether the sisters meet in fact, or would have met, if only the dream had continued — depends on how we interpret the pronominal ambiguity of the climactic sentence.

In "Wives of the Dead," each sister, upon receiving her good news, contemplates and then rejects as cruel waking the other to tell. First Margaret visits Mary, then Mary visits Margaret. The sisters' thoughts are remarkably similar. Declares Margaret, at the door to Mary's room:

> "Poor Mary! . . . Shall I waken her, to feel her sorrow sharpened by my happiness? No; I will keep it within my bosom till the morrow." (64)

And likewise Mary:

> She opened the chamber-door, which had been closed in the course of the night, though not latched,

> advanced to the bedside, and was about to lay her hand upon the slumberer's shoulder. But then she remembered that Margaret would awake to thoughts of death and woe, rendered not the less bitter by their contrast with her own felicity. (66)

Earlier, when Margaret approached her sister's bed, she saw that sleep had transformed Mary's face, giving it "a look of motionless contentment"; she therefore shrinks "from disturbing her sister; "[w]ith a sudden step," writes Hawthorne, "she turn[s] away" (64). More explicitly, however, what Margaret turns away from is "the disclosure she had to make," and the attendant feeling of having been "involuntarily unfaithful" (64). In the final moments of the story, we seem to witness Mary moving toward a similar shrinking back from disclosure. In the final paragraph we find Mary standing over the bed of her sister, solicitous of Margaret's comfort:

> Before retiring, she set down the lamp and endeavored to arrange the bed-clothes, so that the chill air might not do harm to the feverish slumberer. But her hand trembled against Margaret's neck, a tear also fell upon her cheek, and she suddenly awoke. (67)

The difficulty that rests in this melancholy ending arises from the doubled ambiguity of which sister Hawthorne means by "her" in "her cheek," and by "she" in "she suddenly awoke." The possibilities of meaning put into play by this pronominal confusion are very nearly too complex to calculate. Is "she" Mary, waking alone to tears of grief? Or is "she" Margaret, waking to discover Mary looking down at her? Indeed, the "she" might even be a Margaret who wakes alone. Guilty, perhaps, at the sudden asymmetry of fortunes, she may be seeking to restore the household's delicate balance by dream. We've no way of knowing. Once the identity of this final "she" is thrown into doubt, the meaning; of the whole becomes uncertain. For even if we discount Mary's messenger as a figment of imagination, we've no assurance any longer that Margaret's encounter was any more real, though we've had no reason until now to wonder. At play may be, unverifiably, one, none, or a pair of dreamt messengers. Having insinuated a doubt, Hawthorne allows a flood of doubts to overtake and drown our understanding. We may feel perturbed by this, particularly if we recall the opening lines, which bid us hear a story "simple and domestic" enough to have survived a hundred years' retelling (61). Presenting "Wives of the Dead" as a tale derived from a marked moment in history, and specific locale — the first half of the eighteenth century, in Massachusetts — Hawthorne goads us into accepting certain suppositions. We expect, for instance, we are going to hear something true. Only retrospecatively will we realize untruth too can be historical. As dream and as reality, each widow's encounter with her messenger would have roused the interest of friends and neighbors. Hawthorne's particular contribution — the ambiguity of the ending — is what scrapes against our sense of historiographic propriety, against our sense of what a tale consists that survives a hundred years' retelling. We expect, for instance, that even if the "what happened" is unsettled, the points of contention will be clearly defined. Did the husbands return? Did the widows dream their good fortune? If the ending is in doubt, this doubt should be part of the historical record — not the result of an ambiguous turn of phrase on the part of the teller. A story remembered for a hundred years will not resolve itself on anything so literary as a word choice. There is in Hawthorne's tale — we only now appreciate this — a tension between historical facticity and psychological acuity, between the cultivation of a story that explores states of mind at and past the verge of grief's evening, and the simple and domestic incidents of a past time.[4]

Dreaming and waking find their shared thresholds in many another of Hawthorne's sketches. "The Haunted Mind," most notably, recalls "The Wives of the Dead." Here too dreaming functions as an explication of the night. Here too remorse threatens the division between dream and reality:

> In the depths of every heart, there is a tomb and a dungeon, though the lights, the music, and revelry above may cause us to forget their existence, and the buried ones, or prisoners whom they hide. But sometimes, and oftenest at midnight, those dark receptacles are flung wide open. In an hour like this, when the mind has a passive sensibility, but no active strengths; when the imagination is a mirror, imparting vividness to all ideas, without the power of selecting or controlling them; then pray that your griefs may slumber, and the brotherhood of remorse not break their chain. (201-02)

It is our habit to think of inner life as singular, unshareable, something experienced by one person only and knowable only insofar as that one person takes the trouble of divulging the experience in words. Understanding inner life as the scene of existence, as an insecure prison holding a "brotherhood of remorse," Hawthorne's tale brings us to a profound awareness of just how indistinct the boundary between inner and outer life can become, especially in times of crisis. Enclosed for a night within their shared domestic space, the troubled sisters, Margaret and Mary, discover that their inner lives, being chained to a single "brotherhood of remorse," remain intertwined no matter how divergent their individual fates. In this way, inner and outer reality become confused, "imparting vividness to all ideas" — whether unspoken or spoken, whether dreamt or real. However misleading Hawthorne's initial historicizing gesture, however unsatisfying the ambiguity of his ending, Hawthorne's handling of the sisters' inner lives and of the shared interiority of their dwelling stands beyond reproach, a marvelous depiction of hidden household dynamics brought to light by intense grief and extreme shifts of fortune. A portion of Hawthorne's success derives from his vivid conception of the sisters' world, a domestic projection of the "dungeon" and "tomb" buried in each sister's "heart." In this sense, regardless of the ending, Hawthorne's story does function as a dream, as a marking out (with gothic tinge) of "those dark receptacles," namely, the widows' psyches, where "the brotherhood of remorse" strains against slumber. Michel Foucault, in an early text, writes:

> The dream is an existence carving itself out in barren space, shattering chaotically, exploding noisily . . . It is the world at the dawn of its first explosion when the world is still existence itself and not yet the universe of objectivity . . . The dream is situated in that ultimate moment in which existence still is its world; once beyond, at the dawn of wakefulness, already it is no longer its world. (59)

In dreams, writes Foucault, historical subjects find themselves momentarily as if outside history ("in barren space"), acting out an event which is nonetheless historical ("the dawn of the world at its first explosion"), an acting out whereby existence and the site of existence become one. And this, more or less, is what happens in "The Wives of the Dead," regardless of the messengers' reality. That is, Hawthorne carves his tale as if "in barren space" (using words instead of wood and stone), establishing an interior world (the shared home) where one "existence" and another (the widows) are displayed, "shattering chaotically, exploding noisily, " propelled by the "dawn" of a "first explosion" (the trauma of the husbands' deaths) up to and beyond "the dawn of wakefulness" (the end of the story), where a revelation of what actually transpires ("the universe of objectivity") presumably takes place. Hawthorne, of course, doesn't use words like "shatter" and "explode. " He prefers an image of overflow, as when he has Margaret speak "with a fresh burst of tears" (62), or Mary overtaken by "a flood of conviction" (66). Nevertheless, what all these words and all these images suggest, both Hawthorne's and Foucault's, is a troubling of the boundaries between "existence" and "its world," between the sisters and their home. In "The Wives of the Dead," this troubling of the bounds between character and locale first shows in Hawthorne's depiction of marriage as a mode of existence predicated on the sharing of space. "The brothers and their wives," we read, "entering the married state, " join together "in one household," partly shared and partly private — "with equal rights to the parlor, and. exclusive privileges in two sleeping rooms contiguous to it" (62). With the brothers dead and the two widows now joined even more closely, this last spatial division has become eroded. Thus, retiring for sleep, the widows open the doors "of both chambers . . ., so that part of the interior of each" becomes "reciprocally visible" (62). As John L. Seizer notes, the implication is that the widows show "an openness to their inmost selves as well" (312). Functioning here as a dreamscape, architectural interiority both shapes and gives access to the inner lives of the occupants. Thus, while the story's principal tension is the impact one woman's good fortune will have on her still-bereaved sister, the dramatization of this tension lies in each sister's visit to the other's private chamber. That Mary and Margaret both enter such a private chamber, a vulnerable space where dream would claim exclusive privilege, only partly indicates the peculiar blurring of architectural and psychological interiority which Hawthorne accomplishes in this tale. More acutely still, his descriptions of the setting reveal this blurring; through the opacity of Hawthorne's language, we glimpse, as through "fantastic tracery upon a window," a revelation of the relationship between the two women and their world. In his descriptions of the trips to the window, for instance, we see this world as an overflow of sexuality, an overflow each sister intuits as a pleasure and a threat. Taken as a whole, what "Wives of the Dead" appears to reveal — by dreamlike event, by eventful dream — is a secret infidelity, discovered or suspected, dreamt or real, we cannot tell.

Yet strictly speaking, the revelation never takes place. The story's ambiguous ending instead postpones the revelation—irrevocably. Or to put it in the story's own terms, the secrets of the night shrink from being grasped, "like a wounded sufferer from a hand that revives the throb." Ironically, these very words — applied to Margaret early on — provide our first hint that a secret even exists:

> "Come, dearest sister; you have eaten not a morsel to-day," she said. "Arise, I pray you, and let us ask a blessing on that which is provided for us."
>
> Her sister-in-law was of a lively and irritable temperament, and the first pangs of her sorrow had been expressed by shrieks and passionate lamentation. She now shrunk from Mary's words, like a wounded sufferer from a hand that revives the throb.
>
> "There is no blessing left for me, neither will I ask it," cried Margaret, with a fresh burst of tears. "Would it were His will that I might never taste food more." (62)

Later we learn, from the second messenger, that Mary's husband was lost on a ship called the Blessing. Retrospectively, the roles in this exchange will seem reversed. Unthinking Margaret should be the one to mention the ship's name in casual conversation, reviving Mary's suffering. Why, then, this turn on the word "blessing"? And why have Margaret declare she'll "never taste food more"? Could it be that Mary's unconscious reference to her own husband's demise has provoked Margaret's tense (because guilty?) response?

> Yet she trembled at these rebellious expressions, almost as soon as they were uttered, and by degrees, Mary succeeded in bringing her sister's mind nearer to the situation of her own. (62)

Hawthorne's wording ("by degrees") draws a parallel between Mary's handling of her sister's temper and the seafaring trade of the dead husband; at the same time, Margaret's "fresh burst of tears" recalls ominously the "tempestuous Atlantic" where the sailor met his end, that is, where the sailor's ship, the Blessing, "turned bottom upwards", (66). In these two oblique reminders of Mary's husband's death, the true mutuality of the sisters' grief becomes a matter for reasonable suspicion. Dreamt or not, the hidden dynamics Hawthorne reveals are predicated on a shared household's carefully poised symmetries. Hawthorne delineates these symmetries early on, adopting a language contractual in tone, a tone that makes sense above all when construed in light of an unspoken brotherly obligation, biblical in origin. Writes Hawthorne:

> The brothers and their brides, entering the married state with no more than the slender means which then sanctioned such a step, had confederated themselves in one household, with equal rights to the parlor, and claiming exclusive privileges in two sleeping rooms contiguous to it. (62)

Between the two "sleeping rooms" lies situated the hearth, "where the brothers had been wont to sit in young and laughing dignity, as heads of families" — a "happy circle," now empty, adjacent to the window posed vertically over the front door (62). In this elaboration of the story's setting, we are casually told that the house consists of two floors (i.e., two stories, the second one "projecting" [63]); in the same breath, Hawthorne announces, by way of noticing the house's furnishings, the couples" financial condition, masterfully choosing a word ("middling") that quietly suggests the overlapping of fates yet to come:

> The rainy twilight of an autumn day; a parlor on the second floor of a small house, as beseemed the middling circumstances of its inhabitants, yet decorated with little curiosities from beyond the sea, and a few delicate specimens of Indian manufacture, — these are the only particulars to be premised in regard to scene and season. (61)

What bursts the limits of each sister's inner life, forcing the widows to appraise more fully the mutuality of their situation, is the lattice-work of responsibilities, dependence, and risk implicit in their relationship — a legal relationship, which the two maintain in a shared domestic space. As much as the sharing of space, it is the sisters' legal relationship which provokes the encounter with which the story ends. Hawthorne's tale is premised on particulars of time, place, and circumstance which mark the sisters as both historical and fabular — a duplicity of interest which the tale reveals in a number of different ways. The word "premised," for instance, chosen by Hawthorne with characteristic care, alerts us to the tale's twin foundations in architecture and law (premises being both buildings, and the preliminary portions of a deed). Hawthorne delineates his tale's foundations in both senses. I have already noted how architecture gives form to the characters' inner lives, lending the tale an air of dream or fable. Hawthorne also spells out the sisters' legal relationship, evident in the division of rooms and property, and in the fact of marriage. This emphasis on rights and responsibilities helps ground the tale historically. By a similar token, while Hawthorne begins by locating his wives on the shores of Massachusetts, on the eve of the French and Indian War, he proffers details which in their fairy-tale neatness appear to sever the two women from history altogether:

> Two young and comely women sat together by the fireside nursing their mutual and peculiar sorrows, they were the recent brides of two brothers, a sailor and a landsman, and two successive days had brought tidings of the death of each, by the chances of Canadian warfare, and the tempestuous Atlantic. (61)

The insistent repetition of the number two lends an unreal quality to these opening sentences. Two floors, two women, two brothers, two days, a twilight scene — already here, Hawthorne has begun to gather materials for the psychological study to come. Note, for instance, that the widows are "nursing" their grief. Childless, the sisters have only their grief to tend to — an important point, as we shall soon see, and one intimately related to the story's symmetries. To some extent, "The Wives of the Dead" is an algebraic problem, a calculation involving variables, or better yet a problem for calculus, an array of figures seeking a range of answers rather than one solution. For notwithstanding the story's many numerological givens (two widows, two brothers, two bedrooms, two messengers), and notwithstanding the story's computational constraints (one house, one night, one window), definitive solution founders on an indeterminate pronominal reference, the "she" of the final line, a single term with two possible values, each generating a number of permutations. These permutations in turn resolve into two distinct categories: on the one hand, a restoration of symmetries (with both messengers real — or unreal); on the other hand, a final disruption of balance (with one sister's dashed dream becoming the other's miraculous reality). Taken all together, these two general endings suggest an underlying theme: the delicate balance of a household founded on duplicity.

Critics who write on "Wives of the Dead" tend to focus on whether the ending implies an epiphany, a realization that one or both of the messengers are unreal. So far as I know, none addresses the implications of an ending which would rupture the tale's symmetry. Yet the possibility of such rupture is precisely what concerns the sisters themselves. The prospect of one — and only one — husband's survival is in many ways more threatening to the women than the finality of both brothers' deaths. Both women consider this possibility, prompted by a thought of pain and pang of sympathy; exacerbating their apprehensions, perhaps, is a shared but unspoken recollection of the biblical law regarding widows of brothers:

> If brethren dwell together, and one of them die, and have no child, the wife of the dead shall not marry without unto a stranger: her husband's brother shall go in unto her and take her to him to wife, and perform the duty of an husband's brother unto her. (Deut. 25:5)

Though Hawthorne never cites this passage, he does make brief mention of scripture in general. Immediately following the first mention of the brothers' deaths, Hawthorne writes:

> The universal sympathy excited by this bereavement, drew numerous condoling guests to the habitation of the widowed sisters. Several, among whom was the minister, had remained till the verge of evening; when one by one, whispering many comforting passages of Scripture, that were answered by more abundant tears, they took their leave and departed to their own happier homes. (61)

Entering the grieving sisters' shared dwelling, the "whispering" guests leave suggestions of comfort, suggestions "answered" with "more abundant" grieving. But perhaps these tears which answer Scripture answer also the problem of the ending, a problem posed with a single tear's falling: what, if anything, happens in this story? In order to answer this question, we need to review in detail what Hawthorne tells us about the sisters after the two separate for the night. Having crossed twilight's threshold, sharing their grief with their neighbors and then each other, the two sisters retreat alone to "reciprocally visible" bed-chambers to await the sun. Here the widows' converged fates begin to part:

> Thither the widowed ones retired, after heaping ashes upon the dying embers of their fire, and placing a lighted lamp upon the hearth . . . The cold light of the lamp threw the shadows of the furniture up against the wall, stamping them immovably there, except when they were shaken by a sudden flicker of the flame. (62)

The turmoil each sister finds in her own heart, expressed so evocatively in the figure of the hearth, begins in sleep, or fevered wakefulness, to generate a turmoil of ember and ash, shadow and light. The turmoil is not the same for each sister, nor does it find the same expression in Hawthorne's prose. "Sleep," writes Hawthorne, "did not steal upon the sisters at one and the same time" (62). Mary, suffering a grief "quietly borne," sinks into "temporary forgetfulness" (62); when she later wakes, "with a sudden start" from a dream she can't recall, she acts as though in a stupor (65). Margaret, "disturbed and feverish" (62), remains conscious, rising from bed "trembling between fear and eagerness" (63). The two episodes which follow, the sisters' meetings with the messengers, congruent yet different, likewise vary in important particulars. Through this variance Hawthorne registers not only the distinctness of the two women's characters and fates, but an interrelationship between the two only hinted at in the narrative proper. When the sisters retreat to sleep, they leave open their doors and the curtains round their beds so that each can see into the other's chamber. Mary, "all of whose emotions were influenced by her mild, quiet, yet not feeble character" (61), sinks into a presumably peaceful sleep, though later Margaret finds her with "face . . . turned partly inward to the pillow," "hidden there to weep" (64). Margaret, on the other side of the "happy circle," lying awake in bed "listening to the drops of rain, that came down in monotonous succession," finds herself incapable of the "temporary forgetfulness" that comes so easily to her sister (62). Disengagement from both wakefulness and relationship is impossible. As Hawthorne writes, "A nervous impulse continually caused her to lift her head from the pillow, and gaze into Mary's chamber, and the intermediate apartment" (62). In this intermediate space she sees the hearth, and the four chairs belonging to the husbands and their wives, set in their "old positions," but "vacant" (62).

It is in this condition of wakefulness, "groaned in bitterness," that the "knock" first registers upon Margaret's consciousness (63). Yet even as she hears this knocking, her whole manner begins to change; things occur to her with an erotic physicality that suggests — especially in light of the ending — that she never does rise from bed, but instead falls fretfully into sleep. For even while deciding whether or not to answer, Margaret, we learn,

> was breathing hurriedly, and straining her ears to catch a repetition of the summons . . . The knocking was now renewed in slow and regular strokes, apparently given with the soft end of a doubled fist, and was accompanied by words, faintly heard through several thicknesses of wall. (63)

Here, as before, Margaret stares into her sister's room and sees Mary fast asleep — at which point, ostensibly, Margaret leaves her bed and goes to the window. This description, too, Hawthorne gives with sexually charged language, though if previously we are given a surprisingly naturalistic evocation of Margaret masturbating amid the sounds of overheard lovemaking (the "knocking," which comes in "slow and regular strokes," the words "faintly heard through several thicknesses of wall" — a "summons" which has her "straining" to hear, "breathing hurriedly"), now the sexual meaning is veiled in dreamlike innuendo:

> A lantern was reddening the front of the house, and melting the light in its neighboring puddles, while a deluge of darkness overwhelmed every other object. As the window grated on its hinges, a man in a broad brimmed hat and blanket-coat, stepped from under the shelter of the projecting story, and looked upward to discover whom his application had aroused. Margaret knew him as a friendly innkeeper of the town.
>
> "What would you have, Goodman Parker?" cried the widow. (63)

Note, in addition to the lantern's poetic "reddening" and "melting" of the night, the biblical shading of the word "knew," and the suggestion of "widow" in the word "window" (the loud cry of the former and the grating sounds of the latter alike "aroused" by "a man in a . . . blanket-coat"). Note also the words Margaret uses to ask what the messenger's business might be: "What would you have, Goodman Parker?" she cries, with a forwardness and vehemence that suggest more than mere anger at having been roused from bed. What happens in this encounter nonetheless remains indeterminate. Is the widow's cry sounded in a dream, and if so, where does the dream begin? If the knocking is something she hears while awake, could it be she falls asleep at precisely the moment she is said to have arisen? Or might the knocking not signify the beginning of her dream? Could it be, moreover, that in this dream Margaret is again overhearing, or imagining she overhears, another's lovemaking? (Is it, indeed, the knocking at a door she hears?) Are we asked to see in the word "lantern" the figure of a slattern, to imagine the friendly innkeeper as having taken shelter with this lantern/slattern in a dreamlike "deluge of darkness," under the "projecting story" from which Margaret (or Mary?), as "window," is heard grating on her "hinges"? As we read along, the sexual interplay between "Goodman" Parker and "Mistress" Margaret becomes obscure, hidden behind the veil of the news he brings. ("I judged you wouldn't mind being broke of your rest," is what the "honest man" says, ending their interview.) At this he departs,

> and his lantern gleam[s] along the street, bringing to view indistinct shapes of things, and the fragments of a world, like order glimmering through chaos, or memory roaming over the past. (64)

These images describe quite accurately how a dream illuminates the past in "indistinct shapes" and "fragments," showing the mere "glimmering" of "order" before disappearing back into the night. "Margaret staid not to watch these picturesque effects," writes Hawthorne. Instead, "Joy flashed into her heart, and lighted it up at once, and breathless, and with winged steps, she flew to the bedside of her sister." Here, however, "a thought of pain broke in upon her," causing Margaret to feel "involuntarily unfaithful." Three times Margaret looks in on Mary: first, while lying feverishly in bed, unable to sleep; second, while listening with quickened breath to the repetition of the summons; third, flying to her sister's bedside, after her heart lights up with joy. For reasons never explicitly given, Margaret's disturbed thoughts, her arousal by the messenger, and her reception of the messenger's news, all return her attention to Mary's bedchamber. Is her divided attention entirely due to concern for her sister? Hawthorne has carefully depicted Mary as the widow preoccupied with the other's condition, and Margaret as more tempestuous in nature. One possibility is that Margaret desires the return of Mary's husband more than her own. To be sure, the news of her husband's survival is "delightful," but "more delightful and more wild" are other, unnamed possibilities. Returning to bed, writes Hawthorne, Margaret's "mind was thronged with delightful thoughts, till sleep stole on and transformed them to visions, more delightful and more wild, like the breath of winter . . . working fantastic tracery upon a window" (65). Perhaps these wintery visions are of her brother-in-law. Perhaps, unconsciously, she is holding out for a survival even more desired ("fantastic") than her own husband's.

Mary's summons unfolds somewhat differently. All during Margaret's wakeful fever and all during Margaret's encounter with Goodman Parker, Mary has been asleep, "sunk into temporary forgetfulness." Now, with Margaret asleep and night far advanced, Mary awakes with a start from a vision — a vision described in terms vaguely suggestive of Margaret's encounter at the window. "A vivid dream," writes Hawthorne, "had latterly involved her in its unreal life, of which, however, she could only remember that it had been broken in upon at the most interesting point" (65). Here, the word "latterly" recalls the "lattice" of the window. The phrase "broken in upon" recalls the words of Goodman Parker ("I judged you wouldn't mind being broke of your rest"); the phrase also recalls the narrator's earlier words, that "a thought of pain broke in" upon Margaret's happiness. Mary's dream remains mysterious; all we learn is that it is interrupted. But how? By her sudden waking? Or before that, by Margaret's conversation at the window, overheard in the depths of sleep? Indeed, if Margaret's good fortune is itself the "unreal life" of Mary's "vivid dream," Margaret's "thought of pain" might well be what wakes Mary "with a sudden start." Margaret's thought, that is, could well be Mary's own. In any case, at this point Mary begins to perceive a knocking.

Hawthorne's description of her reception of this sound differs markedly from the description of how Margaret hears. Of Mary he writes:

> She listened with imperfect consciousness . . .; and first she deemed the noise a matter of course, like the breath she drew; next, it appeared a thing in which she had no concern; and lastly, she became aware that it was a summons necessary to be obeyed. At the same moment, the pang of recollection darted into her mind . . .; the dim light of the chamber, and the objects therein revealed, had retained all her suspended ideas. (65)

The emphasis here is not sexual but has instead to do with knowledge. She hears first "with imperfect consciousness"; the sound is "deemed" nothing unusual, then "a thing in which she had no concern"; finally, more perfectly "aware" of her circumstance, she perceives the noise as "a summons" and feels "the pang of recollection." For Margaret, the hearthlight is "cheerful radiance" and the lamp-light befitting of reunion. For Mary, this same light reveals "suspended ideas." She then moves to a spot where another has preceded her — the window, left unlocked by accident and yielding easily to the touch. Her predominant emotion appears to be fear. She trembles as she asks "Who's there?" Again, as with Margaret's encounter, there is something unreal in the description:

> The storm was over, and the moon was up; it shone upon broken clouds above, and below upon houses black with moisture, and upon little lakes of fallen rain, curling with the shiver beneath the quick

> enchantment of a breeze. A young man in a sailor's dress, wet as if he had come out of the depth of the sea, stood alone under the window . . . [P]revious to her marriage, he had been an unsuccessful wooer of her own.
>
> "What do you seek here, Stephen?" said she.
>
> "Cheer up, Mary, for I seek to comfort you," said the rejected lover. (65)

Earlier, Mary is described as having (while asleep) "a look of motionless contentment . . ., as if her heart, like a deep lake had sunk down so far within" (64). Now, as if from the wet depths of her own heart, comes her old suitor Stephen, as if he were "the pang of recollection [that had] darted into her mind," a regret come to life to comfort her. Virtuous Mary immediately rejects the offer: "'Stephen, I thought better of you!' exclaimed the widow, with gushing tears, and preparing to close the lattice; for she was no whit inclined to imitate the first wife of Zadig" (66). The eroticism of Margaret's encounter with Goodman Parker is here eschewed in favor of a chaste recitation of the facts. He tells her that her husband is alive and that he (Stephen) has seen the husband himself. "There's the comfort I bring you, Mary, and so good night" (66). Again the end of the encounter is described in terms of light and shadow. "He hurried away, while Mary watched him with a doubt of waking reality, that seemed stronger or weaker as he alternately entered the shade of the houses, or emerged into the broad streaks of moonlight" (66). Like Margaret, Mary's first impulse is to share her news, and like her sister-in-law she enters the other's private chamber. She then remembers, like Margaret before her, the effect her news will have on the household's delicate emotional balance. Yet despite these similarities, Hawthorne's wording brings important differences to light. Thus, while Margaret's fear for Mary involves a sorrow "sharpened" by happiness;

Mary fears for Margaret "thoughts of death and woe, rendered not the less bitter by their contrast with her own felicity" (66). Likewise, while Margaret's response to the messenger's news is breathless flight and a flash of joy, Mary feels "new-born gladness" and "a blessed flood of conviction." The word "blessed," of course, recalls the name of Mary's husband's ship; the phrase "new-born" reminds us of the unspoken brotherly obligation to a childless and widowed sister-in-law. But why is the obligation invoked in this passage as a qualification of Mary's "gladness"? I have already suggested that Margaret desires her brother-in-law's survival even more than that of her own husband. Perhaps Mary, chaste to the end, harbors diametrically opposite thoughts. Perhaps she dreads her brother-in-law's return even more than the death of her husband. Perhaps she even dreads her own husband's return — if it means his returning to a widowed Margaret as well.

If only one of the husbands had come back alive, he would not have been obligated or had the right to perform the duty of a husband's brother in the biblical sense cited above. He would, however, have returned to a home shared with a now-husbandless woman. The household's symmetry would have been broken. Would such a break in symmetry have led to other breaks, other disruptions? And does a thought of these other possible disruptions enter into the minds of the widows when they consider or dream the miraculous returns of their spouses?

In the end, "Wives of the Dead" brings two women to a shuttered window to look beyond themselves, to glimpse the possibility of resurrection. At the same time, having spied through this window, through the "projecting" story of their shared domestic space, this miraculous possibility, the two women are called back to themselves, back also to their relationships — with each other and the dead brothers — and thus, after a long night of grief, and dreamed or actual reprieve, to the possibility of a changed relationship. Earlier, when Margaret bursts forth in lamentation with "rebellious expressions," Mary succeeds "in bringing her sister's mind nearer to the situation of her own." Shortly after this moment of sympathetic alignment, the two sisters part for sleep. What becomes doubtful, then, at night's end, is just how near their situations remain.

The question remains, why does Mary let a tear fall at the story's end? Could it be, as recognition dawns in her, that she's recalling the biblical law concerning brothers and their wives, so that her own husband's survival, as waking reality, brings the fear her sister-in-law will assert an ancient privilege—that her sailor husband will feel compelled to give the landsman's widow a child? Or has she a premonition that this conclusion will come true for another reason? Of course, as already noted, it is possible that the tear isn't Mary's at all. Why, then, should Margaret, asleep with happy dreams, let fall a tear? Why, at the end, is her slumber "unquiet"? Why, earlier, does Margaret become "disturbed and feverish, in proportion as the night advanced with its deepest and stillest hours" (62)? Could the death of Mary's husband at sea, news of which preceded the news of her own husband's death by a day, have awakened in Margaret a growing sense of shame, so that now, recalling "comforting passages of Scripture," her conscience becomes inflamed, marking her as guilty in her various engagements with Mary, rendering Margaret particularly vulnerable to dreams?

My point is not to propose a solution to the ending. The pronominal ambiguity of the final line is ineradicable; the tension between dream and reality, history and fable, is fundamental. For this reason, "Wives of the Dead" demands a style of reading that remains open to possibilities of meaning, not certainties. I would nonetheless emphasize the following points. First, Mary's husband — the sailor — appears to be the focus of both wives' grief. Second, while Mary's handling of Margaret's outburst recalls the sailor's profession, the outburst itself recalls the sailor's demise — suggesting that Margaret is in some way linked to the tragic turn of Mary's life. Third, Mary's summons by messenger emphasizes chasteness and the acquisition of knowledge, while Margaret's summons highlights impetuousness and joy. Fourth, the onanistic imagery of Margaret's dreamlike response to the messenger's knocking implies that her sexual desire is fixed on her sister-in-law's bedroom, while the erotic description of Mary's response suggests instead an untouched reservoir of physical need.[5] Fifth, the legal relationship of the two sisters takes on new psychological resonance in light of the brotherly obligation decreed by the Bible. Finally, if only one husband survives (as each sister has occasion to believe), the household's delicate balance will be irreparably and perhaps disastrously disturbed.

When we first meet Mary and Margaret, they are sitting together by the fireplace. This site, marked by the dead husbands' empty chairs ("two humbler seats... near them, the true thrones of that little empire"), defines, Hawthorne tells us, the shared interiority where the sisters "had exercised in love, a power that love had won" (62-63). That Mary and Margaret's first words of exchange implicate though we don't know this yet — Mary's husband's ship, explains perhaps the strange power that the sisters both exercise and win in love's "empire." This exchange, which gives a premonition of Margaret's disturbed attempt to fall asleep, strains the bonds of sorrow which unite the sisters even more closely than the bonds of marriage:

> United, as they had been, by the relationship of the living, and now more closely so by that of the dead, each felt as if whatever consolation her grief admitted, were to be found in the bosom of the other. They joined their hearts, and wept together silently. (61)

Tenuously, Hawthorne proposes a correlation between the permeability of the sisters' inner lives, and the revelation of hidden household dynamics. The sisters, he writes, find consolation by joining their hearts. More specifically, he writes that each sister allows entry to and confesses — the two meanings of "admit" — precisely those discoveries "found in the bosom of the other." Are these discoveries made in a dream? Certainly they are made as if in a dream — in a shared moment of crisis:

> The dream is no accomplice of sleep. It ascends again the slope that sleep descends, towards life, it goes toward existence, and there, in full light, it sees death as the destiny of freedom. For the dream, as such, and by virtue of the meanings of existence it bears with it, kills sleep and life that falls asleep. (Foucault 54)

Foucault in these words describes aptly the course of Hawthorne's tale. However true or false the news the messengers bring, they bring the sisters to a necessary waking, an encounter with one another and with "a world which secretes its opaque contents and the forms of a necessity that cannot be deciphered" (Foucault 54). Dreamt or real, the messengers are no accomplices of sleep. They murder sleep, and the life that falls asleep. Ultimately, the news of each messenger suggests a threat of rupture in the symmetry determining the legal structure of the household — a threat that retains its force even if the messengers themselves turn out to have been dreamt. In this respect, the significance of the story's ending is not simply that awakening brings consciousness, but that consciousness in its most awakened state brings the sisters to a fuller appreciation of the intertwining of their separate fates. Indeed, calling into question the very notion of self as a singular, self-sustaining interiority, Hawthorne's carefully constructed dream-tale proposes this threat of rupture as a necessary prelude to the "waking reality" whose truest messenger is Hawthorne's own language. Guided by this language — a poetic vocabulary thick with hints of thwarted desire, pregnant with adulterous forebodings — the reader too becomes susceptible of awakening. Susceptible also of remaining asleep, immured in pleasing if unfulfilled dreams.

NOTES

1. Thompson, in *The Art of Authorial Presence* (66-76), provides the broadest overview of the scant critical literature. Noteworthy treatments include Van Doren, *Nathaniel Hawthorne*, 82-84; Lang, "How Ambiguous Is Hawthorne?"; Schubert, *Hawthorne, The Artist*, 110-12; Doubleday, *Hawthorne's Early Tales*, 215-18; Carlson, "The Function of the Lamp in Hawthorne's 'The Wives of the Dead'"; Seizer, "Psychological Romance in Hawthorne's 'Wives of the Dead'"; Christophersen, "Hawthorne's 'The Wives of the Dead': Bereavement and the 'Better Part'"; Friedman, "Hawthorne's Dreaming Wives of the Dead"; Colacurcio, *The Province of Piety*, 100-7; and Harris, "The Wives of the Living?: Absence of Dreams in Hawthorne's 'The Wives of the Dead.'"

2. Moore praises Hawthorne's use of ambiguity as "an intentional masking of meaning" — "an ambiguity of theme," which Moore distinguishes from "sense distorted within a sentence by ambiguous placement of words" (50). In a footnote, he offers "the last sentence of 'The Wives of the Dead'" as an example of the less desirable form of ambiguity — the use of "[a]mbiguous syntax" to "obscure [the] meaning" (136 n. 1).

3. Colacurcio makes the same point, though for him this unascertainability serves as proof that no dreaming can be involved in the principal portions of the plot. Taking issue with Carlson and Lang, and siding with Doubleday, Colacurcio notes, "The problem is not only that this reading requires an entirely dishonest narrator,' but even more drastically that it bungles the story's management of point of view: there is simply no plausible point of transition from one dreaming consciousness to the other" (555 n. 11, citation omitted). Thompson, for

his part, disputes Colacurcio's reading by proposing that the story is "intentionally ambiguous throughout" (69). Further evidence of Hawthorne's intentions may lie in the story's placement in The Snow-Image, where "Wives" immediately follows "Old Ticonderoga," a sketch of just the sort of fort Margaret's husband would have sought in his skirmish on the frontier. The final sentence of "Old Ticonderoga" reads, "Tall trees had grown upon its ramparts, since the last garrison marched out, to return no more, or only at some dreamer's summons, gliding from the twilight past to vanish among realities" (389, emphasis added).

4. Nor would the discovery of a source text mitigate this tension. An old story which resolved the brothers' fates would only underscore Hawthorne's heightening of the tension between objective fact and subjective desire. An old story which didn't resolve the brothers' fates would instead historicize this tension.

5. Though he derives a very different conclusion, McDermott notes this important difference in the erotic treatment of the sisters' responses when he writes, "[Mary's] dream appears . . . as a wish-fulfillment to fill the void in her heart. It pales, however, when compared with Margaret's fierce will" (147).

REFEENCES

Carlson, Patricia Ann. "The Function of the Lamp in Hawthorne's 'The Wives of the Dead.'" *South Atlantic Bulletin* 40:2 (May 1975): 62-64.

Christophersen, Bill. "Hawthorne's 'The Wives of the Dead': Bereavement and the 'Better Part.'" *Studies in Short Fiction* 20 (1983): 1-6.

Colacurcio, Michael J. *The Province of Piety: Moral History in Hawthorne's Early Tales.*

Cambridge: Harvard UP, 1984.

Doubleday, Neal Frank. *Hawthorne's Early Tales, a Critical Study.* Durham: Duke UP, 1972.

Foucault, Michel. "Dream, Imagination, and Existence." Transl. Forrest Williams. In *Review of Existential Psychology & Psychiatry* 19:1 (1984): 29-78.

Friedman, Thomas. "Hawthorne's Dreaming Wives of the Dead." *Cuyahoga Review* 1:2 (Fall 1983): 141-42.

Harris, Mark. "The Wives of the Living?: Absence of Dreams in Hawthorne's 'The Wives of the Dead.'" *Studies in Short Fiction* 29 (1992): 323-29.

Hawthorne, Nathaniel. *Tales and Sketches; A Wonder Book for Girls and Boys; Tanglewood Tales for Girls and Boys.* Ed. Roy Harvey Pearce. New York: The Library of America, 1982.

King James Bible. Deut. 25:5.

Lang, H.J. "How Ambiguous Is Hawthorne?" *Hawthorne: A Collection of Critical Essays*. Ed. A. N. Kaul. Englewood Cliffs: Prentice-Hall, 1966: 86-98.

McDermott, John V. "Hawthorne's The Wives of the Dead." *Explicator* 54:3 (Spring 1996): 145-47.

Moore, Thomas R.A *Thick and Darksome Vell: The Rhetoric of Hawthorne's Sketches*, Prefaces, and Essays. Boston: Northeastern UP, 1994.

Schubert, Leland. *Hawthorne, The Artist: Fine-Art Devices in Fiction*. New York: Russell & Russell, 1963.

Selzer, John L. "Psychological Romance in Hawthorne's 'Wives of the Dead.'" *Studies in Short Fiction* 16 (1979): 311-15.

Thompson, G.R. *The Art of Authorial Presence: Hawthorne's Provincial Tales*. Durham: Duke UP, 1993.

Van Doren, Mark. *Nathaniel Hawthorne*. 1949. Repr. New York: Greenwood P, 1979.

Index